Manhood in the Making

Manhood in the Making

Cultural Concepts of Masculinity

DAVID D. GILMORE

YALE UNIVERSITY PRESS
NEW HAVEN & LONDON

Published with assistance from the Kingsley Trust
Association Publication Fund established by the Scroll
and Key Society of Yale College.

Designed by Nancy Ovedovitz and set in Baskerville
type by The Composing Room of Michigan, Inc.
Printed in the United States of America by Vail-Ballou
Press, Binghamton, New York.

Library of Congress Cataloging-in-Publication Data

Gilmore, David D., 1943–
Manhood in the making : cultural concepts of
masculinity / David D. Gilmore.
    p. cm.
    Includes bibliographical references.
    ISBN 0–300–04646–4 (cloth)
    ISBN 978-0-300-05076-9 (pbk.)
    1. Masculinity (Psychology)—Cross-cultural studies.
2. Machismo—Cross-cultural studies.   3. Men—
Psychology—Cross-cultural studies.   I. Title.
BF692.5.G55 1990
155.3'32—dc20   89–22425
                                        CIP

20 19 18 17 16 15 14 13 12 11

This book is dedicated to
Maggie and Aggie and Julian:
three
tuff
guys.

But when, by what test, by what indication does manhood commence? Physically, by one criterion, legally by another. Morally by a third, intellectually by a fourth—and all indefinite.

—Thomas De Quincey, *Autobiography*

Masculinity is not something given to you, something you're born with, but something you gain. . . . And you gain it by winning small battles with honor.

—Norman Mailer, *Cannibals and Christians*

In human beings pure masculinity or femininity is not to be found in either a physiological or biological sense. Every individual on the contrary displays a mixture of the character-traits belonging to his own and to the opposite sex; and he shows a combination of activity and passivity whether or not these last character-traits tally with his biological ones.

—Sigmund Freud, *Three Essays on Sexuality*

Are you a man?

—Lady Macbeth to her husband, *Macbeth*

Contents

Preface

In his introduction to *Don Quixote*, Cervantes modestly begged the reader's indulgence for the imperfections to follow. "Idle reader," he wrote, "you may believe me without any oath that I would want this book, the child of my brain, to be the most beautiful, the happiest, and most brilliant imaginable. But I could not contravene that law of nature according to which like begets like." Considering the result, Cervantes's modesty may have been disingenuous, but mine is genuine in expressing the same sentiment. Still, like him, I believe I have done my best, though the result be imperfect.

I first became interested in the subject of manhood when I lived in Spain doing anthropological fieldwork in a small town. People there were always talking about "real men" and about being macho, usually in a purely sexual sense, but not always. Hardly a day passed when this subject went unmentioned. Later I found the topic of manliness cropping up in discussions of my experiences with students and with colleagues. Most societies, even in the most unlikely places, I discovered, had some idea about "true" manhood; men everywhere were preoccupied by analogous concepts or anxieties, and the similarities seemed worth exploring. The explosion of feminist writing on sex and gender in the past decade has advanced our knowledge of women's roles but has left these manhood cults and codes virtually untouched. For all these reasons, a retrospective cross-cultural study of manhood and masculinity seemed worthwhile.

This book was hard to research because there is no recognized place to look up "manhood" as a cultural category and compare notes. Clues are few and far between in a vast literature. Consequently, to avoid wasting too much time, I often had to depend upon personal contacts and leads. I want to thank the many people who helped, either by responding to my sometimes importuning requests for information, or by indulging my curiosity about their own fieldwork experiences. The following people deserve a special note of gratitude for their kind forbearance: Bernard Siegel, Carol Ember, T. O. Beidelman, Gail Hershatter, Bill Kelly, Robert Dentan, Donald Tuzin, Ronald Reminick, George Stade, Frank Conant, Paula Brown, Michael Gilmore, Nikos Stamatakis, Nancy Rosenberger, Sarah Uhl, Dennis McGilvray, and Russell Bernard. A particular debt is owed to Mac Marshall, Michael Herzfeld, Thomas Gregor, Paul Spencer, Stanley Brandes, and Gilbert Herdt for providing case studies of exemplary thoroughness, sensitivity, and—one must add—beauty. Without the pathfinding efforts of these heroic explorers in the mysteries of manhood, this book could never have been written.

For help in making the manuscript presentable and more coherent, I owe a great debt to Ellen Graham of Yale University Press, an editor both of meticulous standards and of kind discretion, who was most generous with her time and her encouragement. I am equally indebted to the anonymous reviewer for Yale Press, who responded quickly with constructive advice while also correcting many errors in text. Any remaining errors are my own. I also want to thank my put-upon friends Dan Bates, Lawrence Martin, and Jim Matthews, leading scholars of Turkey, monkeys and pigeons, respectively, who helped me gain partial control over my recalcitrant word processor. A belated word of thanks is also due Ruben E. Reina, my thesis advisor at the University of Pennsylvania back in the early 1970s. A benevolent patriarch and true gentleman, he pushed me through gently but firmly when I resisted, showing me the inspirational power of high (in this case perhaps undeserved) expectations.

Generous grants from the following agencies took me to Spain and Morocco and permitted me free time to ponder the data collected there: the National Institute of Mental Health, the National Science Foundation, the Council for the International Exchange of Scholars, the National Endowment for the Humanities, the American Philosophical Society, and the Wenner-Gren Foundation.

Finally I want to thank my family, who put up with my strange moods and erratic behavior for the past two years. My wife Margaret M. Gilmore, M.D., did her best to ignore the mumbling and cursing emanating from my general direction while keeping things in perspective. My daughter Agatha Emily was a source of inspiration with her lovely art work and soothing piano playing; and my new son, Julian Jay, learned to walk and to say Da-Da at age nine months, thereby setting a sterling example for his floundering and inarticulate father.

✿ ✿ ✿ ✿ ✿

Introduction

Comparison is primary. Even to see a
"culture" involves closure and contrast.
    —James Boon, *Other Tribes, Other Scribes*

This book is about the way people in different cultures conceive and experience manhood, which I will define here simply as the
approved way of being an adult male in any
given society. More specifically it is about why
people in so many places regard the state of
being a "real man" or "true man" as uncertain or precarious, a prize to be won or
wrested through struggle, and why so many
societies build up an elusive or exclusionary
image of manhood through cultural sanctions, ritual, or trials of skill and endurance.

In pursuing these aims from a cross-cultural perspective, the book takes a panoramic
view of notions of masculinity in both Western and non-Western cultures and traditions.
As the subject is the cultural construction and
meaning of sex stereotypes, in this case male
ones, this study fits into the broader current
focus in anthropology on sex roles and gender. But it limits itself to the ideology of masculinity, a subject that I think has been unjustly neglected in today's growing feminist
literature in cultural anthropology. My feeling is that while women's roles are being reex-
amined fruitfully and necessarily in this liter-

ature, masculinity, though equally problematic, still suffers from the "taken for granted" syndrome. As Judith Shapiro (1979: 269) has said of the burgeoning feminist literature in anthropology, "the focus is on women; the social and cultural dimensions of maleness are often dealt with implicitly rather than explicitly. Moreover, much of the recent cross-cultural research is not only about women, but by women, and in some sense, for women." I think both sex roles and stereotypes need consideration, partly because of the light each reflects on the other; hence this book on manhood, its many guises, its experiences, its meanings. This book then is about men but certainly not for men only.

In keeping with the venerable tradition of culture sampling in anthropology, I have tried to provide extended cases of male ideologies from each of the basic socioeconomic types or categories recognized in contemporary culture theory. There are examples from hunting-gathering bands, horticultural and pastoral tribes, peasants, and postindustrial civilizations, in no particular order and without any evolutionary framework in mind. All the inhabited continents are represented by ethnographic examples (again in no particular order), and there are examples of manly ideals from warrior and pacifist societies, from egalitarian and stratified ones, and from matrilineal, patrilineal, and bilateral kinship systems. The sample is thus fairly broad, but no ethnographic sampling can ever hope to achieve closure, and I recognize the absence here of extended cases from aboriginal North America, the Arctic, Australia, northern Europe, and, I am sure, other places. Presumably someone else better versed in the literature of these areas will someday rectify these omissions.

Using ethnographic field data and secondary literature from this relatively wide sample, I try to trace the theme of what it means to "be a man"—a common enough exhortation in societies around the world. On the basis of the ethnographic material, I suggest that there is something almost generic, something repetitive, about the criteria of man-playing, that underlying the surface variation in emphasis or form are certain convergences in concepts, symbolizations, and exhortations of masculinity in many societies but—and this is important—by no means in all. I will speak here of tendencies or parallels in male imagery around the world, a ubiquity rather than a universality. As we proceed, I will attempt to provide some tentative answers to why these widespread resemblances in male images, this replicate "deep structure of masculinity," as some researchers have called it (Tolson 1977:56), should exist in otherwise dissimilar cultures. These explanations will incorporate some aspects of psychoanalytic theory, using some recently developed neo-Freudian ideas about the development of male gender identity, but I will argue later that such psychological theories must be applied in tandem with materialist perspectives, that is, taking into account the way that intrapsychic dynamics relate to the social organization of production. Thus it will soon become evident that my approach here is basically, for want of a better word, a functional one. I will argue that manhood ideals make an indispensable contribution both to the continuity of social systems and to the psychological integration of men into their community. I regard these phenomena not as givens, but as part of the existential "problem of order" that all societies must solve by encouraging people to act in certain ways, ways that facilitate both individual development and group adaptation. Gender roles represent one of these problem-solving behaviors.

Let me state here emphatically that this study is not meant to be a contribution to the philosophical debate about functional*ism* in the social sciences. A crude Malinowskian functionalism, based almost exclusively on human biology and given over to one-to-one correspondences, is clearly, as its detractors have shown, teleological and circular when applied uncritically. Although indebted both to Malinowski and to Radcliffe-Brown's classic concept of social structure, my view of functional interpretation tries to penetrate the meeting point between manifest and latent functions dialectically. It does this by trying to show how a piece of behavior works as a strategy of adaptation under certain conditions while simultaneously reconciling individual and social needs through the feedback of sanction and reward. Thus variant cases, such as we will consider in chapter 9, can be made comprehensible by the same interpretive framework rather than simply standing as negative examples. However, since this book is intended as a tentative first step in the direction of synoptic masculinity studies, an area of research still in its infancy, my conclusions should be regarded as exploratory rather than definitive, as I will be the first to admit.

As we shall see in the following chapters, ideas and anxieties about masculinity as a special-status category of achievement are widespread in societies around the world, being expressed to varying degrees, but they do not seem to be absolutely universal. There are exceptions: cultures where manhood is of minimal interest to men, or where the subject is entirely elided as a symbolic category among members of both sexes. In chapter 9 I will try to account for these anomalous cases in accordance with the interpretive model I have proposed.

Because of the trajectory of my own anthropological training, my research for the meaning of manhood began long ago in Andalusia (southern Spain), one of the most culturally conservative parts of that country. There I found a pervasive concern among men about their masculinity and a cultural ideal of manhood (an image supported by public opinion among most women as well as men). What I found particularly interesting about the Andalusian male image (*machismo,* as it is called in a word that has worked its way into English and many other languages) was in fact this contextual universality, that it was held to be valuable and indispensable by society as a whole and was therefore an integral component of traditional Spanish culture for both sexes. This cultural hypostasis of the male image, which I believe exists to a degree in many societies, led me to believe that the manhood ideal is not purely psychogenetic in origin but is also a culturally imposed ideal to which men must conform whether or not they find it psychologically congenial. That is, it is not simply a reflection of individual psychology but a part of public culture, a collective representation. If true, there must be sociocultural as well as psychodynamic reasons for its salience, and these therefore must be amenable to comparative anthropological analysis. Thus I believe the best way to approach the subject is through a methodological hybrid combining both a cultural materialism and an analytic personality psychology.

A psychological anthropologist, Robert LeVine (1973), has called this dual modality the "two systems" approach. He regards the individual as having to balance two sets of demands as a member of society. The first stems from his own psychic conflicts; the second derives from without as a result of his need for cultural conformity and acceptance. The individual's behavior then is seen as a compromise solution to these separate and sometimes opposing pressures. My use of this scheme is functional to the extent that it regards conditioned behavior as a response to, or strategy for solving, inherent problems of human existence. Following the principle of Ockham's Razor, it seeks the most parsimonious explanation: the one that explains the most by the least.

From our starting point in Andalusia, and more broadly the Mediterranean world of which Andalusia is a part, we move to consider other cultures far distant. We will take a look at other societies where inspirational male imagery is equally pervasive but expressed in different ways and to different degrees of intensity. We travel to Micronesia, Melanesia, equatorial Africa, aboriginal South America, South and East Asia, with side trips to the Middle East, North America, Britain, and ancient Greece. In all these places, living up to a highlighted image of manhood is a frequent theme, although often articulated at lower social decibels than, for example, in southern Spain, Sicily, or Mexico. Given its limitless venue, this book is an exercise in comparative culture study without geographic or linguistic boundaries. Admittedly, I have written it from a male perspective, using data collected mainly (but not exclusively) by male anthropologists simply because these are the only data we have at present. But it considers male gender identity a problematic, a puzzle, an unresolved cryptogram or enigma; it takes nothing for granted, and it incorporates field data from Spain gathered by a female co-worker.

A PREPARATORY NOTE ON PROCEDURES

Before we start looking at data, I would like to address briefly the question of comparative methods in order to avoid methodological problems later. How does one go about comparing ideals of gender in different cultures without tearing features from their natural context? How does one measure the normative variables without resorting to apriorism? Although cultural anthropology touts itself as the comparative science par excellence, there has never really been general agreement on any procedure that might be called the ethnographic "comparative method" (cf. Kuper 1983:197). In the succeeding chapters, I will follow the lead of S. F. Nadel (1951), one of the founding fathers of anthropology, whose comparative procedure has been put to good use recently by Fredrik Barth in a cross-cultural study of ritual practices in New Guinea (1987). Barth's resuscitation of Nadel is a good place to begin.

As Barth points out, Nadel's comparative goal is synthetic rather than typological. Nadel sees the comparative study of cultural variation as the critical component of anthropological analysis, in a sense its raison d'être. Although he acknowledges the importance of holistic or systemic description of separate cultures, he stresses that the heart of the anthropological procedure lies in the comparative testing of propositions stating necessary interconnectedness between *certain features* of such systems. Moreover, Nadel rejects a ceteris paribus clause, that is, he argues that for the observer to arrive at a valid conclusion about the meaning of statistical covariation, the miscellaneous features of society should specifically *not* be equal. Otherwise the correlations depicted as covariation may simply reflect some other, unrevealed factor in these surrounding features.

Nadel's procedural methods, put to good empirical use by

Barth in his study of the Mountain Ok people, are valuable because they permit us to test the continuities underlying the flux of temporal variability, to probe beneath exterior patterns and to identify the nature of the obscured features that seem to provide the order upon which the visible similarities rest. By observing patterns of variation in their context, we may be able to highlight the replication of features otherwise masked and to observe how they relate systematically in varying contexts (Barth 1987:10–11). Thus we may provisionally identify the comparative method to be followed here as identifying the empirical extent of order and its underlying forces through comparisons of variations and their relations. Instead of comparing replicate "things" placed side by side, we are comparing the variable components or criteria which constitute the things as congeries of empirical categories, in this case, the components of masculine gender ideology.

❀ ❀ ❀ ❀ ❀ 1

The Manhood Puzzle

There are continuities of masculinity that
transcend cultural differences.
—Thomas Gregor, *Anxious Pleasures*

Are there continuities of masculinity across
cultural boundaries, as the anthropologist
Thomas Gregor says (1985:209)? Are men
everywhere alike in their concern for being
"manly?" If so, why? Why is the demand
made upon males to "be a man" or "act like a
man" voiced in so many places? And why are
boys and youths so often tested or indoctri-
nated before being awarded their manhood?
These are questions not often asked in the
growing literature on sex and gender roles.
Yet given the recent interest in sexual ster-
eotyping, they are ones that need to be considered if we are to understand both sexes
and their relations.

Regardless of other normative distinctions
made, all societies distinguish between male
and female; all societies also provide institutionalized sex-appropriate roles for adult
men and women. A very few societies recognize a third, sexually intermediary category,
such as the Cheyenne *berdache,* the Omani
xanith, and the Tahitian *mahu* (which we will
examine later), but even in these rare cases of
androgynous genders, the individual must
make a life choice of identity and abide by

prescribed rules of sexual comportment. In addition, most societies hold consensual ideals—guiding or admonitory images—for conventional masculinity and femininity by which individuals are judged worthy members of one or the other sex and are evaluated more generally as moral actors. Such ideal statuses and their attendant images, or models, often become psychic anchors, or psychological identities, for most individuals, serving as a basis for self-perception and self-esteem (D'Andrade 1974:36).

These gender ideals, or guiding images, differ from culture to culture. But, as Gregor and others (e.g. Brandes 1980; Lonner 1980; Raphael 1988) have argued, underlying the surface differences are some intriguing similarities among cultures that otherwise display little in common. Impressed by the statistical frequency of such regularities in sexual patterning, a number of observers have recently argued that cultures are more alike than different in this regard. For example, Gregor (1985:200) studied a primitive Amazonian tribe and compared its sex ideals to those of contemporary America. Finding many subsurface similarities in the qualities expected of men and women, he concludes that our different cultures represent only a symbolic veneer masking a bedrock of sexual thinking. In another study, the psychologist Lonner (1980:147) echoes this conclusion. He argues that culture is "only a thin veneer covering an essential universality" of gender dimorphism. In their comprehensive survey of sex images in thirty different cultures, Williams and Best (1982:30) conclude that there is "substantial similarity" to be found "panculturally in the traits ascribed to men and women."

Whether or not culture is only a thin veneer over a deep structure is a complicated question: as the rare third sexes show, we must not see in every culture "a Westerner struggling to get out" (Munroe and Munroe 1980:25). But most social scientists would agree that there do exist striking regularities in standard male and female roles across cultural boundaries regardless of other social arrangements (Archer and Lloyd 1985:283–84).

The one regularity that concerns me here is the often dramatic ways in which cultures construct an appropriate manhood—the presentation or "imaging" of the male role. In particular, there is a constantly recurring notion that real manhood is different from simple anatomical maleness, that it is not a natural condition that comes about spontaneously through biological maturation but rather is a precarious or artificial state that boys must win against powerful odds. This recurrent notion that manhood is problematic, a critical threshold that boys must pass through testing, is found at all levels of sociocultural development regardless of what other alternative roles are recognized. It is found among the simplest hunters and fishermen, among peasants and sophisticated urbanized peoples; it is found in all continents and environments. It is found among both warrior peoples and those who have never killed in anger.

Moreover, this recurrent belief represents a primary and recurrent difference from parallel notions of femaleness. Although women, too, in any society are judged by sometimes stringent sexual standards, it is rare that their very status as woman forms part of the evaluation. Women who are found deficient or deviant according to these standards may be criticized as immoral, or they may be called unladylike or its equivalent and subjected to appropriate sanctions, but rarely is their right to a gender identity questioned in the same public, dramatic way that it is for men. The very paucity of linguistic labels for females echoing the epithets "effete," "unmanly," "effeminate," "emasculated," and so on, attest to this archetypical difference between sex judgments worldwide. And it is far more assaultive (and frequent) for men to be challenged in this way than for women.

Perhaps the difference between male and female should not be overstated, for "femininity" is also something achieved by women who seek social approval. But as a social icon, femininity seems to be judged differently. It usually involves questions of body ornament or sexual allure, or other essentially cosmetic behaviors that enhance, rather than create, an inherent quality

of character. An authentic femininity rarely involves tests or
proofs of action, or confrontations with dangerous foes: win-or-
lose contests dramatically played out on the public stage. Rather
than a critical threshold passed by traumatic testing, an either/or
condition, femininity is more often construed as a biological
given that is culturally refined or augmented.

TESTS OF MANHOOD: A SURVEY

Before going any further, let us look at a few examples of this
problematic manhood. Our first stop is Truk Island, a little atoll
in the South Pacific. Avid fishermen, the people of Truk have
lived for ages from the sea, casting and diving in deep waters.
According to the anthropologists who have lived among them,
the Trukese men are obsessed with their masculinity, which they
regard as chancy. To maintain a manly image, the men are
encouraged to take risks with life and limb and to think "strong"
or "manly" thoughts, as the natives put it (M. Marshall 1979).
Accordingly, they challenge fate by going on deep-sea fishing
expeditions in tiny dugouts and spearfishing with foolhardy
abandon in shark-infested waters. If any men shrink from such
challenges, their fellows, male and female, laugh at them, calling
them effeminate and childlike. When on land, Trukese youths
fight in weekend brawls, drink to excess, and seek sexual conquests to attain a manly image. Should a man fail in any of these
efforts, another will taunt him: "Are you a man? Come, I will
take your life now" (ibid.:92).

Far away on the Greek Aegean island of Kalymnos, the people
are also stalwart seafarers, living by commercial sponge fishing
(Bernard 1967). The men of Kalymnos dive into deep water
without the aid of diving equipment, which they scorn. Diving is
therefore a gamble because many men are stricken and crippled
by the bends for life. But no matter: they have proven their
precious manhood by showing their contempt for death
(ibid.:119). Young divers who take precautions are effeminate,
scorned and ridiculed by their fellows.

These are two seafaring peoples. Let us move elsewhere, to inland Black Africa, for example, where fishing is replaced by pastoral pursuits. In East Africa young boys from a host of cattle-herding tribes, including the Masai, Rendille, Jie, and Samburu, are taken away from their mothers and subjected at the outset of adolescence to bloody circumcision rites by which they become true men. They must submit without so much as flinching under the agony of the knife. If a boy cries out while his flesh is being cut, if he so much as blinks an eye or turns his head, he is shamed for life as unworthy of manhood, and his entire lineage is shamed as a nursery of weaklings. After this very public ordeal, the young initiates are isolated in special dormitories in the wilderness. There, thrust on their own devices, they learn the tasks of a responsible manhood: cattle rustling, raiding, killing, survival in the bush. If their long apprenticeship is successful, they return to society as men and are only then permitted to take a wife.

Another dramatic African case comes from nearby Ethiopia: the Amhara, a Semitic-speaking tribe of rural cultivators. They have a passionate belief in masculinity called *wand-nat*. This idea involves aggressiveness, stamina, and bold "courageous action" in the face of danger; it means never backing down when threatened (Levine 1966:18). To show their wand-nat, the Amhara youths are forced to engage in whipping contests called *buhe* (Reminick 1982:32). During the whipping ceremonies, in which all able-bodied male adolescents must participate for their reputations' sake, the air is filled with the cracking of whips. Faces are lacerated, ears torn open, and red and bleeding welts appear (ibid.:33). Any sign of weakness is greeted with taunts and mockery. As if this were not enough, adolescent Amhara boys are wont to prove their virility by scarring their arms with red-hot embers (Levine 1966:19). In these rough ways the boys actualize the exacting Amhara "ideals of masculinity" (Reminick 1976:760).

Significantly, this violent testing is not enough for these virile Ethiopians. Aside from showing physical hardihood and courage in the buhe matches, a young man must demonstrate his

potency on his wedding night by waving a bloody sheet of mar-
ital consummation before the assembled kinsmen (ibid.:760–
61). As well as demonstrating the bride's virginity, this ceremonial defloration is a talisman of masculinity for the Amhara
groom. The Amhara's proof of manhood, like that of the Trukese, is both sexual and violent, and his performances both on
the battlefield and in the marriage bed must be visibly displayed,
recorded, and confirmed by the group; otherwise he is no man.

Halfway around the world, in the high mountains of Melanesia, young boys undergo similar trials before being admitted into
the select club of manhood. In the New Guinea Highlands, boys
are torn from their mothers and forced to undergo a series of
brutal masculinizing rituals (Herdt 1982). These include whipping, flailing, beating, and other forms of terrorization by older
men, which the boys must endure stoically and silently. As in
Ethiopia, the flesh is scored and blood flows freely. These Highlanders believe that without such hazing, boys will never mature
into men but will remain weak and childlike. Real men are
made, they insist, not born.

PARALLELS

To be sure, there are some contextual similarities in these last
few examples. The Amhara, Masai, and New Guinea Highlanders share one feature in common beyond the stress on manhood: they are fierce warrior peoples, or were in the recent past.
One may argue that their bloody rites prepare young boys for
the idealized life of the warrior that awaits them. So much is
perhaps obvious: some Western civilizations also subject soft
youths to rough hazing and initiations in order to toughen them
up for a career of soldiering, as in the U.S. Marines (Raphael
1988). But these trials are by no means confined to militaristic
cultures or castes. Let us take another African example.

Among the relatively peaceful !Kung Bushmen of southwest
Africa (Thomas 1959; Lee 1979), manhood is also a prize to be
grasped through a test. Accurately calling themselves "The

Harmless People" (Thomas 1959), these nonviolent Bushmen have never fought a war in their lives. They have no military weapons, and they frown upon physical violence (which, however, sometimes does occur). Yet even here, in a culture that treasures gentleness and cooperation above all things, the boys must earn the right to be called men by a test of skill and endurance. They must single-handedly track and kill a sizable adult antelope, an act that requires courage and hardiness. Only after their first kill of such a buck are they considered fully men and permitted to marry.

Other examples of stressed manhood among gentle people can be found in the New World, in aboriginal North America. Among the nonviolent Fox tribe of Iowa, for example, "being a man" does not come easily (Gearing 1970:51). Based on stringent standards of accomplishment in tribal affairs and economic pursuits, real manhood is said to be "the Big Impossible," an exclusive status that only the nimble few can achieve (ibid.:51–52). Another American Indian example is the Tewa people of New Mexico, also known as the Pueblo Indians. These placid farmers, who are known today for their serene culture, gave up all warfare in the last century. Yet they subject their boys to a severe hazing before they can be accounted men. Between the ages of twelve and fifteen, the Tewa boys are taken away from their homes, purified by ritual means, and then whipped mercilessly by the Kachina spirits (their fathers in disguise). Each boy is stripped naked and lashed on the back four times with a crude yucca whip that draws blood and leaves permanent scars. The adolescents are expected to bear up impassively under the beating to show their fortitude. The Tewa say that this rite makes their boys into men, that otherwise manhood is doubtful. After the boys' ordeal, the Kachina spirits tell them, "You are now a man. . . . You are made a man" (Hill 1982:220). Although Tewa girls have their own (nonviolent) initiations, there is no parallel belief that girls have to be *made* women, no "big impossible" for them; for the Tewa and the Fox, as for the other people above, womanhood develops naturally, needing no cultural intervention, its predestined arrival at menarche commemorated rather than forced by ritual (ibid.:209–10).

Nor are such demanding efforts at proving oneself a man confined to primitive peoples or those on the margins of civilization. In urban Latin America, for example, as described by Oscar Lewis (1961:38), a man must prove his manhood every day by standing up to challenges and insults, even though he goes to his death "smiling." As well as being tough and brave, ready to defend his family's honor at the drop of a hat, the urban Mexican, like the Amhara man, must also perform adequately in sex and father many children. Such macho exploits are also common among many of the peasant and pastoral peoples who reside in the cradle of the ancient Mediterranean civilizations. In the Balkans, for instance, the category of "real men" is clearly defined. A real man is one who drinks heavily, spends money freely, fights bravely, and raises a large family (Simic 1969, 1983). In this way he shows an "indomitable virility" that distinguishes him from effeminate counterfeits (Denich 1974:250). In eastern Morocco, true men are distinguished from effete men on the basis of physical prowess and heroic acts of both feuding and sexual potency; their manly deeds are memorialized in verses sung before admiring crowds at festivals, making manhood a kind of communal celebration (Marcus 1987:50). Likewise, for the Bedouin of Egypt's Western Desert, "real men" are contrasted with despicable weaklings who are "no men." Real Bedouin men are bold and courageous, afraid of nothing. Such men assert their will at any cost and stand up to any challenge; their main attributes are "assertiveness and the quality of potency" (Abu-Lughod 1986:88–89). Across the sea, in Christian Crete, men in village coffee shops proudly sing paeans to their own virility, their self-promotion having been characterized as the "poetics of manhood" by Michael Herzfeld (1985a:15). These Cretans must demonstrate their "manly selfhood" by stealing sheep, procreating large families, and besting other men in games of chance and skill (ibid.).

Examples of this pressured manhood with its almost tal-

ismanic qualities could be given almost indefinitely and in all
kinds of contexts. Among most of the peoples that anthropologists are familiar with, true manhood is a precious and elusive
status beyond mere maleness, a hortatory image that men and
boys aspire to and that their culture demands of them as a measure of belonging. Although this stressed or embattled quality
varies in intensity, becoming highly marked in southern Spain,
Morocco, Egypt, and some other Mediterranean-area traditions,
true manhood in other cultures frequently shows an inner insecurity that needs dramatic proof. Its vindication is doubtful,
resting on rigid codes of decisive action in many spheres of life:
as husband, father, lover, provider, warrior. A restricted status,
there are always men who fail the test. These are the negative
examples, the effete men, the men-who-are-no-men, held up
scornfully to inspire conformity to the glorious ideal.

Perhaps these stagy routes to manhood seem bizarre to us at
first glance. But none of them should surprise most Anglophone
readers, for we too have our manly traditions, both in our popular culture and in literary genres. Although we may choose less
flamboyant modes of expression than the Amhara or Trukese,
we too have regarded manhood as an artificial state, a challenge
to be overcome, a prize to be won by fierce struggle: if not "the
big impossible," then certainly doubtful.

For example, let us take a people and a social stratum far
removed from those above: the gentry of modern England.
There, young boys were traditionally subjected to similar trials
on the road to their majority. They were torn at a tender age
from mother and home, as in East Africa or in New Guinea, and
sent away in age sets to distant testing grounds that sorely took
their measure. These were the public boarding schools, where a
cruel "trial by ordeal," including physical violence and terrorization by elder males, provided a passage to a "social state of
manhood" that their parents thought could be achieved in no
other way (Chandos 1984:172). Supposedly, this harsh training
prepared young Oxbridge aristocrats for the self-reliance and
fortitude needed to run the British Empire and thereby man-

ufactured "a serviceable elite as stylized as Samurai" (ibid.:346). Even here, in Victorian England, a culture not given over to showy excess, manhood was an artificial product coaxed by austere training and testing.

Similar ideas motivated educators on both sides of the Atlantic, for example, the founders of the Boy Scouts. Their chartered purpose, as they put it in their pamphlets and manuals, was to "make big men of little boys" by fostering "an independent manhood," as though this were not to be expected from nature alone (cited by Hantover 1978:189). This obsessive moral masculinization in the English-speaking countries went beyond mere mortals of the day to Christ himself, who was portrayed in turn-of-the-century tracts as "the supremely manly man," athletic and aggressive when necessary, no "Prince of Peace-at-any-price" (Conant 1915:117). The English publicist Thomas Hughes dilated rhapsodically about the manliness of Christ (1879), while his colleagues strove to depict Christianity as the "muscular" or "manly" faith. Pious and articulate English Protestants loudly proclaimed their muscular religion as an antidote to what Charles Kingsley derided as the "fastidious maundering, die-away effeminacy" of the High Anglican Church (cited in Gay 1982:532). Boys, faiths, and gods had to be made masculine; otherwise there was doubt. The same theme runs through much British literature of the time, most notably in Kipling, as for example in the following lines from the poem "If":

> If you can fill the unforgiving minute
> With sixty seconds worth of distance run,
> Yours is the Earth, and everything that's in it,
> And—which is more—you'll be a Man, my son!

Consequent only to great deeds, being a Kiplingesque Man is more than owning the Earth, a truly imperial masculinity consonant with empire building. The same theme of "iffy" heroism runs through many aspects of popular middle-class American culture today. Take, for example, the consistent strain in U.S.

literature of masculine *Bildungsroman*—the ascension to the exalted status of manhood under the tutelage of knowledgeable elders, with the fear of failure always lurking menacingly in the background. This theme is most strongly exemplified by Ernest Hemingway, of course, notably in the Nick Adams stories, but it is also found in the work of such contemporaries as William Faulkner and John Dos Passos, and in such Hemingway epigones as Studs Terkel, Norman Mailer, James Dickey, Frederick Exley, and—the new generation—Robert Stone, Jim Harrison, and Tom McGuane. This "virility school" in American letters (Schwenger 1984:13), was sired by Papa Hemingway (if one discounts Jack London) and nurtured thereafter by his acolytes, but it is now in its third or fourth generation and going strong (for a feminist view see Fetterly 1978).

In contemporary literary America, too, manhood is often a mythic confabulation, a Holy Grail, to be seized by long and arduous testing. Take, for example, this paradigmatic statement by Norman Mailer (1968:25): "Nobody was born a man; you earned manhood provided you were good enough, bold enough." As well as echoing his spiritual forebears, both British and American, Mailer articulates here the unwritten sentiments of the Trukese, the Amhara, the Bushmen, and countless other peoples who have little else in common except this same obsessive "quest for male validation" (Raphael 1988:67). Although some of us may smile at Mailer for being so histrionic and sophomoric about it, he nevertheless touches a raw nerve that pulsates through many cultures as well as our own. Nor is Mailer's challenge representative of only a certain age or stratum of American society. As the poet Leonard Kriegel (1979:14) says in his reflective book about American manhood, "In every age, not just our own, manhood was something that had to be won."

Looking back, for instance, one is reminded of the cultural values of the antebellum American South. Southerners, whatever their class, placed great stress on a volatile manly honor as a defining feature of the southern character, a fighting principle.

Indeed, Bertram Wyatt-Brown, in his book *Southern Honor* (1982), has argued convincingly that this touchy notion was a major element behind southern secessionism and thus an important and underrated political factor in U.S. history. A defense of southern "manliness" was in fact offered by Confederate writers of the time, including the South Carolina firebrand Charles C. Jones, as one justification for regional defiance, political separation, and, finally, war (cited in McPherson 1988:41). And of course similar ideals are enshrined in the frontier folklore of the American West, past and present, as exemplified in endless cowboy epics.

This heroic image of an achieved manhood is being questioned in America by feminists and by so-called liberated men themselves (Pleck 1981; Brod 1987). But for decades, it has been widely legitimized in U.S. cultural settings ranging from Italian-American gangster culture to Hollywood Westerns, private-eye tales, the current Rambo imagoes, and children's He-Man dolls and games; it is therefore deeply ingrained in the American male psyche. As the anthropologist Robert LeVine (1979:312) says, it is an organization of cultural principles that function together as a "guiding myth within the confines of our culture." But given the similarities between contemporary American notions of manliness and those of the many cultures discussed above, can we drop LeVine's qualifying phrase about "the confines of our culture"? Can we speak instead of an archetype or "deep structure" of masculinity, as Andrew Tolson (1977:56) puts it? And if so, what explains all these similarities? Why the trials and the testing and the seemingly gratuitous agonies of man-playing? Why is so much indoctrination and motivation needed in all these cultures to make real men? What is there about "official" manliness that requires such effort, such challenge, and such investment? And why should manhood be so desirable a state and at the same time be conferred so grudgingly in so many societies? These are some of the questions I want to consider here. Only a broadly comparative approach can begin to answer them.

MANHOOD AND GENDER ROLE

Let us pause at this point to take stock. What do we know so far about the origins of such gender imagery? Until very recently, studies of male and female were wedded to a persistent paradigm derived from mechanistic nineteenth-century antecedents. Most pervasive was the idea of generic types, a Universal Man counterpoised to a Universal Woman—a sexual symmetry supposedly derived from self-evident dualisms in biology and psychology (Katchadourian 1979:20). Freud, for example, held that anatomy was destiny, and Jung (1926) went so far as to develop universal principles of masculinity and femininity which he conveyed as "animus" and "anima," irreducible cores of sexual identity. Western literature and philosophy are full of such fundamental and supposedly immutable dualisms (Bakan 1966); they are also found in some Asian cosmologies, for example, the Chinese Yin and Yang, and in countless sets of binary oppositions both philosophical and scientific (e.g., Ortner 1974). What could be a neater polarity than sex? Our view of manhood in the past was often a simple reflection of these polar views of male and female "natures" or "principles." This view had some scientific support among biologists and psychologists, many of whom held that the aggressiveness of masculinity, including the testing and proving, was merely a consequence of male anatomy and hormones: men seek challenges because they are naturally aggressive. That is simply the way they are; women are the opposite. Period.

The way we look at sex roles, however, has changed drastically in the past two decades. Although appealing to many, sex dualisms and oppositions are definitely out of fashion, and so are sexual universals and biological determinisms. Part of the reason, aside from the recent movement away from static structural dualisms in the social sciences generally, lies in the feminist revolution of the past twenty years. Starting in the 1960s, the feminist attack on the bipolar mode of sexual thinking has shaken this dualistic edifice to its roots; but to be fair, it was never very sturdy to begin with. For example, both Freud and Jung accepted an inherent mixture of masculinity and femininity within each human psyche. Although he distinguished male and female principles, Jung to his credit admitted the existence of animus and anima to degrees in all people; bisexuality was in fact one of the bedrocks of Freud's psychological reasoning. In every human being, Freud (1905:220) remarks, "pure masculinity or femininity is not to be found either in a psychological or a biological sense. Every individual on the contrary displays a mixture."

Moreover, feminists of various backgrounds and persuasions (see, for example, Baker 1980; Sanday 1981; Otten 1985) have convincingly demonstrated that the conventional bipolar model based on biology is invalid and that sex (biological inheritance) and gender (cultural norms) are distinct categories that may have a relationship but not an isomorphic identity. Most observers would agree that hormones and anatomy do have an effect on our behavior. The biological anthropologist Melvin Konner has convincingly shown this in his book, *The Tangled Wing* (1982). Assessing the latest scientific and clinical literature in this highly acclaimed survey, Konner concludes that testosterone (the main male sex hormone) predisposes males to a slightly higher level of aggressivity than females (see also Archer and Lloyd 1985:138–39). But, as Konner freely admits, biology does not determine all of our behavior, or even very much of it, and cultures do indeed vary to some degree in assigning sex roles, measured in jobs and tasks. Discrete concepts of masculinity and femininity, based on secondary sex characteristics, exist in virtually all societies, but they are not always constructed and interfaced in the same way. Gender is a symbolic category. As such, it has strong moral overtones, and therefore is ascriptive and culturally relative—potentially changeful. On the other hand, sex is rooted in anatomy and is therefore fairly constant (Stoller 1968). It is now generally accepted, even among the most traditional male researchers, that masculine and feminine principles are not inherent polarities but an "overlapping continuum" (Biller and Borstelmann 1967:255), or, as Spence and Helmreich put it (1979:4), "orthogonal dimensions."

Still, as we have seen from the examples above, there exists a recurrent cultural tendency to distinguish and to polarize gender roles. Instead of allowing free play in sex roles and gender ideals, most societies tend to exaggerate biological potentials by clearly differentiating sex roles and by defining the proper behavior of men and women as opposite or complementary. Even where so-called "third sexes" exist, as for example the Plains Indian berdache and the Omani xanith, conventional male and female types are still strongly differentiated. So the question of continuities in gender imaging must go beyond genetic endowment to encompass cultural norms and moral scripts. If there are archetypes in the male image (as there are in femininity), they must be largely culturally constructed as symbolic systems, not simply as products of anatomy, because anatomy determines very little in those contexts where the moral imagination comes into play. The answer to the manhood puzzle must lie in culture; we must try to understand why culture uses or exaggerates biological potentials in specific ways.

PREVIOUS INTERPRETATIONS

Some feminists and other relativists have perceived the apparent contradiction between the theoretical arbitrariness of gender concepts and the empirical convergence of sex roles. Explanations have therefore been offered to account for it. The existing explanations are interesting and useful, and I do not argue against them on the grounds of logical consistency. Rather, I think that the wrong questions have been asked in this inquiry. Most explanations have been phrased in one of two ways, both ideologically satisfying depending upon one's point of view, but neither getting us very far analytically.

First, the question has been phrased by the more doctrinaire Marxists and some radical feminists in an idiom of pure conflict theory. They see gender ideology as having a purely exploitative function. Thus they ask, inevitably, cui bono? Since many male ideologies include an element of gender oppressiveness, or at least hierarchy (in the view of liberated Western intellectuals), some of these radicals regard masculine ideologies as masks or justifications for the oppression of women. They see male ideologies as mystifications of power relationships, as examples of false consciousness (see, for example, Ortner 1981; Godelier 1986). This explanation is probably true for some cases, at least as a partial explanation, especially in some extreme patriarchies where male dominance is very pronounced. But it cannot be true as a universal explanation, because it cannot account for instances in which males are tested for manhood but where there is relative sexual equality. We have seen one example of this in the African Bushmen (Thomas 1959; Lee 1979; Shostak 1981). Although these nonsexist foragers are often held up by feminists as a model of sexual egalitarianism (Shostak 1981), Bushmen boys must prove their manhood by hunting prowess. They must also undergo tests of hardiness and skill from which girls are excluded (see chapter 5). Their manhood is subject to proof and, conceptually, to diminishment or loss. The same is true of the Fox and the Tewa of North America. So if a conception of manhood has no oppressive function in these societies, what is it doing there? It seems that the conflict theorists are missing something.

The second idiom of explanation is equally reductionistic. Here, biological or psychological processes are given analytical priority. There are two forms of biopsychological reductionist argument. The first is biological/evolutionary à la Lionel Tiger in *Men in Groups* (1971). Tiger holds that men worry about manhood because evolutionary pressures have predisposed them to do so. Once we were all hunters, and our success and therefore the survival and expansion of the group depended upon our developing genetically determined "masculine tendencies," aggression and male bonding being principal among them. This sociobiological argument is useful in certain cases, again, most notably in the violent patriarchies. But it is demonstrably false as a universal explanation because there are many societies where "aggressive" hunting never played an important role, where men do not bond for economic purposes, where violence and war are devalued or unknown, and yet where men are today concerned about demonstrating manhood. Further, this argument commits the historical fallacy of proposing a historical explanation for a cultural trait that persists under changed circumstances.

The second genetic reductionism is the standard psychoanalytic one about male psychic development. It is based squarely on an orthodox reading of Freud's Oedipus complex and its derivative, castration anxiety. This orthodoxy has been challenged recently with a neo-Freudian viewpoint stressing other aspects of male development, which I find much more powerful and to which I will return later. The standard psychoanalytic view holds that men everywhere are defending against castration fears as a result of identical oedipal traumas in psychosexual development. Masculinity cults and ideals are compensations erected universally against such fears (Stephens 1967; Kline 1972).

In this view, the norms of masculinity are projected outward from the individual psyche onto the screen of culture; public culture is individual fantasy life writ large. I think this explanation is useful in some cases but supererogatory. More damaging, it fails to give proper weight to social constraints that enforce male conformity to manhood ideals; as we shall see, boys have to be encouraged—sometimes actually forced—by social sanctions to undertake efforts toward a culturally defined manhood, which by themselves they might not do. So the explanation cannot be one based solely on psychic projections. Moreover, the orthodox psychoanalytic view can also be demonstrated to be false at a universal level, for there are empirical exceptions to the culture of manhood. There are a few societies that do not place the usual stress on achieving a masculine image; in these exceptional "neuter" societies, males are freed from the need to prove themselves and are allowed a basically androgynous script, which, significantly, they find congenial. As these exceptions do exist (see chapter 9), the answer to the masculinity puzzle must have a social side to it, because formal variation cannot be explained on the basis of a psychological constant such as castration anxiety.

SOME HELP FROM THE POST-FREUDIANS

At this point we have to call upon some alternative models of male psychosexual development that accommodate social and relational factors. A psychological theory of masculinity that I find useful and that I will refer to in the following chapters derives in part from recent work by the post-Freudian ego psychologists. The list of relevant theorists and their works is long but may be reduced here to Erik Erikson, Ralph Greenson, Edith Jacobson, Margaret Mahler, Gregory Rochlin, Robert Stoller, and D. W. Winnicott.

The basic idea here concerns the special problems attached to the origin of masculinity as a category of self-identity distinct from femininity. The theory begins with the assumption that all infants, male and female, establish a primary identity, as well as a social bond, with the nurturing parent, the mother. This theory already departs from the classic Freudian assumption that the boy child has from the first a male identity and a natural heterosexual relationship with his mother that culminates in the oedipal conflict, that the boy's identity as male is axiomatic and unconflicted. This new theory goes on to posit an early and prolonged unity or psychic merging with the mother that Freud (1914) discussed under "primary narcissism," a period when the infant fails to distinguish between self and mother. The argument is that the physical separation of child and mother at birth does not bring with it a psychological separation of equivalent severity or finality.

As the child grows, it reaches the critical threshold that Mahler (1975) has called separation-individuation. At this juncture its growing awareness of psychic separateness from the mother combines with increased physical mobility and a motoric exercise of independent action, for example, walking, speaking, manipulating toys. These independent actions are rewarded socially both by parents and by other members of the group who want to see the child grow up (Erikson 1950). Boys and girls alike go through these same trial stages of separation, self-motivation, encouragement and reward, and proto-personhood; and both become receptive to social demands for gender-appropriate behavior. However, according to this theory, the boy child encounters special problems in the crucible of the separation-individuation stage that impede further progression toward independent selfhood.

The special liability for boys is the different fate of the primal psychic unity with the mother. The self-awareness of being a separate individual carries with it a parallel sense of a gender identity—being either a man or a woman, boy or girl. In most societies, each individual must choose one or the other unequivocally in order, also, to be a separate and autonomous person recognizable as such by peers and thus to earn acceptance. The special problem the boy faces at this point is in overcoming the previous sense of unity with the mother in order to achieve an independent identity defined by his culture as masculine—an effort functionally equivalent not only to psychic separation but also to creating an autonomous public persona. The girl does not experience this problem as acutely, according to this theory, because her femininity is reinforced by her original symbiotic unity with her mother, by the identification with her that precedes self-identity and that culminates with her own motherhood (Chodorow 1978). In most societies, the little boy's sense of self as independent must include a sense of the self as different from his mother, as separate from her both in ego-identity and in social role. Thus for the boy the task of separation and individuation carries an added burden and peril. Robert Stoller (1974:358) has stated this problem succinctly:

> While it is true the boy's first love object is heterosexual [the mother], he must perform a great deed to make this so: he must first separate his identity from hers. Thus the whole process of becoming mas-

culine is at risk in the little boy from the day of birth on; his still-to-be-created masculinity is endangered by the primary, profound, primeval oneness with mother, a blissful experience that serves, buried but active in the core of one's identity, as a focus which, throughout life, can attract one to regress back to that primitive oneness. That is the threat latent in masculinity.

To become a separate person the boy must perform a great deed. He must pass a test; he must break the chain to his mother. He must renounce his bond to her and seek his own way in the world. His masculinity thus represents his separation from his mother and his entry into a new and independent social status recognized as distinct and opposite from hers. In this view the main threat to the boy's growth is not only, or even primarily, castration anxiety. The principal danger to the boy is not a unidimensional fear of the punishing father but a more ambivalent fantasy-fear about the mother. The ineradicable fantasy is to return to the primal maternal symbiosis. The inseparable fear is that restoring the oneness with the mother will overwhelm one's independent selfhood.

Recently, armed with these new ideas, some neo-Freudians have begun to focus more specifically on the puzzle of masculine role modeling cults. They have been less concerned with the questions of gender identity and castration anxiety than with the related questions of regression and its relation to social role. In a recent symposium on the subject, the psychoanalyst Gerald Fogel (1986:10) argues that the boy's dilemma goes "beyond castration anxiety" to a conflicted effort to give up the anaclitic unity with the mother, which robs him of his independence. In the same symposium, another psychoanalyst (Cooper 1986:128) refers to the comforting sense of omnipotence that this symbiotic unity with the mother affords. This sense of omnipotence, of narcissistic completeness, sensed and retained in fantasy as a blissful experience of oneness with the mother, he argues, is what draws the boy back so powerfully toward childhood and away from the challenge of an autonomous manhood. In this view, the struggle for masculinity is a battle against these regressive wishes and fantasies, a hard-fought renunciation of the longings for the prelapsarian idyll of childhood.

From this perspective, then, the manhood equation is a "revolt against boyishness" (Schafer 1986:100). The struggle is specifically "against regression" (ibid.). This revisionist theory provides us with a psychological key to the puzzle of manhood norms and ideals. Obviously, castration fear is also important from an individual point of view. But manhood ideologies are not only intrapsychic; they are also collective representations that are institutionalized as guiding images in most societies. To understand the meaning of manhood from a sociological point of view, to appreciate its social rather than individual functions and causes, regression is the more important variable to consider. The reason for this is that, in aggregate, regression poses a more serious threat to society as a whole. As we shall see, regression is unacceptable not only to the individual but also to his society as a functioning mechanism, because most societies demand renunciation of escapist wishes in favor of a participating, contributing adulthood. Castration anxiety, though something that all men may also need to resolve, poses no such aggregate threat to social continuity. In sum, manhood imagery can be interpreted from this post-Freudian perspective as a defense against the eternal child within, against puerility, against what is sometimes called the Peter Pan complex (Hallman 1969). We will return to this argument at various times in this book.

Let us now begin our quest by looking at some examples of manhood imagery. Our first stop is the cradle of Western civilizations, the Mediterranean Basin, specifically Spain. There the road to manhood is a hard one that all men must travel whether they like it or not.

❄ ❄ ❄ ❄ ❄ 2

Performative Excellence: Circum-Mediterranean

In Glendiot idiom, there is less focus on "being a good man" than on "being *good at* being a man"—a stance that stresses *performative excellence,* the ability to foreground manhood by means of deeds that strikingly "speak for themselves."
—Michael Herzfeld, *The Poetics of Manhood*

The lands of the Mediterranean Basin have for centuries been in close contact through trade, intermarriage, intellectual and cultural exchange, mutual colonization, and the pursuit of common regional interests (Braudel 1972; Peristiany 1965; Davis 1977). The use of terms such as *Mediterranean* or *Circum-Mediterranean* (Pitt-Rivers 1963; Giovannini 1987) to categorize these lands is not meant to imply a "culture area" as that term has been used in American ecological anthropology—for Mediterranean societies are as diverse and varied as anywhere else in the world—but rather to serve as a concept of heuristic convenience in ethnographic analysis and comparison (Pitt-Rivers 1977:viii). Although not representing a unity in the sense of cultural homogeneity (Herzfeld 1980), many Mediterranean societies place importance on "certain institutions" (Pitt-Rivers 1977:ix) that invite comparison. Aside from obvious resemblances in ecology, settlement patterns, and economic adaptations, what seems to provide a basis of comparison more than anything else is, in fact, a shared image of manhood. In his magisterial survey, *People of the Mediterranean,* John Davis (1977:22) writes,

> Many observers assert the unity of the Mediterranean on various grounds, some of them more plausible than others. At a straightforward, noncausal level, anthropologists, tourists, even Mediterranean people themselves notice some common cultural features: attitudes, elements of culture that are recognizably similar in a large proportion of Mediterranean societies, and that are readily intelligible to other Mediterranean people. "I also have a moustache," is the phrase happily recorded by J. G. Peristiany. . . . In an emblematic way, it serves to denote not only manliness, which is so common a concern around the Mediterranean, but also a style of anthropological argument.

This invocation of the mustache, of course, is shorthand for saying I am a man, too, the equal of any, so afford me the respect of the hirsute sex. By appealing to this common denominator, the statement is both a warning and an evocation of the fiercely egalitarian (and competitive) values shared by many otherwise diverse peoples of the region.

In the Mediterranean area, most men are deeply committed to an image of manliness because it is part of their personal honor or reputation. But this image not only brings respect to the bearer; it also brings security to his family, lineage, or village, as these groups, sharing a collective identity, reflect the man's reputation and are protected by it. Because of its competitive, sexually aggressive aspects, Mediterranean male imagery has been perceived, at least in some of the Latin countries, as self-serving, disruptive, and isolating, a matter of "personal vice" and a "social evil" (Pitt-Rivers 1961:118). This is part of a distancing stereotype shared by many northern visitors who for their own reasons assume the south to be "different" (Herzfeld 1987). But this overlooks the very important and often constructive group implications of the male image as it exists in many

Mediterranean societies and which, as we shall see later, is not so different in effect from masculine imagery elsewhere. I want to explore the implications of these male ideals in this chapter as the first step in our quest for the meaning of manhood.

We begin our discussion of masculine imagery in the Mediterranean societies by taking a negative example. This is the man who is not "good at being a man," in Michael Herzfeld's felicitous phrase above. What does he lack? Let me start by describing such a case from my own fieldwork in the Andalusian pueblo of Fuenmayor (a pseudonym). Although the following discussion is geared to southern Spain and to other areas in the northern littoral of the Mediterranean, much of what I say here relates to parts of the Islamic Middle East as well.

LORENZO

Like many other men in the Mediterranean area with whom they share the common sensibilities alluded to by Davis, the Andalusians of Spain's deep south are dedicated to proving their manliness publicly. Even more than other Iberians, they are fervent followers of what the Spanish critic Enrique Tierno Galván (1961:74–76) has called a quasi-religious Hispanic "faith in manhood." If you measure up in this regard, you are "very much a man" (*muy hombre*), "very virile" (*muy macho*), or "lots of man" (*mucho hombre*). If not, you are *flojo,* a weak and pathetic impostor. The polysemous term *flojo* literally means empty, lazy, or flaccid; it is used also to describe a dead battery, a flat tire, or some other hopeless tool that does not work. It connotes flabby inadequacy, uselessness, or inefficiency.

Our example, Lorenzo, was a callow fellow in his late twenties, a perennial student and bachelor. A gentle character of outstanding native intelligence, Lorenzo was the only person from Fuenmayor ever to have attended graduate school to pursue a doctorate, in this case in classic Castilian literature. But he was unable for various reasons ever to complete his dissertation, so he remained in a kind of occupational limbo, unable to find suitable work, indecisive and feckless. Because of his erudition, unusual in such backwater towns, Lorenzo was generally acknowledged as a sort of locally grown genius. Many people had high hopes for him. But the more traditionally minded people in town were not among his admirers. They found him reprehensible for their own curmudgeonly reasons, for in the important matter of gender appropriateness, Lorenzo was considered highly eccentric, even deviant. "A grave case," one townsman put it.

People pointed first to his living arrangements. Oddly, even perversely, Lorenzo stayed indoors with his widowed mother, studying, reading books, contemplating things, rarely leaving his cramped scholar's cloister. He had no discernible job, and as he earned no money, he contributed nothing concrete to his family's impoverished larder, a fact that made him appear parasitic to many. He lived off his uncomplaining old mother, herself hardworking but poor. Withdrawn and secretive, Lorenzo made no visible efforts to change this state of affairs; nor did he often, as other men are wont to do, enter the masculine world of the bars to drink with cronies, palaver, debate, or engage in the usual convivial banter. When he did, he drank little. Rarely did he enter into the aggressively competitive card games or the drunken bluster that men enjoy and expect from their fellows.

Perhaps most bizarre, Lorenzo avoided young women, claiming not to have time for romance. Along with his other faults, Lorenzo was actually intensely shy with girls. This is a very unusual dereliction indeed, one that is always greeted with real dismay by both men and women in Spain. Sexual shyness is more than a casual flaw in an Andalusian youth; it is a serious, even tragic inadequacy. The entire village bemoans shyness as a personal calamity and collective disgrace. People said that Lorenzo was afraid of girls, afraid to try his luck, afraid to gamble in the game of love. They believe that a real man must break down the wall of female resistance that separates the sexes; otherwise, God forbid, he will never marry and will sire no heirs. If that happens, everyone suffers, for children are God's gift to family, village, and nation.

Being a sensitive soul, Lorenzo was quite aware of the demands made upon him by importuning kith and kin. He felt the pressure to go out and run after women. He knew he was supposed to target a likely wife, get a paying job, and start a family. A cultural rebel by default or disinclination, he felt himself to be a man of modern, "European" sensibilities. Above all, he wanted to remain beyond that "stupid rigmarole" of traditional southern expectations, as he called it. He was clearly an agnostic in regards to Tierno Galván's Spanish faith in manhood.

One evening, after we had spent a pleasant hour talking about such things as the place of Cervantes in world literature, he looked up at me with his great, sad brown eyes, and confessed his cultural transgressions. He began by confiding his anxieties about the aggressive courting that is a man's presumed function. "I know you have to throw yourself violently at women," he said glumly, "but I prefer not to," adding, "It's just not me." Taking up his book , he shook his head and cast his mournful eyes to the ground with a shrug, awaiting a comforting word from a sympathetic and, he believed, enlightened foreigner. It was obvious he was pathologically afraid of rejection.

Because he was a decent and honest man, Lorenzo had his small circle of friends in the town. Like Lorenzo, they were all educated people. Given to introspective brooding, he was the subject of much concern among them. They feared he would never marry, bachelorhood being accounted the most lamentable fate outside of blatant homosexuality, which is truly disgusting to them. With the best intentions in mind, these people often took me aside to ask me if I did not think it was sad that Lorenzo was so withdrawn, and what should be done about him? Finally, one perceptive friend, discussing Lorenzo's case at length as we often did, summed up the problem in an unforgettable phrase that caused me to ponder. He expressed admiration for Lorenzo's brains, but he noted his friend's debilitating unhappiness, his social estrangement; he told me in all seriousness and as a matter obviously much considered that Lorenzo's problem was his failure "as a man." I asked him what he meant by this, and he explained that, although Lorenzo had pursued knowledge with a modicum of success, he had "forgotten" how to be a man, and this forgetting was the cause of his troubles. This friend laid the blame for Lorenzo's alienation squarely on a characterological defect of role-playing, a kind of stage fright. Shaking his head sadly, he uttered an aphoristic diagnosis: "Como hombre, no sirve" (literally, as a man he just doesn't serve, or work). He added, "Pobrecito, no sirve pa' na'" (poor guy, he's totally useless).

Spoken by a concerned friend in a tone of commiseration rather than reproach, this phrase, "no sirve," has much meaning. Loosely translated, it means that as a man Lorenzo fails muster in some practical way, the Spanish verb *servir* meaning to get things done, to work in the sense of proficiency or serviceability. There is a sense of the measurable quantity here—visible results. But what are these practical accomplishments of Andalusian manliness? Let me digress briefly in order to place Lorenzo and his apostasy from Tierno's "faith" in the broader context of the Circum-Mediterranean area by offering some comparisons from across the sea.

MANLY SERVICES

Lorenzo's friends made a connection between manhood and some code of effective or "serviceable" behavior. This echoes Chandos's (1984:346) description of the British public-school elite, the English locution connoting utility being both etymologically and conceptually cognate to the Spanish *sirve*. But more than simply serving, this behavior in Lorenzo's community had to be public, on the community stage, as it were. A man's effectiveness is measured as others see him in action, where they can evaluate his performance. This conflation of masculinity and efficaciousness into a theatrical image of performing finds powerful echoes in other Mediterranean lands. Let us take, for example, Greece. Luckily we have excellent data for that country, thanks to the untiring efforts of Michael Herzfeld. There, too, the manly man is one who performs, as Herzfeld has it, center stage. His role-playing is manifested in "foregrounded" deeds, in actions that are seen by everyone and therefore have the potential to be judged collectively. As Herzfeld says of the Greeks he studied, the excellent man, the admired man, is not necessarily a "good" man in some abstract moral sense. Rather he is *good at being a man*. This means not only adequate performance within set patterns (the male script); it also means publicity, being on view and having the courage to expose oneself to risk. In addition, it means decisive action that works or serves a purpose, action that meets tests and solves real problems consensually perceived as important.

A subtle and perceptive fieldworker, Herzfeld (1985a) describes for the village of Glendi in Crete—an island of Mediterranean cultural synthesis—the archetype of social acceptance that is most relevant to the present case. To be a man in Crete and Andalusia means a pragmatic, agential modality, an involvement in the public arena of acts and deeds and visible, concrete accomplishments. This showy modality has nothing to do with the security or domestic pleasures of the home or with introspection. These things are associated with self-doubt, hesitancy, withdrawal into the wings, that is, with passivity. It is here that Lorenzo, back in Spain, has been deficient. He is, above all else, a recessive man, staying demurely at home, avoiding life's challenges and opportunities. Manhood at both ends of the sea seems to imply a nexus of gregarious engagement, a male praxis endlessly conjoined on the stage of community life.

If we go back in time we find some intriguing echoes. The ancient Greeks also admired an outgoing, risk-taking manliness of effective action. They also judged a man not for being good but for whether or not he was useful in the role he played on the communal stage—an "efficient or defective working part of the communal mechanism" (Dover 1978:108). Their agonistic view of life is the ethos that informs the restless heroism of the Homeric sagas with a call to dramatic, even grandiose, gestures (Gouldner 1965). But this image is also associated with ideals of manly virtue that the ancient Greeks, like some of their modern descendants, held and still hold dear in it vulgar manifestation as *filotimo,* masculine pride or self-esteem (Herzfeld 1980:342–45). The Spaniards or Italians might call this right to pride by some cognate of "honor," *honra* or *onore,* or perhaps respect. It conveys a self-image deeply involved with the endless search for worldly success and fame, for approbation and admiration in the judgmental eyes of others. This emphasis on the dramatic gesture appears early in Greek culture. It shows up in Homer, in the *Iliad* most visibly: in Achilles' willingness to trade a long, uneventful life for a brief one filled with honor and glory, and in Agamemnon's willingness to trade several months of his life for an honorable death on the battlefield at Troy (Slater 1968:35).

This quest for fame and for the glorious deed as a measure of masculine virtue took on a life of its own in the ancient eastern Mediterranean world. Indeed, in the flourishing Athens of the fifth century B.C., male life seems to have been an unremitting struggle for personal aggrandizement—for "fame and honor, or for such goals as could lead to these (wealth, power, and so forth)" (ibid.:38). Despite the Greek emphasis on moderation that we cherish today, this obsessive glory-seeking grew more and more a part of Greek masculine ideals, to the point where the chronicler Thucydides was motivated to chastise his countrymen: "Reckless audacity came to be considered the courage of a loyal ally; prudent hesitation specious cowardice; moderation was held to be a cloak for unmanliness" (1951, iii:82). One mythological model of this manly man covered in glory, the embodiment of this Greek ideal, is the intrepid and wily traveller Odysseus.

The *Odyssey* is a parable of this kind of dramatized manliness uniting practical effect and moral vision. Its hero sets forth, engaging in countless struggles, surviving through physical strength and clever stratagems fair and foul. After innumerable encounters with the dangers and monsters of the world, he returns triumphantly in the final act to succor wife and kin, the ultimate heroic Greek male. Odysseus is no saint; he is portrayed as a trickster and manipulator. But his tricks "work." They have the desired end: the rescue of the endangered wife left at home, Penelope, and the restoration of the family's honor, threatened by the opportunistic suitors. The Homeric epic captures in legend the thrust of this peripatetic, pragmatic, and serviceable Mediterranean manhood.

From a psychological point of view, it is clear that this ancient morality of man-acting has something to do with the cultural encoding of impulse sublimation. An inspirational model of right action, it directs energies away from self-absorption and introspection toward a strategy of practical problem-solving and worldly concerns. The manly image in ancient Greece as well as in modern Andalusia is an inducement toward ceaseless enterprise judged by measurable ends. In an important sense, it is more than simply the sublimation of libido and aggression into culturally-approved channels of practical achievement; it is also the encouragement to resist their opposites: indolence, self-doubt, squeamishness, hesitancy, the impulse to withdraw or surrender, the "sleepiness" of quietude (symbolized in Greek legend by death by drowning—a universal metaphor for returning to the womb). As well as a commitment to commanding action in an agonistic context, an aggressive stance in service to proximate goals—what Gouldner has called the Greek contest system—manliness in much of the Mediterranean world can be called a social agoraphilia, a love for the sunlit public places, for crowds, for the proscenium of life. Such open contexts are associated not only with exposure and sociability but also with risk and opportunity, with the possibility of the grand exploit and the conspicuous deed. We can thus describe Lorenzo's first failure as a man as a refusal to sally forth into the fray.

A NORTHERN PARALLEL

This phototropic manly adventurism is not confined to the Mediterranean cultures by any means. In the north of Europe, too, didactic tales pitting risk-taking against withdrawal abound, attesting to a widespread European archetype. There is a very telling parallel, for example, in the story of the knight Tannhäuser as borrowed by Wagner from the sixteenth-century *Volkslied von Tannhäuser* by Jobst Gutknecht. In the old German legend, the hero, in a moment of moral weakness, has been granted his heart's desire to live with Venus in her fabulous mountain, the Venusberg. His every desire is immediately fulfilled by the voluptuous goddess and her attendants, the Naiads and Sirens. But he is alone and estranged and has grown weary of this barren subterranean paradise. Wagner's version begins in a gloomy cave, where Tannhäuser is engaged in a violent internal struggle. Should he remain a happy but passive captive, his needs instantly gratified by the goddess and her minions, or should he renounce all this and return to the sunlit world of conflict and danger? After much hesitation, the hero renounces the decadent pleasures of the engulfing Venus, who would deprive him of his chance at battling the world. "I must return to the world of men. I stand prepared for battle," he sings, "even for death and nothingness" (I, i). Tannhäuser's achievement in abandoning the goddess, like Odysseus's triumph over the Sirens, is a means of moral regeneration through the acceptance of existential struggle. The knight has mastered the most primitive of the demands of the pleasure principle—the temptation to drown in the arms of an omnipotent woman, to withdraw into a puerile cocoon of pleasure and safety. As in the *Odyssey,* the scene of the great decision is one in which water imagery abounds: murky grottos, dim pools, misty waterfalls.

German culture, too, at least in its prewar manifestations, had its "real man" traditions, ideals of manly courage deriving from martial Prussian prototypes. In fact, "masculinism" is deeply ingrained in the Teutonic ideal, and not only its militaristic or Wagnerian manifestations, as Klaus Theweleit has shown in his book on Weimar culture, *Male Fantasies* (1987:55).

SEX AND MARRIAGE

It is, of course, a commonplace version of this kind of mighty inner struggle against self-withdrawal that Lorenzo had become embroiled in and that he seemed to be losing in Spain. But there is more at stake here than a show of self-mastery and competitive fitness. There is also sex; or rather, an aggressive role in courtship. Lorenzo's friends bemoaned his failure to go out and capture a wife. "As a man he does not serve" refers explicitly to wife-capture and phallic predation.

In some Muslim areas, for example, rural Turkey (Bates 1974) and the southern Balkans (Lockwood 1974), this predation often takes the form of actual bride theft or prenuptial rape, often involving kidnapping or violence. Such things used to occur also in parts of southern Italy, where some men first raped and then married reluctant brides. Wife-by-capture is still common in parts of rural Greece (Herzfeld 1985b). This assertive courting, minus the violence, is an important, even essential requirement of manhood in Spain as well. It is a recurrent aspect of the male image in many parts of southern Europe, whereas it seems less critical in the northern countries.

Most of what we know about Mediterranean ideas of manhood, in fact, concerns their more expressive components—more precisely, their sexual assertiveness (Pitt-Rivers 1977): the *machismo* of Spain and the *maschio* of Sicily (Giovannini 1987) are examples. There is also the *rajula* (virility) complex of Morocco (Geertz 1979:364), which has been likened specifically to Hispanic *machismo* by a female anthropologist (Mernissi 1975:4–5). There are parallels in the Balkans, which anthropological observers Simic (1969, 1983) and Denich (1974), male and female scholars respectively, independently identify with the *machismo* of Hispanic culture. A real man in these countries is forceful in courtship as well as a fearless man of action. Both sex and economic enterprise are competitive and risky, because they place a man against his fellows in the quest for the most prized resource of all—women. Defeat and humiliation are always possible.

In Sicily, for instance, masculine honor is always bound up with aggression and potency. A real man in Sicily is "a man with big testicles" (Blok 1981:432–33); his potency is firmly established. Among the Sarakatsani of Greece, also, an adult male must be "well endowed with testicles" (J. K. Campbell 1964:269), quick to arousal, insatiable in the act. Such beliefs also hold true for much of Spain, especially the south (Pitt-Rivers 1965, 1977; Brandes 1980, 1981; Mitchell 1988), where a real man is said to have much *cojones,* or balls. Such big-balled men, naturally, tower over and dominate their less well-endowed and more phlegmatic fellows.

Yet there is more to this than competitive lechery (which, incidentally, is not as highly regarded in the Muslim countries, for in Islam unbridled lust is held to be socially disruptive and immoral for both sexes [Bates and Rassam 1983:215]). This extra dimension is important for a deeper understanding of the social matrix of Circum-Mediterranean ideas of manhood that I mentioned above. Even in those parts of southern Europe where the Don Juan model of sexual assertiveness is highly valued, a man's assigned task is not just to make endless conquests but to spread his seed. Beyond mere promiscuity, the ultimate test is that of competence in reproduction, that is, impregnating one's wife. For example, in Italy, "only a wife's pregnancy could sustain her husband's masculinity" (Bell 1979:105). Most importantly, therefore, the Mediterranean emphasis on manliness means results; it means procreating offspring (preferably boys). At the level of community endorsement, it is legitimate reproductive success, more than simply erotic acrobatics—a critical fact often overlooked by experts on Mediterranean honor who stress its disruptive or competitive elements (Pitt-Rivers 1977:11). Simply stated, it means creating a large and vigorous family. Promiscuous adventurism represents a prior (youthful) testing ground to a more serious (adult) purpose. Sexuality and economic self-sufficiency work in parallel ways.

In southern Spain, for example, people will heap scorn upon a married man without children, no matter how sexually active he may have been prior to marriage. What counts is results, not the preliminaries. Although both husband and wife suffer in prestige, the blame of barrenness is placed squarely on him, not his wife, for it is always the man who is expected to initiate (and accomplish) things. "Is he a man?" the people sneer. Scurrilous gossip circulates about his physiological defects. He is said to be incompetent, a sexual bungler, a clown. His mother-in-law becomes outraged. His loins are useless, she says, "no sirven," they don't work. Solutions are sought in both medical and magical means. People say that he has failed in his husbandly duty. In being sexually ineffectual, he has failed at being a man.

BEYOND SEX: PROVISIONING

Aside from potency, men must seek to provision dependents by contributing mightily to the family patrimony. This, too, is measured by the efficiency quotient, by results (Davis 1977:77). What counts, again, is performance in the work role, measured in sacrifice or service to family needs. What has to be emphasized here is the sense of social sacrifice that this masculine work-duty entails. The worker in the fields often despises manual labor of any sort, because it rarely benefits him personally. For example, the rural Andalusians say that work is a "curse" (D. Gilmore 1980:55), because it can never make a man rich. For the poor man, working means contracting under humiliating conditions for a day-wage, battling with his fellows for fleeting opportunities in the work place, and laboring in the fields picking cotton and weeding sunflowers from dawn to dusk. Synonymous with suffering, work is something that most men will freely admit they hate and would avoid if they could.

Yet for the worker, the peasant, or any man who must earn his bread, work is also a responsibility—never questioned—of feeding dependents. And here, as in matters of sex and fatherly duty, the worker's reputation as a citizen and a man is closely bound up with clearly defined service to family. A man who shirks these obligations renounces his claim to both respectability and manhood; he becomes a despised less-than-man, a wastrel, a *gamberro*. The latter term means an irresponsible reprobate who acts like a carefree child or who lives parasitically off women. Although it is true that women in Andalusia are often wage-earners too, the husband, to be a real man, must contribute the lion's share of income to support wife and family like a pillar and to keep the feminine machine of domestic production running smoothly. A man works hard, sometimes desperately, because, as they say, *se obliga,* you are bound to your family, not because you like it. In this sense, Spanish men are, as Brandes notes (1980:210), like men everywhere, actively pursuing the breadwinning role as a measure of their manhood. The only difference is that they rarely get pleasure or personal satisfaction from the miserable work available to them.

In southern Italy, much the same attitude is found. John Davis (1973:94–95) writes of the town of Pisticci: "Work is also justified in terms of the family of the man who works: 'If it were not for my family, I'd not be wearing myself out' (*non mi sacrifico*). The ability of a husband to support his wife and children is as important a component of his honour as his control of his wife's sexuality. Independence of others, in this context, thus implies both his economic and sexual honour. . . . Work, then, is not regarded as having any intrinsic rewards. Men work to produce food and some cash for their families."

This sacrifice in the service of family, this contribution to household and kin, is, in fact, what Mediterranean notions of honor are all about. Honor is about being good *at being a man,* which means building up and buttressing the family or kindred—the basic building blocks of society—no matter what the personal cost: "[Mediterranean] honor as ideology helps shore up the identity of a group (a family or a lineage) and commit to it the loyalties of otherwise doubtful members. Honor defines the group's social boundaries, contributing to its defense against the claims of equivalent competing groups" (Schneider 1971:17).

The emphasis on male honor as a domestic duty is wide-spread in the Mediterranean. In his seminal survey of the literature, John Davis, like Jane Schneider in the quote above, finds confirmation for his view of masculine honor as deriving from work and economic industry as much as from sexual success: "It should be said at the outset that honour is not primarily to do with sexual intercourse . . . but with performance of roles and is related to economic resources because feeding a family, looking after women, maintaining a following, can be done more easily when the family is not poor" (1977:77).

Sometimes this kind of economic service can be quantified in terms of money or other objects of value, or it can be expressed in material accumulations that are passed on to women and children, such as dowries. For example, Ernestine Friedl (1962), writing about a Greek peasant village in contemporary Boeotia, describes the honor of fathers as grounded in their ability to provide large dowries in cash and valuables to their daughters. This success assures them of the best in-laws, contributes to family prestige, and consequently enhances their image as provider. Manhood is measured at least partly in money, a man's only direct way of nourishing children. Manhood, then, as call to action, can be interpreted as a kind of moral compunction to provision kith and kin.

MAN-THE-PROTECTOR

After impregnating and provisioning comes bravery. Being a man in Andalusia, for example, is also based on what the people call *hombría*. Technically this simply means manliness, but it differs from the expressly virile or economic performances described above. Rather, hombría is physical and moral courage. Having no specific behavioral correlatives, it forms an intransitive component: it means standing up for yourself as an independent and proud actor, holding your own when challenged.

Spaniards also call this *dignidad* (dignity). It is not based on threatening people or on violence, for Andalusians despise bullies and deplore physical roughness, which to them is mere buffoonery. Generalized as to context, hombría means a courageous and stoic demeanor in the face of any threat; most important, it means defending one's honor and that of one's family. It shows not aggressiveness in a physical sense but an unshakable loyalty to social group that signals the ultimate deterrent to challenge. The restraint on violence is always based on the capacity for violence, so that reputation is vital here.

As a form of masculine self-control and courage, hombría is shown multitudinously. For example, in Fuenmayor, a group of young men may wander down to the municipal cemetery late at night after a few drinks to display their disdain for ghosts. They take with them a hammer and a nail or spike. Posturing drunkenly together, they pound the nail into the cemetery's stucco wall. Challenging all manner of goblins and ghouls, they recite in unison the following formula to the rhythm of the hammer blows:

Aquí hinco clavo	I here drive a spike
del tio monero	before goblin or sprite
venga quién venga,	and whatever appear,
aquí lo espero!	I remain without fear!

The last man to run away wins the laurels as the bravest, the most manly. Sometimes adolescents will challenge each other to spend a night in the cemetery in a manner of competitive testing, but otherwise hombría is nonconfrontational, as the defiance is displaced onto a supernatural (nonsocial) adversary. Nevertheless, as the above example shows, it is competitive and, like virility and economic performance, needs proof in visible symbols and accomplishments. Hombría judges a man's fitness to defend his family. Pitt-Rivers (1961:89) has depicted it best: "The quintessence of manliness is fearlessness, readiness to defend one's own pride and that of one's family." Beyond this, hombría also has a specifically political connotation that enlarges its role in Spain.

For the past century, Spain, and Andalusia in particular, has been a land of political struggle. Class consciousness is strong as a result of deep antagonism between landowners and laborers (Martinez-Alier 1971). Hombría among the embattled workers and peasants has taken on a strongly political coloration from this class opposition: loyalty to social class. Among peasants and workers, manliness is expressed not only by loyalty to kindred but also by loyalty to the laboring class and by an active participation in the struggle for workers' rights. For example, workers are very manly who uphold laborers' rights by refusing to back down in labor disputes. This was an especially courageous act under the Franco dictatorship but is still admired today among the committed. Charismatic labor leaders—especially those jailed and beaten by the Franco police, as was Marcelino Camacho, the head of the underground Workers' Commissions—are highly admired as being very virile. In their group they are men with "lots of balls," envied by men, attractive to women. In the eyes of their political enemies they may be hated, but they are also respected and feared.

A concrete example: there was in Fuenmayor the famous case of the militant agitator nicknamed "Robustiano" (the Robust One), so called for his athletic build and his formidable courage. After the Civil War, when his left-leaning family was decimated by the Nationalists in the postwar persecutions, he had openly defied the Franco police by continuing his revolutionary activities. Beatings, threats, and blackballing had no effect. After each return from jail he took up the struggle anew, winning admiration from all sides, including his jailers. Despite torture, he never betrayed his comrades, always taking police abuse stoically as a matter of course. Robustiano developed a huge and loyal following; today he is remembered as one of the martyrs who kept up the workers' spirits during the dark days of the dictatorship. Beyond this, people remember Robustiano as a real man, an apotheosis of the Andalusian ideal of manhood.

Apart from politics, this call to dramatic action in defense of one's comrades finds echoes throughout the Mediterranean region where social class is less important than other primordial ties, as among patrilineal peoples of the African littoral. For example, among the Kabyles of Algeria, according to Bourdieu (1965, 1979a), the main attribute of the real man is that he stands up to other men and fiercely defends his agnates. "All informants give as the essential characteristic of the man of honour the fact that he *faces* others," Bourdieu remarks (1979a:128). A real man suffers no slights to self or, more importantly, to family or lineage. Nearby, in eastern Morocco, true men are those who stand ever ready to defend their families against outside threats; they "unite in defense of their livelihoods and collective identity" (Marcus 1987:50).

Likewise, among the Sarakatsani shepherds of modern-day Greece (J. K. Campbell 1964:269–70), the true man is described as *varvatos*, clearly cognate to the Italian *barbato*, bearded or hairy. Aside from indicating strength and virility (the facial hair again), this also "describes a certain ruthless ability in any form of endeavour" in defense of his kindred. Virile Sarakatsani shepherds are those who meet the demands of pastoral life in which "'reputation' is impossible without strength" (ibid.:317). In this way the Sarakatsani man gains the respect of competitors and fends off threats to his domain. Thus he maintains his kindred's delicate position in a tough environment. "The reputation for manliness of the men of the family is a deterrent against external outrage" (ibid.:271). Campbell sees this stress on manliness in essentially functional terms. "Here again," he writes (ibid.:270), "we see the '*efficient*' aspect of manliness" (emphasis added).

Man-the-protector is everywhere encountered in the Mediterranean area. Throughout, bureaucratic protections are weakly developed, states are unstable, feuding is endemic, and political alignments, like patronage, are shifting and unreliable. Because of the capriciousness of fortunes and the scarcity of resources, a man ekes out a living and sustains his family through toughness and maneuvering. For example, in Sicily, *"un vero uomo"* (a real man) is defined by "strength, power, and cunning necessary to protect his women" (Giovannini 1987:68). At the same time, of course, the successfully protective man in Sicily or Andalusia garners praise through courageous feats and gains renown for himself as an individual. This inseparable functional linkage of personal and group benefit is one of the most ancient moral notions found in the Mediterranean civilizations. One finds it already in ancient seafaring Greece in the voyager Odysseus. His very name, from *odyne* (the ability to cause pain and the readiness to do so), implies a willingness to expose oneself to conflict, risk, and trouble and to strive against overwhelming odds in order to achieve great exploits. "To be Odysseus, then, is to adopt the attitude of the hunter of dangerous game: to deliberately expose one's self, but thereafter to take every advantage that the exposed position admits; the immediate purpose is injury, but the ultimate purpose is recognition and the sense of a great exploit" (Dimrock 1967:57).

But Odysseus's ultimate goal is not simply one vainglorious exploit after another. All his wayfaring heroism is directed at a higher purpose: to rescue wife and child and to disperse the sinister suitors who threaten them both. The real man gains renown by standing between his family and destruction, absorbing the blows of fate with equanimity. Mediterranean manhood is the reward given to the man who is an efficient protector of the web of primordial ties, the guardian of his society's moral and material integuments.

AUTONOMOUS WAYFARERS

The ideals of manliness found in these places in the Mediterranean seem to have three moral imperatives: first, impregnating one's wife; second, provisioning dependents; third, protecting the family. These criteria demand assertiveness and resolve. All must be performed relentlessly in the loyal service of the "collective identities" of the self.

One other element needs mention. The above depend upon something deeper: a mobility of action, a personal autonomy. A man can do nothing if his hands are tied. If he is going to hunt dangerous game and, like Odysseus, save his family, he needs absolute freedom of movement. Equally important as sex and economic resourcefulness is the underlying appeal to independent action as the starting point of manly self-identity. To enter upon the road to manhood, a man must travel light and be free to improvise and to respond, unencumbered, to challenge. He must have a moral captaincy. In southern Spain, as reported by Brandes (1980:210), dependency for an Andalusian peasant is not just shameful; it is also a negation of his manly image. Personal autonomy is the goal for each and every man; without it, his defensive posture collapses. His strategic mobility is lost, exposing his family to ruin. This theme, too, has political implications in Spain.

An example comes from George Collier's account of the Spanish Civil War in an Andalusian village. Collier (1987:90) points out the role played by masculine pride in the labor movements of workers and peasants in western Andalusia. He describes the critical political connotations of what he calls the "cultural terms in which Andalusians relate autonomy to masculine honor" and the virtues attached to asserting this masculinity (ibid.:96). Collier's discussion of the violent conflicts between landowners and laborers during the Second Republic (1931–36) in the pueblo of Los Olivos (Huelva Province) shows that a driving force behind their confrontations was this issue of personal autonomy. The peasants and workers were defending not only their political rights but also their self-image as men from the domineering tactics of the rich and powerful. Autonomy permitted them to defend their family's honor. Encumbered or dependent, they could not perform their manly heroics. Their revolutionism, as Collier brilliantly shows, was as much a product of a manhood image as their political and economic demands. This was particularly true of southern Spain, but Collier sees this mixture of political ideology and masculine self-image as something more widely Mediterranean:

> Villagers in Los Olivos held to the ideal of masculine autonomy characteristic of property relations and the system of honor in the agrarian societies of the Mediterranean. . . . The prepotent male discouraged challenges by continually reasserting this masculinity and potential for physical aggression while he guarded against assaults on the virtue of his women and stood up to others to protect his family's honor. . . . The ideal of masculine autonomy thus charged employer-employee relations with special tension. In having to accept someone else's orders, the employee implicitly acknowledged his lack of full autonomy and his vulnerability to potential dishonor. (Ibid.:96–97)

To be dependent upon another man is bad enough, but to acknowledge dependence upon a woman is worse. The reason, of course, is that this inverts the normal order of family ties, which in turn destroys the formal basis for manhood. For instance, in Morocco, as reported by Hildred Geertz (1979:369), the major values of *rajula,* or manly pride, are "personal autonomy and force," which imply dominating and provisioning rather than being dominated and provisioned by women. There is in deed no greater fear among men than the loss of this personal autonomy to a dominant woman.

In Morocco there is in fact a recurrent anxiety that a man will fall under the magical spell of a powerful woman, a demonic seductress who will entrap him forever, as Venus entrapped Tannhaüser, or as Circe attempted to enslave Odysseus, causing him to forget his masculine role (Dwyer 1978). The psychological anthropologist Vincent Crapanzano has written an entire book about a Moroccan man who lived in terror of such a demonic female *jinn.* He tells us that this anxiety is widespread: "This theme of enslavement by a woman—the inverse of the articulated standards of male-female relations, of sex and marriage—pervades Moroccan folklore" (1980:102). There, as in Spain, a man must gain full and total independence from women as a necessary criterion of manhood. How can he provide for dependents and protect them when he himself is dependent like a child? This inversion of sex roles, because it turns wife into mother, subverts both the man and the family unit, sending both down to corruption and defeat.

SEXUAL SEGREGATION

Many of these themes—activity versus passivity, extroversion versus introversion, autonomy versus dependence—are expressed in the physical context of Mediterranean rural community life. The requirement that the male separate conclusively from women could be no more clearly expressed than in the prohibitions against domesticity that pervade the ethnographic literature. In many Mediterranean societies (D. Gilmore 1982:194–96), the worlds of men and women are strictly demarcated. Male and female realms are, as Duvignaud says of Tunisia, "two separate worlds that pass without touching" (1977:16). Men are forced by this moral convention of spatial segregation to leave home during the day and to venture forth into the risky world outside. Like Lorenzo, a man hiding in the shadows of home during the daytime is immediately suspect. His masculinity is out of place and thus questionable. A real man must be out-of-doors among men, facing others, staring them down. In Cyprus, for example, a man who lingers at home with wife and children will have his manhood questioned: "What sort of man is he? He prefers hanging about the house with women" (Loizos 1975:92). And among the Algerian Kabyle described by Bourdieu (1979b:141), his fellows will malign a homebody for much the same reason: "A man who spends too much time at home in the daytime is suspect or ridiculous: he is 'a house man,' who 'broods at home like a hen at roost.' A self-respecting man must offer himself to be seen, constantly put himself in the gaze of others, confront them, face up to them (*qabel*). He is a man among men." So we can see the manly image working to catapult men out of the refuge of the house into the cockpit of enterprise.

ANOTHER ECCENTRIC

To conclude, I will describe another negative case from Andalusia that illustrates these last points. There was a man in
Fuenmayor who was a notorious homebody and whose family
suffered the consequences. Alfredo was a rubicund little merchant with the non-Castilian surname Tissot (his ancestors had
emigrated from Catalonia generations earlier). A sedentary man
of middle age, he operated a small grocery establishment from
out of his home—nothing unusual for men with small retail
businesses. But Alfredo was unusual in that he rarely ventured
out from his home, where he lived with his wife and two pretty
grown daughters.

In Andalusia, as in Cyprus or Algeria, a man is expected to
spend his free time outdoors, backslapping and glad-handing.
This world is the street, the bar, the fields—public places where
a man is seen. He must not give the impression of being under
the spell of the home, a clinger to wife or mother. While out,
men are also expected to become involved in standard masculine
rivalries: games of cards and dominoes, competitive drinking
and spending, and contests of braggadocio and song. Although
aware of such expectations, Alfredo resisted them, because, as
he confided to me one day, such socializing was a waste of time
and money—you have to spend money in the bars; you have to
buy rounds of drinks for the company of fellows, and you have
to tipple and make merry. You have to boast and puff yourself
up before your cronies. All this conviviality was expensive and
boring, so the chubby grocer stayed at home with his family. He
read books and watched television at night or went over his
accounts.

Like all other townsmen, Alfredo was under the scrutiny of
public opinion and was accountable as a man. Although grudgingly admitting his modest business acumen (said however to be
based on his wife's capital), the townspeople did not accept his
lame excuses for inappropriate comportment. As a descendant
of distrusted ethnic outsiders (Catalans are known as a race of

workaholics and misers), he was expected to display strange attitudes, but his refusal to enter the public world of men in favor of home was greeted with outrage and indignation. Especially vilified was his stinginess with both time and money, which was felt as an insult to the other men of the pueblo, a calculated withdrawal from the male role, which demands not just familiar provisioning but a certain degree of generosity in the wider society. A man of means is expected to spend freely and thus to support his community. People say such a man owes something to the town. Alfredo's withdrawal damaged both his own prestige and that of his family, which suffered equally in the public spotlight.

One hot afternoon, as I was walking past the Tissot house with a group of friends, my companions made passing comments on Alfredo's strangeness. "What kind of man is he," they muttered, pointing at his sealed and cloistered house, "spending his time at home?" Glowering ominously, they likened him to a mother hen. They offered colorful explanations for his contemptible secretiveness, alluding to certain despicable character traits such as cheapness and egoism. But beyond these picayune moral defects, my informants found something truly repulsive in the merchant's domesticity, furtiveness, and sedentariness. They suggested a basic failure at a deeper level in the most important thing of all: man-acting. Carrying this character assassination further, my informants left the realm of observable fact and ventured into gossipy speculation, which is common in such matters of serious deviance. Unequivocal explanations are deemed necessary when deeply-felt customs are violated.

The men then told me their suspicions about Alfredo. In the telling I could feel a palpable relaxation of their anxiety about him, for they had reduced the deviance to root causes that they could scapegoat and consensually reject in a way that corroborated their own self-image. It all boiled down to Alfredo's failure as a man. This was shown incontrovertibly, as in the case of Lorenzo, by his shadowy introversion. As a consequence of his withdrawn uxoriousness, in the minds of his fellows, the Tissot household, bereft of sexual respectability, was held necessarily to be abnormal in terms of sexual functioning. Its very existence was, therefore, by local standards, attributable to aberrant practices. Since Alfredo was not a real man, as his community had decided, then his daughters, by logical extension, could not be the product of his own seed. The explanation that tied all together (since the eccentric Catalan was also known as a moderately wealthy man) was that he was a panderer and a pimp for his wife, and his daughters and his wealth were the result of her secret whoring. The villagers had thus conceptually, if inaccurately, reversed provider and dependent roles in this ugly and ridiculous slander. The associated success of insemination was stolen by a hostile act of imagination. Poor Alfredo was utterly incapable of combatting this malicious attack because he had cut himself off from male communication, so he and his family suffered from the slights and contempt reserved for deviants.

Hypothetically classified as unnatural, then, Alfredo's inexplicable character traits fell into a kind of preordained order of the man-who-is-no-man. For example, there was the matter of his cooking. He was known to help wife and daughters in the kitchen, cutting, chopping, and so on, performing tasks absolutely unnatural to the male physiology and musculature. Andalusians recognize that there are professional chefs, but they are men who have learned a trade to earn a living, and so they retain their claim to manhood. At home, even chefs do not cook; their wives do. But Alfredo was said to help eagerly out of his own perverted volition. "Is he a man?" people scoffed, "cooking, hanging about in the kitchen like that?" The Andalusians believe fervidly that male and female anatomy provide for different, complementary skills. It was true that Alfredo helped in the kitchen. Since he invited me into his home (in itself an act of unusual, even deviant hospitality), I saw him. He never hid this indictable bit of information from me. I came to know him fairly well on these occasions. Being a didactic and helpful sort of man in a fussy way, he instructed my wife and myself in the proper preparation of certain specialties of Spanish cuisine, providing precise, often compulsive directions for grinding ingredients to make a tasty gazpacho. I learned how to whip up a savory, if smelly, garlic soup in the gleaming Tissot kitchen. He always watched that everything was done in the proper order. For example, the bread always went in the pot after you added the vinegar: no improvising here. Beaming maternally, the homebody took pride in his knowledge of local recipes and in my vocal appreciation of his culinary skills.

But his fellows in the streets laughed at him, scorning his hurried excuses, grimacing disgustedly when I spoke of him, holding both him and his superfluous wife in contempt. The placid pleasure Alfredo took in his own odd domesticity hastened his withdrawal from manly assemblages and activities. The introverted grocer failed to make it as a man by local standards. This failure in turn robbed his family of respectability, plunging them all into disrepute, so that, for example, his two daughters had to find fiancés in other towns. Alfredo's fatal flaw was that he failed even to present himself for the test of manhood. He failed, most decisively, to separate: his public identity was blurred by the proximity of women. He had withdrawn into a sheltered cocoon of domesticity, self-indulgently satisfied with good food and easeful luxury, unwilling or afraid to enter the risky ring of manhood. This withdrawal made the other men uncomfortable, so they conceptually emasculated him and stole his family's honor, placing them all beyond the pale and obviating the threat they represented.

And yet, Alfredo was for other men a subject of endless discussion and debate. Perhaps, despite their protestations, there was something about him that, though also repellent, attracted these tough, virile men? Or possibly he represented to them some contumacious principle—living well without visibly working, perhaps—that caused ambivalent feelings that had to be expunged through projection and denial? To explore this issue further, let us pull up stakes and move on to another place and another culture.

Looking for Manhood:
Truk Island

All men were once boys, and . . . boys are
always looking for ways to become men.
                    —James Dickey, *Deliverance*

Andalusian manhood requires an erotic and
economic competence and a willingness to
"engage," to take risks. Manhood comes
gradually, cumulatively; there are no chronological markers, except perhaps, marriage,
which signifies adulthood for both sexes. Or
at least marriage provides an opportunity,
not always seized, as in the case of Tissot.

In Spain there is no formal recognition of
manhood. There are no investment ceremonies, no visible emblems, no curtain calls.
Endorsed rather than ordained, manhood remains forever in doubt, requiring daily demonstration. One observer (Murphy 1983) has
called the boy's passage "riteless," feckless,
and amorphous—yet pressured. This ambiguity is true of many other Latin countries
and of their Muslim neighbors, too. In Morocco, for example, David Hart writes that
male puberty is socially recognized "only in a
tacit fashion"; he notes that this is "true of all
Muslim society" (1976:124). For Mediterranean peoples, with a few exceptions (see
chapter 6), achieving manhood is an indi-

vidual venture of searching and testing, textured by the web of social relations, the imagery inspirational rather than emblematic.

Letting the boy sink or swim is one way of structuring his passage. Other societies rely on various rituals that guide boys along a preordained collective highway. In this chapter we will look at one society, Truk Island,* that, like Spain, provides little or no ritual confirmation, leaving each man to find his own way. In chapter 4 we will examine another such society, the aboriginal Mehinaku of Brazil. Following this, we switch gears and study a few societies that commemorate manhood through chronological markers. By whichever method attained, manhood is a matter of storm and stress, of challenges and trials.

TRUCULENT TRUKESE

If you travel halfway around the world from the Mediterranean, you find yourself somewhere in the middle of the South Pacific. Because of the myriad tiny islands there, this part of the terraqueous globe is called Micronesia, a place of microcosms. Among these archipelagos, described sensuously by the anthropologist Mac Marshall (1979), lies the little flyspeck of Truk, a United States Trust Territory administered briefly by the United Nations after the Second World War. Truk is the stereotypical tropical paradise, its verdant landscapes now blighted somewhat by American industrial refuse, but still beautiful and fecund. As the slang phrase has it, Truk "grows on you," sometimes literally (ibid.:6).

The geologically complex atoll surrounding Truk Island is unique in the world, caused by the massive collapse of a gigantic volcanic mountain range gradually sinking into the surrounding sea over eons of time. Adding to this mountainous bulkhead is the growth of a coral reef that encircles Truk Lagoon. The dozen or so inhabited islands that rise above the quiet waters are the only physical remnants of the rim of this once-giant volcano

*"Truk Island" is used for convenience. Technically, the correct term is "Truk Island group," which includes the entire atoll.

peak. Visually inviting and colorful, Truk is a lovely natural stage for the unfolding of manhood, a drama played out with life-or-death intensity.

One of the atoll islands within this lagoon is called Moen. It encompasses just over seven square miles of land, much of it near-vertical mountainous terrain, its highest peak rising 1,214 feet above the sea's level in the lagoon. Moen Island is a district center for Truk, a hub of activity, relatively speaking, on the tiny and remote trust territory. Its population has grown considerably since the Americans took over in 1945. Just before the war, there were only 2,115 people on Moen. By 1967 this number had more than doubled, and six years later, in 1973, the population had nearly doubled again, to 9,562 (Kay 1974). Marshall provides an estimate of eleven thousand persons for the later 1970s (M. Marshall 1979:7). It appears that Moen is a thriving community relative to more outlying islands.

Once a tribal people, the Trukese are acculturated to Western ways but still maintain remnants of their aboriginal kinship system. They practice traditional matrilineal inheritance and matrilocal residence patterns, living in extended matriclans. Clanship is still of critical importance to them. As we shall see, it also plays a role in their notions of masculinity.

As a tyro in cultural anthropology, landlubber Mac Marshall went to Moen in the 1970s to study the effects of beer-drinking on the youth of Truk. Alcoholism had been identified since the early 1900s as a chronic form of social pathology among the young islanders, many of whom succumb to its pernicious effects by their early twenties. Most young men pass through a turbulent adolescent period of heavy drinking. This is, in fact, a requisite phase of the male life cycle deeply ingrained in the culture. Worse, when they drink, usually on weekends, they fight in violent mêlées, often causing serious injury with clubs and knives and the kung fu kicks that seem to have captured their imagination. Hence the title of Mac Marshall's monograph (1979) on Truk: *Weekend Warriors*. Most of these youths eventually overcome their early addiction to alcohol and violence, settling down to constructive family life. But the few who do not create a headache both for themselves and for the island administration. Interestingly, most of the older men and women of all ages eschew drink; moreover, they never fight physically, so that the police problem is confined to young men. Marshall went to Moen Island as an expert in the role of drinking in culture and as a student of alcohol abuse, wishing to isolate its causes in the broader culture, perhaps to help in its amelioration. As often happens, he left a changed but wiser man.

When Marshall left Moen in 1976, the focus of his study had shifted because he had become more aware of the role of alcohol in the overall Trukese scheme of things. After a few months on the atoll, Marshall had become an expert on Trukese concepts of masculinity. He found the people there obsessed with it, and he discovered that he was unable to study any aspect of their culture without first acquiring a passable comprehension of what it meant to be a man on Truk. Prepared at first to find causes of drink in anomie, unemployment, or any of the usual explanations, he found instead the root cause in the Trukese cult of *pwara,* the native term for manliness. Rather than an end, drinking is one stepping-stone to a male image. This pwara concept, not necessarily with its linked drinking component, has resonances in other parts of the world. In many respects, Marshall remarks (1979:56), it resembles the machismo of Spain, Latin America, and the Mediterranean lands. These haunting echoes of Hispanic culture made it, for me, the second step toward the masculinity problem.

SOME HISTORY: TRUK AND THE WORLD

Today the young Trukese are macho drinkers and brawlers, but in the past they were fierce warriors. They fought among themselves for glory and booty, and they quickly dispatched any helpless Western sailor unlucky enough to be shipwrecked on the island. Their reputation as "Dread Hogoleu," merciless killers, was known far and wide (ibid.:37). This chronic violence was, in the past, a major avenue for the establishment of a man's reputation on the island and a principal prop of his claim to manhood, which he consolidated through battlefield exploit. Although this emphasis on the brave deed set the stage for what followed, its expression has changed in these more peaceable times.

Western contact dates to 1565. In that year, the Spaniards made contact with the remote island when the ship *San Lucas* put in briefly for a quick reconnaissance. They claimed the islands for the Spanish crown, duly recorded in official archives, but they never developed their putative possession or settled there. Following this initial probe, Truk was happily ignored for 250 years, until Manuel Dublon made a brief call aboard the brig *San Antonio* in 1814; this visit had no noticeable effect on local culture. Spanish influence was therefore negligible, except on paper. The Trukese were left to their own devices until the heyday of European imperialism in the late nineteenth century. At that point, the colony-starved Germans moved in, only to be replaced later by the Japanese. By 1900, the previously innocent islanders had acquired rum and other intoxicants through sporadic contact with sailors and traders reckless enough to barter with the dread natives.

After formally annexing Truk in 1885, the Germans proved to be less laissez-faire than their absentee predecessors. In a successful effort to colonize their new possession, they stamped out native warfare with draconian police measures. They also settled in force, exploiting the atoll for its rich deposits of phosphorus and copra. During this period also, waves of Western missionaries from various countries and denominations took up the challenge of Christianizing the Trukese and stamping out harmful native practices, such as raiding, indecency, and the use of ardent spirits. This they did with degrees of success: all Trukese are either Catholic or Protestant today and are mostly modest in their sexual bearing. But the young men continue to drink to excess. After World War I, as Pacific allies of the victors, the Japanese displaced the Germans, holding on to the islands as strategic enclaves until their defeat in the next war. Shortly afterward, the Americans came in with televisions, baseball, and beer cans. As one can surmise from all this, Truk has had a spotty history of encounters with civilization.

MALE AND FEMALE LIFE CYCLES

Despite the stress on proving one's masculinity, the Trukese life cycle provides an ambiguous route to this goal, making its achievement doubtful. There is no telling early on that male and female are such important concepts in the Trukese view. Infants of either sex are considered to be more or less neuter. The Trukese language does not label sex at this stage, providing only a single generic term, *monukön,* for infant (M. Marshall 1979:84). The Trukese in fact do not distinguish sex seriously until comparatively late, about age three or four, and toddlers are not treated differently by sex to any significant degree. By the age of four, however, everything changes drastically and pressures begin to mount on both sexes for sex-appropriate conduct.

At that time, children begin to be socialized differently—a process that gradually takes on rigid dimensions. As they grow up, children play in mixed-sex groups for some time, but as they approach their teens, they begin to encounter strong sanctions for sexual segregation. More or less at the beginning of puberty, boys and girls begin the transformation into the appropriate young adult category: *anuön* for young men and *faapwin* for young women in the Trukese dialect. At this point, too, public interactions with the opposite sex become very much constrained and circumspect, as both sexes begin to drift sharply apart under parental and community pressure. The road to manhood (as well as to womanhood) begins to beckon.

As the physical separation of the sexes continues, there begins a process of thorough role differentiation in work, education, moral values, and even in the way males and females are supposed to speak and think. When they reach puberty, young boys are expected to engage in strenuous economic activities involving "strength and potential risk" (ibid.:84). These include deep-sea fishing, clambering up the tall breadfruit trees to gather the fruit, and so on. Girls and young women assist in food preparation but never participate in these subsistence pursuits, which are considered too dangerous for females. As girls learn to cook, sew, and perform other domestic chores, boys learn to fight, roaming freely over the village and countryside looking for excitement and challenges.

The same conceptual division in sexual domains that we encountered in some Mediterranean societies obtains here. Trukese women, who are said to have "weak thought," are expected to be submissive and are encouraged to avoid risks and to shun danger. This means that they have to stay close to home, in fact, indoors, most of the time. Thus while men, propelled by their "strong thought," sally forth fearlessly to conquer demons, women sit demurely at home. "Masculinity is public and assertive. Femininity is private and acquiescent" (ibid.:83).

By the time they are thirteen, male youths begin to drink alcohol, always in groups. "Real men" are supposed not only to drink, but to drink heavily. They also start to smoke tobacco—two indulgences absolutely denied to girls. As they reach their middle teens, boys begin to participate in weekend brawls and to confront danger, both from other boys and from nature, as a matter of course. It is felt that boys should begin to seek opportunities for displaying strong thought. This strong thought, also called manly thought, which we will hear about again, entails an aggressive, adventurous bravado and is shown by acts of public derring-do. It seems largely to involve seeking challenges, taking daredevil risks with life and limb, and landing effective punches. Most important in strong thought is its competitive element, the injunction to stay on or near the top of the social heap (ibid.:58). To be strong, a Trukese man must not be bested by another. In Trukese eyes, a real man must not be outdone in any activity or lack anything that someone else possesses. Strong thought expresses the pervasive egalitarian current that runs through Trukese culture. "By means of strong thought and its demonstration through acts of bravery . . . one proves oneself at least as

good as others (and ideally, just slightly better)" (ibid.:58). Thus
one avoids losing to others, losing face. Meanwhile, the girls
collaborate in these efforts at combative masculine display by
bestowing their favors on youths who prove themselves real men
by fighting and competing.

Strong thought involves an unhesitating determination to
match or outdo other males specifically where any kind of physical risk or challenge is involved. Competitive drinking is one such
risky enterprise, but it is just another part of a "larger complex of
masculine risk-taking" (ibid.:58). Other such challenging pursuits, aside from fighting, are gambling, sporting showdowns,
and competitions over material wealth. Material one-upmanship
is critical because the Trukese are very much into keeping up with
the Joneses. There is in fact a pervasive acquisitive strain in the
culture. Given the active striving on the part of so many young
men to build public images, there are bound to be winners and
losers in any such confrontation, physical or economic. When a
fight or a competition over status occurs, someone is usually
bested by his opponent and humiliated; he must then seek to
recoup his standing. Marshall (ibid.:60) explains: "When competition exists for possession of material goods that demonstrate
one's manly thought, those who cannot purchase a new car, a
motorboat, a Polaroid camera, or an expensive diving watch lose
to those who can obtain these goods. When a member of one's
lineage or district has been humiliated, beaten, or otherwise
mistreated by outsiders, the score must be evened."

Trukese male competitions therefore involve acquiring wealth
in a never-ending spiral as well as fighting and drinking. Also
worthy of note is that male bellicosity includes a strong element of
group loyalty that tends to enhance kinship solidarity and afflu-
ence in the showing. All such rivalries for consumer goods benefit
not only the individual who gains prestige but his entire lineage as
well, because the latter, as a corporate group, shares in the wealth
and status of its members. In fact, Marshall takes some care to
emphasize the collective focus of Trukese male competitions and
to place them in their historical context of traditional clan rival-

ries (ibid.:61). He compares Trukese feuding to the Hatfields and the McCoys in American folklore, noting that most interlineage and interdistrict warfare in aboriginal Truk consisted of a seesaw battle among clans—not merely individuals acting alone—to remain one-up. When the other side took the advantage, one could not rest until vengeance was had by all. This feuding mentality, combined with a constant need to vindicate personal, lineage, and district reputations, remains strong in Truk today. "A good person comes to the aid of his kinsmen, showing courage and manly thought as needs be. Traditionally and presently, one's rights are enforced mainly by the strength of support one can muster from one's relatives. Coming from a large lineage with a reputation for bravery makes it less likely that one will be trifled with by others" (ibid.:161). Marshall makes this corporate aspect of male rivalries clear through numerous case studies of violence in which the antagonists tend to square off in groups whose solidarity is determined by clan or district identifications. The battles thus follow the lines set up by "primary kinship loyalties" (ibid.:72), reinforcing primordial ties and clan boundaries. The collective focus of this feud-type conflict is of course not unique to Truk. As we have seen from the Mediterranean material and as others have noted in passing (Schneider 1971; Black-Michaud 1975; Meeker 1979; Boehm 1984), there is clearly some sort of connection between male assertiveness and the existence of segmentary lineage organization or endemic feuding between symmetrical corporate units. We will see more evidence of this when we look at East Africa and New Guinea.

What is specific to Truk is that the violence of pwara (manliness) is a passing stage confined entirely to adolescence. After marriage, at age thirty or so, the Trukese male is expected to transcend his earlier carousing and to settle down to a mature and responsible role as husband and father. The aggressiveness built into his character remains but finds other, more sober outlets: procreativity, learning, respectfulness toward elders, and career success. It is clear that pwara is a kind of basic training for a challenging, demanding male adulthood and is not an end in itself.

Finally, after pointing out the differences between the aggressive male and the reticent female in Trukese culture, Marshall summarizes these categories by means of a scheme of binary oppositions (ibid.:85):

Male	*Female*
Public	Private
Assertive	Acquiescent
Confronts danger	Shuns danger
Takes risks	Avoids risks
Right hand/strength	Left hand/weakness
Strong thought	Weak thought
Should smoke tobacco	Should not smoke tobacco
Should drink liquor	Should not drink liquor

There may be some oversimplification here, as is common in such strictly binary inventories of cultural traits. Still, by the time they are sixteen or seventeen, boys and girls have fully incorporated this basically dichotomous scheme of values as the stuff of their self-identity. Boys have learned to fight, compete, and accumulate consumer goods, girls to sew and cook. The youths have hived off from their neuter beginnings and are well along the rocky road to Trukese manhood.

BEING A MAN

There is no single line that, once passed, confers manhood. The threshold is in the eye of the beholder, a fuzzy demarcation always in need of testing. As Marshall says (ibid.:93), Trukese youths must "work hard" to avoid seeming womanly by demonstrating time and again in a public forum the purity of their strong thought. Ritual does not help them: there are no developmental sequences or ceremonies; nor are there chronological markers as there are for girls, who are officially women at menarche (ibid.:65). One moves according to one's own pace, hoping the community will notice approvingly.

Above all, what is demanded is cultural competence or effectiveness in practical everyday affairs. There are various contexts in which this male omniproficiency must be shown other than fighting, amassing consumer goods, and defending relatives. Marshall remarks that the boys must begin to develop verbal skills or strength as orators, show their learnedness by mastering the formal educational system and/or the wage employment sector of the economy, and begin to sire children and have a number of successful love affairs (ibid.:97).

Aside from being tough and brave, a real man is also expected to be respectful to his elders and to women. In fact, next to bravery, the trait of "*mosonoson* 'respectfulness' is held in highest esteem" (ibid.:57). Educational success is also important for a man. One of the attributes that Trukese seek and admire most is *tipetchem* (learnedness or intelligence). The major way of showing this trait today is to be successful in the formal educational system and subsequently to obtain a desirable government job based on one's educational skills. Marshall adds (ibid.:60), "To fail to be *tipetchem* is to be *tiperoch* 'unschooled or ignorant', a status that brings shame on oneself and one's family."

Beyond this generalized call to mastery of skills and respectfulness to older people, Trukese manhood entails other, more expressive behavioral desiderata. These have been amply described by Marshall and his predecessors on Truk Island, John Caughey (1970) and Ward Goodenough (1949). The first thing they mention is that men are supposed to protect and defend women and dependents against all dangers. Trukese men are strongly, almost obsessively, protective of their women, a fact that visitors have commented on since first contacts were made with the islands. The first foreigner to write of his impressions was the Russian traveler Frederic Lutke, who stayed in the area in 1828. During his visit he and his sailors were warned by the islanders in the most vehement terms to stay away from the women. Only once during their month's stay were they allowed to carry on a brief conversation with two girls. Lutke was at a loss to explain what he called an "extraordinary defensiveness" of the women on the part of the men (ibid.:82).

Ten years later, in 1838, when the French explorer Dumont d'Urville landed in Truk Lagoon, his sailors were baffled to find only men waiting for them in the village. Most of the females, one of the officers writes, must have been hidden away or whisked off to another island well in advance of the foreigners' coming. This extreme solicitude on the part of Trukese men for their women does not, as has been argued, necessarily imply earlier unhappy experiences with rape-minded foreign sailors, for Trukese are inclined to be protective of their females even today when such dangers no longer threaten (Hezel 1973:59).

After this protectiveness toward women comes the Trukese stress on fisticuffs and toughness. Young Trukese men feel they must battle each other to show bravery, to "vindicate manhood in physical combat" (M. Marshall 1979:97). A man who absorbs insults is not a man at all. A common instigation to combat is to insinuate, "Come, are you a man?! I will take your life now" (ibid.:92–93). A man who refuses such invitations is goaded: "Go, wear a woman's clothes" (Caughey 1970:45). What seems to matter most is not winning the fight necessarily, although that counts, but rather the readiness to engage or to respond to challenge and the show of indifference to pain. A real man cares nothing about personal injury, laughing at the sight of his own blood. In fighting, win or lose, if he acquits himself bravely in the heat of combat, a man corroborates his claim to manhood, simultaneously bolstering his group's reputation for strength. An honorable defeat is not itself a loss of face; what seems to matter most is to show a willingness to receive blows, to shed blood. Bruises and scars only add to a man's prestige and that of his lineage.

Because it gives them courage and numbs the senses, the excessive drinking is usually a preliminary to the requisite fighting. Drinking, often with abandon, is highly valued among young men in Truk as a show of ruggedness. Not to drink indicates an unwillingness to face risks, to play the game of death, "to be macho" (ibid.:91). Drinking, then, is the lubricant of the masculine pose, the facilitator or catalyst, and on a symbolic plane, it is also an important signal of intent to uphold a manly reputation, and thus a warning.

FISTICUFFS: AN EXAMPLE

At this point let us examine one of the many extended case examples of Trukese weekend brawling. The case involves a young battler from Moen Island whom Marshall calls "Napoleon" (1979:72–73), for reasons that will soon become clear. Although many Trukese men are big, and nearly all are husky and muscular, scrappy Napoleon was slight of build, short of stature, and young in years (age twenty). He, perhaps more than others, had to work to prove his manhood. The anthropologist encountered him one day when Napoleon was in a surly mood. It was a Sunday afternoon and Napoleon, already tipsy, had been swigging gin from a bottle with several others on the outskirts of the village.

Already on the verge of an outburst, Napoleon was weeping openly while his paternal aunt scolded him in front of several women and children for drinking. In the midst of this humiliating lecture, the young man, visibly shaken, rose abruptly and walked about twenty yards to where a group of sober men was seated beneath some coconut palms. Approaching this inoffensive group, Napoleon singled out the only older one among them, a man of corpulent build in his late forties who had married into the village from a distant district and who was a member of a rival clan.

> Unprovoked, Napoleon walked up to this man and struck him in the chest. Surprised but not stunned, the man did not fight back and one of the young men in the group who was related to Napoleon tried to get Napoleon to leave. . . . Fed up with this brazen attack, another young man in the group—a clan brother of the one just struck— grappled ever so briefly with Napoleon, lifted him bodily in the air,

and flung him hard to the ground where he lay moaning with the wind knocked out of him. (M. Marshall 1979:73)

After a moment's pause, Napoleon's drinking companions hurried over to intervene, helping their friend to his feet and leading him away as he screamed vengeance at those he had attacked. Violently shrugging off his comrades and filling the air with imprecations and threats, Napoleon ripped off his shirt, tore it in half, and threw it to the ground, shouting that he was going to get a knife to carve up the man who had just beaten him. Finally, as the enraged youth rushed off toward his house to fetch his promised weapon, the women who had been watching told the group of men who had been attacked to leave, which they did, thus ending the minidrama.

Marshall's account of the episode suggests that Napoleon had been goaded into an obstreperous display of violence after being scolded by an older woman, his aunt. Having suffered a public rebuke at the hands of a female, he had been made to appear childish and impotent. Humiliated, he felt obliged to recoup his masculine self-esteem by dominating a larger man from another district. He initiated a fight he knew he could not win. His opponent, sorely tested, was defended by his own clan, the battle escalating briefly into a clan confrontation. The instinctual motivation for Napoleon, as for all those involved, was not to win but to counteract the damage or supposed damage to self-image by showing bravery to a mixed audience. Simply mauling someone was good enough.

Marshall provides countless other examples of such "message" fighting. In one case (ibid.:77), a man is slashed deeply in a knife fight, and, although bleeding profusely from venous wounds, he wins plaudits among his peers by refusing medical treatment, shrugging off the pain. His self-control is rewarded by universal praise: "Others viewed this stoicism with admiration as an act of daring and bravery." Scars such as these are worn proudly by weekend warriors; they may even be self-inflicted for show as well as earned in fights. In the old days, for example, Trukese warriors used to intimidate opponents by slowly and ostentatiously cutting their own arms to show their unflinching bravery. Obviously they cared more to make an impression on enemies than to win, as wounding themselves could not have enhanced their fighting capability. One pugnacious fellow, an informant for Marshall, "has a large scar on his arm of which he is exceedingly proud" (ibid.:77). Reading all this, one cannot help thinking of the dueling scars displayed by Prussian and Austrian youths in the nineteenth and early twentieth centuries. These scars were also shown off as proofs not necessarily of victory but of bravery and self-discipline. In many other cultures, too, the battle injury or scar is the man's red badge of courage, the emblem of manhood. It shows the disdain for personal injury upon which all feats of daring rest. Victory naturally helps but is not essential. According to John Caughey, "The classic test of *pwara* is a challenge to fight. The person of *pwara* shows no fear in such a situation. He guides himself, it is said, by the following reckless disdain for self preservation. . . . 'He does not show fear of people, knives, of pain, or of death. He does not show fear of anything'" (1970:17).

As I said, these Trukese battles often break out between men of different villages, lineages, or districts. On the other hand, aggression against close kinsmen is "forbidden" and rarely occurs (M. Marshall 1979:74). In sum, such fighting vindicates not only the individual's manhood but also augments "his lineage's or district's reputation for strength vis-à-vis others" (ibid.:61). In this sense, the fighting strengthens the defensive posture of the entire group. In the same way, Prussian dueling was not mere bravado but prepared young men for an exacting military role in later life.

INTERPRETATIONS

Musing on all this Trukese truculence, Marshall arrives at a not very surprising sociohistorical interpretation: brawling on Truk is a substitute for the outlawed warfare and raiding, which were the means in the past by which Trukese youths took risks, played "the game of death," and thereby gained their manhood (1979:91). Taken on its obvious merits, this seems plausible enough. One should add to this that it is also a means of impressing the girls, who are deeply moved by the youths' violent exploits, previously in war, today in fisticuffs. After one particularly brutal encounter, for example, Marshall heard three young women discuss the fight "with excitement and admiration" (ibid.:91). Naturally, none of this feminine interest is lost on the boys, who see public fighting as a means of making conquests.

Aside from the elimination of warfare under German colonial rule, a problem facing the Trukese boys in their quest for vindication is their structural dependence on women. Because of their matrilineal kinship pattern, Trukese men have some difficulty in physically escaping female control and emotionally separating from mothers. In the distant past, they lived in men's clubs and could proudly play the role of self-directed warrior without interference. Nowadays, because of the elimination of warfare and the retention of their traditional matrilocal residence pattern, they have lost this traditional independence and find themselves beholden, like Napoleon, to older women. Commonly today the boys live with their elder sisters, aunts, and mothers before they marry, and they feel dependent upon women and surrounded by them. As exemplified by Napoleon above, fighting among themselves is obviously one way they have chosen to assert their endangered masculine pride. This leads to what Caughey (1970:5) calls the "paradoxical status" of the Trukese male. The effort to attain independence leads to a cult of flamboyant and obviously compensatory risk taking.

ECONOMIC ELEMENTS IN PWARA

The drunken weekend fighting is of course the most flamboyant sign of manliness on the island, but it is important to keep in mind its other, more sociable aspects. As we have seen, Trukese manhood comes also from competence in worldly pursuits and

is important in acquiring prestige goods as well. Because of the
scarcity of resources on the island and the highly competitive
ethos, this practical competence requires a certain measure of
moral courage. As Marshall puts it, for a Trukese man, establishing a reputation "as a competent man is a risky business in
itself in Greater Trukese Society" (1979:59). The reason is that
the avenues of economic success are severely limited, and men
must fight for what is available. As in other such resource-poor
contexts, success is not assured and must be continually sought
in struggle (ibid.:59). This identification of economic success
with risk taking is based on the material constraints of island life,
which require that men range far and wide to gain a livelihood,
often by besting others in competitive contests.

Before colonization, men fought and died to capture booty;
they also had to go on risky deep-sea fishing expeditions in
order to feed their families. Especially for outer islanders, where
voyaging and navigation were of greater importance than in
Truk Lagoon, taking part in open ocean canoe trips was a frequent means of showing the competence that conferred manhood. Men continue this heroic tradition today by setting out in
small outboard motorboats from Truk proper to such distant
islands as Nama or Losap. "These boats are much less seaworthy
than the sailing canoes, and young men often undertake such
voyages with limited fuel, a single motor, no oars or sails, and
nothing aboard but liquid refreshments . . . , risking the open
sea in a small craft . . . to show bravery. Several other risky or
dangerous endeavors occupy young Trukese men. . . . A way for
exhibiting bravery on Piis-Losap is to spearfish in the deepwater
passes and areas outside the reef where large sharks are common" (ibid.:59).

It is clear that such death-defying traditions, although theatrical like the fisticuffs, had and still have a utilitarian value in
this society. Although this correlation of act and consequence
cannot be a complete or sufficient explanation for either, the
adaptive value is certainly a necessary part of any explanation of
the daredevil tradition. Men have a high level of production

goals set for them by their culture. These involve danger necessarily, and the manhood ideology encourages acceptance of such
challenges without hesitation. If a man rejects this provider's
role, he is said to be useless and to be dependent like a woman or
like a child (Caughey 1970:69). In encouraging risk taking and
stoicism, pwara is clearly a preparation for life's severities.

SEX AND MARRIAGE

Fighting, drinking, and defying the sea are not the only measures
of manhood. A Trukese man must prove competence in another
arena: sex. This sexual element reminds Marshall of masculine
honor in some Mediterranean countries: "Out of a need to prove
themselves strong masculine figures, Trukese males strive to
conquer women sexually to show assertiveness. . . . The personal
reputation carried by every Trukese male is not unlike the concept of *honor* or *face* found in countries where *machismo* is a
dominant masculine value" (ibid.:90–91).

To maintain face in the sexual act, the Trukese man must be
the initiator, totally in command. The success of the sexual act
depends entirely upon his performance; in every love affair he
is sorely tested. Like the Andalusians and the Italians, a Trukese
man must be potent, having many lovers, bringing his partners
to orgasm time and again. Interestingly, this erotic ability is,
again, phrased in an idiom, not of love or charm, but of pure
physical competence. If he fails to satisfy her, the woman laughs
at him; he is shamed for being ineffectual. Ward Goodenough
(1949:619), a predecessor of Marshall's on Truk, has written of
this, "Intercourse is often likened to a contest in which the partner who first achieves an orgasm is said to lose to the other. The
men say that a woman may laugh at a man if he fails to satisfy
her." And, significantly, his failure to perform is rewarded by
jibes and insults that liken him to a baby because he is incapable
of performance. The standard insult for a man who performs
badly is the advice to "take the breast . . . like a baby" (Caughey
1970:95).

Like fighting and breadwinning, sexual intercourse is thus also a risky business for Trukese men, a question of winning or losing, for the man can either do the job or not, depending on how his organ "works." Moreover, in Thomas Gladwin's phrase, intercourse is a contest in which "it is only the man who can lose and not the woman" (1953:308). So the men must perform as best they can, but, as we have seen before, simple stamina is not all that matters when it comes to the sexual side of masculine efficiency. Sexual competence must lead to marriage, procreation, and ultimately the expansion of the primary group. Fathering many children, whether in or out of wedlock, is a critical sign of manly strength for Trukese men (M. Marshall 1979:91). Along these same lines, a man traditionally could demonstrate his personal power by possessing and impregnating more than one wife, although Christian teachings have now put an end to polygyny on Truk. Having more than one wife "showed that a man was of such unusual capacity that he could take on several burdensome social relationships at the same time, or, better, that he was able to turn what was customarily a subordinate relationship to another lineage into an equal or dominant one" (Caughey 1970:226).

ECHOES ABROAD

The Trukese weekend warriors, so wrapped up in proving themselves competent wherever there is risk or opportunity, resemble the Andalusians with their machismo and the Greeks with their manly selfhood. There are similar demands for success in economic pursuits, sex, and defense of dependents and social boundaries. There is a similar conjoining of personal adaptation and corporate utilities in the blueprint of a serviceable manhood. The image of the manly man is counterposed to the negative example of the child at the breast who can do nothing right.

Marshall uses Mexican machismo as his single point of comparative reference. The resemblance between pwara and Hispanic ideals of manliness is certainly striking, at least on the surface and in its sexual emphasis, but this kind of hyper-masculinity holds sway in many other societies, not just Mexico and Spain, where manhood is construed in slightly different ways. For example, the Trukese have impressed some anthropological observers as being very much like Americans as portrayed in Hollywood films, especially Westerns. One such writer (Mahoney 1974:32) has recorded his impressions of the atmosphere in the island bars as follows. Once or twice an evening, he reports, there is a moment when one senses social "electricity" flashing: during the sudden silence that follows the entrance into the bar of men from a particular village or rival island faction; when nearby voices suddenly rise loudly in argument; or when a rock crashes upon the tin roof of the restaurant and everyone present jumps to his feet, "prepared to do battle with someone, though with whom he is not quite sure."

The similarities with the Wild West hold for other parts of North America less associated with cowboy lore, for example, parts of Appalachia or northeastern urban ghettoes, both of which have their manhood codes, or even, it appears, parts of rural Canada. Noel Dyck, a Canadian sociologist, has explored the relation between masculinity and barroom brawling in a western Canadian town he calls Parklund (1980). In various bars there, men engage in a form of ritualized "scrapping" by which they demonstrate they are real men, just as on Truk. Their working assumption is that the measure of a man's masculinity and worth is his willingness and ability to "look after himself" in a fight (ibid.:194). A man has to do what a man has to do, they state, as a matter of obvious principle; and that means defending yourself when threatened or challenged. A brave scrapper is praised as a man "who can take care of himself," while a failure is ridiculed as a "chicken-shit bastard," a "mark," and a "boy" (ibid.:194). Once a man establishes his reputation as a tough guy by entering and winning a few fights, other men respect him and seek him out as a friend and a partner in work—mainly logging and other outdoor jobs that require strength and courage. The brawling, rather than being a waste of energy, is a testing ground that gains a man both prestige and opportunities; he shows to one and all that he can "take it" and fend for himself.

As on Truk, scrapping in Canada is a youthful stage of proving, superseded by a more constructive maturity. Dyck reports that most fights occur between men aged eighteen to twenty-five. After this phase most men settle down to enjoy their status as "hard men" while continuing to visit the bars to socialize and drink. In addition, marriage signals a change in a man's involvement in the scrapping. After marriage, most men either assume a nonfighter's role while drinking in the bars or else they drop out of the bar scene altogether to attend to their domestic responsibilities (ibid.:195). Dyck points out that the man's reputation is not based only on his physical prowess but also on his courage, his fairness in fighting, and his self-assurance in dealing with other men—character traits obviously favorable to survival and success in a rugged frontier environment.

This kind of barroom scrapping-cum-reputation building is probably universal in blue-collar subcultures in the industrial West, in both urban and rural settings (see Leary 1976). Rather than being unusual, therefore, the Trukese men resemble these other rugged, aggressive males who also live in challenging environments; this seems to point to a widely shared tough-guy pose that deters attack by bluff. The strategy is a belligerent one, but the fighting is only a temporary stage that may paradoxically obviate violence later on by fending off threats. This bluff quality, of course, is one of the underpinnings of machismo everywhere it is found. But machismo, seen as the willingness to respond to a challenge, and as found in Truk, Mexico, or the American West, is in my opinion only an exaggerated version of a much more widespread male defensiveness in dangerous contexts. Although the flamboyant aspects of these machismos have been played up in the literature, they are only surface features overlaying an infrastructure of serious social obligations. Beneath the posturing and the self-promotion lies a residue of practical expectations that men everywhere shoulder to some extent. The histrionic displays should not blind us to the deeper structure of a stressed manhood with similar ends: the need to establish and defend boundaries.

But now it is time to move on. The Trukese example points to interesting parallels in vastly separated parts of the world. Observations made in Truk and in the Mediterranean cultures, as well as analogs noted above in the Hollywood Western and in Canada, provide a key to further explorations into manhood by making us think comparatively and by provoking questions about the relation of individual men to the social and natural contexts. One cannot escape the impression that the Trukese men, with their concerns about a sturdy masculine image that advertises a readiness to tangle, would feel at home not only in the American West, the Canadian prairie, or some urban settings in the northeast, but also, as we shall see, in a stone-age Indian tribe in the middle of the Amazon rain forest. What is so striking is the sense of masculinity as a pose that is deeply conflicted, pressured, and forced, a mask of omnicompetence and an almost obsessive independence. Trukese pwara is worn on the outside by youths, loosely, like an ill-fitting coat. The youths experience a relentless anxiety, not that they will fail, for that is part of the testing, but that the external mask will suddenly fall away, revealing the trembling baby within.

❄ ❄ ❄ ❄ ❄ 4

Performance Anxiety: Mehinaku

Thy mother's son! Like enough and thy father's shadow. So the son of the female is the shadow of the male.
—Shakespeare, *Henry IV, Part 2*

Moving now to the New World and the Mehinaku Indians of central Brazil, we begin to glimpse the deeper psychological roots of this inspirational manhood imagery and its consequences. The author of the Mehinaku ethnographies, Thomas Gregor, is a sophisticated and gifted student of psychoanalysis as well as of cultural anthropology. As we follow his description of male identity among the Mehinaku, I digress briefly to consider his psychological theories. Such considerations will help prepare the way for more detailed discussion later of the relation between psychodynamic and cultural factors in the etiology of an omnicompetent masculinity.

Let me remark at the outset that Gregor's vision of manhood is based squarely on the Freudian orthodoxy that I discussed in chapter 1. Using standard psychoanalytic theories, Gregor develops a comprehensive theory of a "Universal Male" (1985:chap. 11). That I do not fully accept this global archetype will become apparent later on. My main hesitation is the allegation of a universal resolution to identical psychic conflicts regardless of environment. Gregor argues that "beneath the veneer of cultural differences," men everywhere experience similar endopsychically-engendered conflicts (ibid.:200). These internal contradictions give rise to continuities in expressions of manhood that "transcend cultural boundaries" (ibid.:209). This hypothetical male archetype, however, like Marshall's, is drawn from exiguous data, being ethnographically restricted to a comparison of the Mehinaku themselves and modern U.S. culture as a single point of reference. Thus, although it opens the issue and, unlike the Truk study, provides an added dimension of psychodynamics, it does not in my opinion provide sufficient comparative evidence to justify the claim of universality. However, signaling a visible start in comparative studies of manhood, Gregor's work remains among the most powerful anthropological contributions to the subject.

THE SETTING

The Mehinaku Indians are aborigines living in the remotest part of the world's greatest remaining rain forest in central Brazil. Fishing, hunting, and cultivating shifting manioc gardens with a stone-age technology, they are little affected by white culture even today. In this sense they are quite different from the oft-colonized Trukese, who have seen too much of Westerners and other would-be colonizers. Concealed by the murky backwaters of the Xingu River, a major tributary of the Amazon, the Mehinaku are surrounded by impassable streams and waterfalls that block all navigation, making their territory inaccessible to all but the most determined outsiders. Even today the nearest white Brazilian settlement, Xavantina, a frontier village itself, is almost 175 miles away to the southeast over thickly forested country. Because of this unusual geographical isolation, some of these Indians have managed to retain their aboriginal culture almost completely (Gregor 1977:13).

The distribution of Mehinaku culture is locally limited by impenetrable topographical barriers. Close by, three wild smaller rivers meet to form the treacherous Xingu. Along with their innumerable tributaries, these streams form a huge alluvial depression of about twenty-five thousand square miles, creating one of the wildest and least populated forests in the world. Living in a small, restricted zone of this wilderness, the various Xingu tribes, of which the Mehinaku are but one branch, exploit several ecological microsystems. The first is a narrow zone of fruit-bearing riverine trees; further inland are flood plains ranging in size from a few feet to several miles. Past these flood plains are miles upon miles of dense forest along whose margin, still never far from water, the Xingu peoples have cut their manioc gardens. Further still are more flood plains, swamps, and other muddy rivers, all emptying into the mighty Amazon (ibid.:13–14).

The humid environment is one of relative natural abundance, but the technological level of the Mehinaku severely limits their economic productivity. For one thing, much of the area around their settlements is unsuitable for their kind of slash-and-burn farming. Moreover, during the extended wet season, much surrounding land is inundated by river waters. Some of it is permanently under water or else too swampy to be used for gardens. Gregor (ibid.:17) estimates that nearly half the land around the Mehinaku village he studied cannot be cultivated for such reasons. In addition, the Indians are unable to use almost a third of the remaining dry land near their village because of large colonies of voracious ants (the leaf cutter, *sauva*, *A. Cephalotes*). Several attempts to plant gardens on the periphery of the village ended in disaster when these ravenous insects completely devoured the crops in bud. These problems are not everyday ones, but combined with geographical limitations inherent in primitive slash-and-burn horticulture and a stone-age technology, they have kept the Mehinaku at a bare subsistence level.

Protected for ages by their inhospitable environment, the Mehinaku were first contacted by the outside world in 1887 by the German explorer Karl von den Steinen, who had set out with a pack train of oxen and mules to explore the headwaters of the Xingu River. As Gregor describes this first intrusion of Westerners into Mehinaku society, both sides acquitted themselves rather poorly. Possibly frightened by his unexpected discovery, the German started barking incomprehensible orders, pointlessly shooting bullets into an Indian house, and finally distributing metal tools that totally nonplussed the Indians. Meanwhile the "savages," as von den Steinen referred to them, melted away in terror into the jungle, their women smearing their bodies with ashes so as to look ugly and thereby avoid being carried off as concubines by the weird white raiders. Although nonviolent themselves, the Mehinaku were familiar with the war and raiding practices of more bellicose neighboring peoples. As we shall see, their tribal motto could be "make love, not war."

After the inauspicious beginning with von den Steinen, relations with the outside world have improved somewhat in the ensuing century. Living today on a government-protected reservation, the Xingu National Park, the Mehinaku are now more accessible to outsiders, and the ethnographer Gregor lived among them for a number of years with relative ease. Through government assistance, the Mehinaku have radios linking them to the Brazilian Indian Agency in São Paulo. The Indians now use some modern steel tools, and medicines are made available to them by missionaries. Nevertheless, despite such technological "improvements," the society and the lifeways of the Mehinaku, like those of other tribes in the region, remain remarkably unchanged from the time that von den Steinen visited them in 1887. The visitor passing through their villages still senses that he or she has stepped into a stone-age society, into what Gregor (1985:11), perhaps committing an "allochronism" (Fabian 1983), calls "a distant time and place." Like other deeply held beliefs, their ideas about gender and manhood are essentially timeless, inherited with little change from their most ancient antecedents. If the acculturated Trukese display a patchwork of indigenous and imported customs, the Mehinaku, by contrast, exhibit a relatively pristine way of life.

Like the other Xingu Indians of central Brazil, the Mehinaku have a bilateral kinship pattern, practicing classificatory cross-cousin marriage and observing affinal avoidances. In their kinship patterns and their material culture and economy they are very similar to nearby tribes that also exploit the resources of the upper Xingu River. These tribes are many: the Auití, Kamaiurá, Trumaí, Kuikuru, and Kalapalo, among others (Gregor 1977:18). Like the Trukese, all these people have a strict division of labor by sex, with the men going forth beyond the village to fish and occasionally to hunt, ranging far and wide, while the women remain at "home" in crowded huts, taking care of children and doing other domestic chores. As the Mehinaku depend on river and lake fish for most of their animal protein, the men are expected to go on long fishing expeditions to distant waters, over rough and hazardous terrain, sometimes staying away for days or weeks. These trips expose the men to attack by the more warlike tribes of the vicinity, whom the Mehinaku refer to disdainfully as "wild Indians."

Like the Trukese, the Mehinaku men are very concerned about their manhood. For them, manliness is a status equivalent to the highest social virtue. As with the Greeks described by Herzfeld, a man's prestige comes not necessarily from being a good man in some abstract moral sense but from being good at being a man, from the ardency of his role playing. The Mehinaku would understand Herzfeld's statement about "foregrounding" acts of manhood without much necessary commentary. Still, there are some fascinating Mehinaku wrinkles. Before we get into these, let me repeat that, unlike the Trukese, the Mehinaku fight no wars and were never warriors. They are self-consciously a nonviolent people, regarding not only warfare but also displays of anger as morally repugnant (Gregor 1977:189). Even in their famous and beloved wrestling matches, which we will examine shortly, strict rules of decorum are observed. Their wrestling is spirited and aggressive, but there are few injuries other than minor scrapes and bruises.

Despite such serene and restrained behavior, the Mehinaku are fiercely competitive people at other levels. For one thing, they are "surprisingly acquisitive" and "very materialistic" (ibid.:118). Each man tries hard to outperform the others in fishing prowess and in accumulating property such as tools and imported consumer goods. Moreover, surprisingly, Gregor reports that theft is rampant in the village he studied. Men steal unabashedly from their neighbors and then trade the loot in other villages, or they steal food and eat it in secret. So endemic is this intravillage pilfering that a man fears to leave any item of value outdoors for more than a few minutes, lest it be gone when he returns. Perhaps, then, given this slightly paranoid and larcenous ethos, it should come as no surprise that the Mehinaku are ardent believers in witchcraft, imagining malevolent intentions all around them. Gregor notes that all men have been accused at one time or another of witchcraft and that a suspected witch may be brutally murdered by his outraged fellows. He provides one grisly example of the latter, which occurred shortly before he entered the field (ibid.:206–07). An informant, Keje, described the incident to him as follows: Keje led a band of avengers, who cornered the suspected witch. "He [the witch] tried to run, but I grabbed him from behind. The others held back. I shouted, 'Are you women? Kill him!' They clubbed him on the head with sticks and machetes until he fell down groaning. We buried him nearby." Such gruesome incidents are rare, but they reflect some of the underlying stresses and strains in Mehinaku culture and society.

MAKE LOVE, NOT WAR

Aside from forceful action, as in the above incident (egged on, significantly, by allegations of effeminacy), probably most important to the Mehinaku as a measure of maleness is sexual performance. The Mehinaku, as Gregor describes them, are unusually preoccupied by sex, the men complaining they can never get enough of it and talking about it all the time. Sexual exploits and joking are constant items of male banter. Responding to all this public highlighting of sexuality, a Mehinaku man wants to show himself an adequate lover so he can claim normalcy. Sexu-

al "function," in the ethnographer's words (1985:137), is a pass-
port to acceptance generally as a man and indeed a critical part
of the Mehinaku masculinity syndrome that defines adult male
status. Like the Trukese, a man who fails to bring his wife or
lover to orgasm, fails to satisfy his partner, fails to beget children, is ridiculed and publicly shamed, becoming not just a figure of fun but an outcast in a more inclusive sense. Everyone
learns quickly of his disgrace. "A man's sexual failures are common knowledge, and his reputation as a lover rides precariously
on the shifting currents of community gossip" (ibid.:137).

Considering all this pressure to perform, the Mehinaku are
very much concerned about sexual potency, possibly more so
than the Trukese. Because it relegates them to the trash heap of
society, impotence is a powerful focus of concern to the men and
the source of much curative magic and anxiety. The Mehinaku
men are stricken constantly by what Gregor calls "performance
anxiety" (ibid.:138), living under constant pressure to measure
up to strict standards, for they know that matters of sexual competence quickly become public knowledge in a society where
"kiss and tell" is the rule rather than the exception. As sexual
dysfunction is a critical blow to a man's reputation, the men have
developed an elaborate system of magical therapy. Gregor re-
counts numerous magical and medical cures for impotence, and
he shows in considerable detail how it haunts all adult men day
and night (ibid.:140). Some of these impotence cures involve
rubbing animal or plant materials directly on the penis; other
cures involve painful scarification of the penis and other forms
of ritual treatment. These treatments make the penis "angry" by
homeopathic magic; after being thus woken up, it performs
well.

Sexual vigor is critical but insufficient to prove manhood.
Also important to a man's image is worldly achievement. This
means accumulating goods in the form of utensils and food. The
successful man who works hard wins the sexual laurels as well,
the reason for which is simple. Men are forever trading food,
mainly fish, and other scarce commodities, such as soap, to wom-

en for sexual favors (1977:133), so there is a direct correlation between material and erotic achievement, both of which, in turn, lead to a coveted manly reputation. This kind of sex-for-lucre exchange is rampant, because Mehinaku men believe that women are by nature less interested in sex than they are and have to be seduced or lured into it. In reality this may not be true (Gregor tends to agree with his informants that men are more highly sexed than women universally), but the women's seeming coyness is also attributable to a moral double standard that constrains them in sexual matters more than men. "All men," says one typical Mehinaku man, Ketepe, "like sex. But women are different." Women are "stingy" with their vaginas, he concludes, to general male agreement (1985:33). Nevertheless, women are easily seduced by offers of meat, fruit, and Western consumer goods, all of which are in short supply in this subsistence economy. In sum, a poor man, or a bad worker who cannot produce, can make few sexual conquests in the face of female indifference or resistance, so he forfeits a spotless masculine image, thus being consigned to a low position in the prestige hierarchy. The rich man has many wives and lovers and thus much prestige; the poor man has few. Characteristically, this reminds Gregor of nothing so much as modern American society: "As in our own society, men who are socially successful are more attractive to women as sexual partners" (ibid.:36). Again, this may or may not be true in an objective sense, but it is certainly a widespread impression among both the general public and sociologists who have studied the issue (David and Brannon 1976).

WORK AND INDUSTRY

To be recognized as a he-man, the Indian must demonstrate other kinds of hyperactivity as well. A good Mehinaku man must be "vigorous, energetic, and hard working" (Gregor 1985:193). An image of industriousness, with strongly economic overtones, is very important. Appearances are critical, and at all times a man should at least look energetic. When in the men's house he should appear lively and boisterous. He should be the first one up in the morning, blowing on his fire, rousing his sleepy children from their hammocks and marching them down to the stream for their daily cold bath. While other villagers are still sleeping, the vigorous he-man has already left to clear a distant garden, to hunt game along trails miles from the village, or to fish on a hard-to-reach lake (ibid.:192).

The way that people judge a man's industry is based on a number of such criteria. More than anything else, they judge him by his willingness to go on these long and arduous fishing trips to distant lakes and streams, often over treacherous terrain, where the vicious "wild Indians" may lurk in ambush. These dangerous expeditions are viewed as a civic duty and as evidence of "good citizenship" because of the importance of fish in the protein-poor Mehinaku diet (1977:192). The connection that the Indians make between economic efficiency, civic duty, and manliness is impressed early and often upon little boys. For example, if a boy sleeps late, lounges about, or, most egregiously, refuses to accompany his father on one of these fishing expeditions, he is chastened not so much as a wastrel but as a "little girl," or a "lover of infants' games" (ibid.:276). In addition, a lazy boy is warned that when he grows up he will be undesirable to women (ibid.:276). As we have seen, this is a serious warning that implies not only sexual rejection but also a future of disgrace and social isolation. Thus manliness is inculcated as a part of a more inclusive ethic of Mehinaku social responsibility.

PHYSICAL APPEARANCE

The physical appearance of a man counts, too. As among the Trukese, a Mehinaku man should be muscular and athletic—both anatomical evidence of fitness. The ideal Mehinaku man, Gregor notes (1985:36), is physically impressive, big and tall, and moves with grace and commanding confidence. He radiates self-assurance. Tall men are indeed more successful as measured in material pursuits than short men, as Gregor's fieldnotes show; whether this comes from inner resources or from external approbation is unclear from his account. "On the average," he writes, "tall men are more likely than short men to sponsor rituals, be wealthy, have many girlfriends, and become village chiefs" (ibid.:36). After having quantified the issue by a village survey, Gregor points out that in his village the three tallest men had nearly twice as many mistresses as the three shortest men, even though their average ages were greater (1977:198). In contrast, the puny or uncoordinated man is scorned as worthless and sexually undesirable and has much less chance to realize his manhood (1985:144). The small man is called *peritsi,* an abusive term connoting ugliness that is seldom uttered without a sneer or laugh. Scorned by women and rejected by prospective parents-in-law, the puny peritsi is a feeble wrestler, an improvident fisherman, an ineffective leader. Gregor gives one example of such a contemptible figure named Ahiri that bears repeating:

> Ahiri is . . . considered a *peritsi.* The shortest man in the village, less than five feet tall and shorter than many of the women, he is . . . abused behind his back. Many of the men conduct affairs with his wife and show contemptuously little concern about hiding their indiscretions. They not only make passes at her when her husband is nearby but flirt with her in his presence. To them a very short man does not merit respect. His size is a justification for taking advantage of him; not only is it safe to abuse him and to have relations with his wife, it is also what he deserves. (1977:198)

The frequent humiliations suffered by the peritsi remind Gregor again of his own North American culture, where small or physically unprepossessing men are similarly handicapped and ill-treated. That bigness should be the measure of a man should come as no surprise to Westerners, Americans in particular. Gregor is undoubtedly right to say, "Our own prejudice against short men is built into courtship, the chances of finding a good job, and even language, where a rich vocabulary of abuse impugns the short man" (1985:36). Others have argued the case on the basis of statistical research. The sociologist Saul Feldman (1975), who expressly studied the issue in the United States, has argued that "heightism" affects our social relations, sexual patterns, employment opportunities, political success, and even our earning power. The political aspect was certainly demonstrated in the U.S. presidential campaign of 1988, when the relative height of the candidates became a major issue in the Bush-Dukakis debates! In North America, among these Amazonian Indians, and elsewhere, this size = manliness equation carries over to comparisons of the sexual organ itself. The penis must be large and impressive—another common male anxiety in many parts of the world.

GENEROSITY

Sheer size therefore gives a boost to the aspiring Mehinaku he-man but is again only a necessary, not sufficient, criterion for validating manhood. This anatomical bulk must be put to practical use in daily tasks. Aside from phallic adequacy, Mehinaku men must show muscular coordination to earn their laurels by constantly creating wealth in food and distributing it by sponsoring feasts. No matter how big and impressive he looks physically, the Mehinaku he-man is afraid of seeming inadequate in producing the goods. This fear of economic inadequacy is one that always haunts him, spurring him on to greater and greater efforts. In fact, the men have a horrendous anxiety about appearing slothful or lethargic; laziness is as bad as impotence because it is equally sterile. One of the ways they combat this ever-present fear is by frequently sponsoring tribal rituals, which require large-scale expenditures of labor and accumulated wealth in the form of food. Above all, a man must appear not only energetic and serious in the food quest but also generous and selfless with his spoils. When he returns from a long, exhausting fishing trip, he is expected to appear immediately in the village plaza, where the people are gathered expectantly. On stage in this way he ostentatiously displays his catch prior to distributing it unsparingly. The hallmark of the real man is that he is selfless: he eats with his kinsmen and friends assembled around him and always shares his food (1977:190). On the other hand, the man who is stingy with food eats alone. "He sneaks back from a fishing trip and enters the village unseen to avoid sharing his catch." The worst kind of man in Mehinaku thought is one who is lazy, stingy, greedy, evasive, and who eats more than his share (ibid.:202). Such parasitic men are despised as effeminate and ostracized as freeloaders; the people assume they are mendacious, immature, and furtive as well. Thus the improvident male unites all Mehinaku defects. Perhaps the Mehinaku make a (unconscious?) connection between the man who is stingy with food and the woman who is stingy with her vagina, in this way furthering the unmanly connotations of economic selfishness? In any case it is clear from Gregor's description that, among the Mehinaku, a real man is a giving soul, ambitious but generous, a committed team player who pulls his own weight.

WRESTLING

As is true in many societies that enjoy sports (Messner 1987), the Mehinaku have developed symbolic frames of reference in competitive games and gladiatorial contests by which a man can demonstrate his worth against his fellows. Among the Mehinaku, the main sport is wrestling. All men are expected to wrestle, to play hard, and, if possible, to win. There are matches and exhibitions every day, and challenge duels are constantly being arranged. Every man "wants to be a champion" (Gregor 1985:95). Because it symbolizes all other skills, wrestling ability is, above all, the measure of a man and a symbolic arena for self-promotion (ibid.:96). A powerful wrestler, say the villagers, is impressive, or frightening (*kowkapapai*). Likened to the powerful anaconda in the quickness of his holds and the lightning way he hobbles his opponents, he commands their fear and respect. The women say the wrestling champion is beautiful (*awitsiri*), and he is in demand as a paramour and husband. Triumphant in politics as well as in love, the champion wrestler embodies the "highest qualities of manliness" (ibid.:145). Not so respected is the loser. A poor wrestler, no matter what his other virtues may be, is regarded as a fool. As he flails about on the wrestling ground, the men shout sarcastic advice from the bench in front of the men's house, urging him to stop eating dirt and to lift his back off the ground before it is broken. The women are less vocal as they watch the matches from the doorways and make muffled jokes, but they too criticize him in private. None of them is satisfied to have a loser or a coward as a husband or lover (ibid.:96).

As in Truk, where the women also watch the brawlers from the sidelines, the Mehinaku men engage in these daily combats largely for feminine approval. Success in beating others means success with the opposite sex. Women shout encouragement from the sidelines and coyly make themselves available to the winners. It is interesting here, also, that as successful wrestlers embody the highest qualities of manliness, the losers in wrestling contests are likened to inadequate little boys. The man who loses a wrestling match is said to become "a master of little boys' games" and to resemble a helpless child (ibid.). Among the Mehinaku, defeat and victory in sports are therefore more than tickets in an inconsequential lottery; nor is wrestling simply a recreation. The contests indicate a man's worth as a functioning adult and are indelible signals of his potential. Avoiding participation in the wrestling matches or losing abjectly are not superficial failings but severe character deficiencies, a betrayal of civic duties. People are not reticent about informing the noncombatant of his obvious deficiencies, showering him with abuse and sending him to the trash heap of society.

Cowardice or incompetence on the mat carries an additional penalty, because it also means being spurned by available females. It is only by playing the game with courage that a Mehinaku man can win and keep a wife, for she will despise him and betray him if he fails to measure up. Mehinaku sexual norms provide for the tacit approval of the wife who cuckolds a poor wrestler; knowing this, most such women carry on adulterous affairs while their husbands sulk helplessly. It is clear that one of the qualities being touted on the public stage is a sense of responsiveness to collective ideals, measured by a willingness to compete forcefully for the culture's highest prizes. A man who fails in the sporting arena, it is assumed, suffers from an inbred character deficiency and will also fail as a farmer and fisherman; he is therefore a poor choice as a husband or lover. This man will have few children to support him later on in life, few sons to revere him and carry on his name, and so he will experience an ever-dwindling status, a progressive social marginalization as irreversible as the physical debilities of old age.

INSIDE/OUTSIDE

The Mehinaku are concerned about the geographic place of men in the village setting. They have the usual public/private split in community space and the usual gender boundaries and barriers. Forcing men out into open spaces where they can be seen, the Mehinaku image of manhood also prohibits a lingering or withdrawal in the confines of home, pushing men into exposed arenas where they must compete or lose face and perhaps suffer the humiliation of being cuckolded. Inside the village, men seek to make a dramatic appearance on center stage. In contrast to the reticent women, men are continually involved in conduct that is more or less deliberately on display in central village areas for the benefit of the rest of the tribe. While gathered in the center of things, they self-consciously strut and preen, wrestle, engage in florid oratory, and gather for important political decisions—"all in full public view" (1977:165). The women, on the other hand, are engaged in domestic affairs in the nonpublic regions, behind the houses, deliberately avoiding the central plaza, which is reserved for men.

The wrestling ground, for example, is symbolically situated in the exact center of the village clearing, an open place "associated with masculinity" (ibid.:24). Participation in this and other forms of open and aboveboard male activity thus entails a culturally enforced removal from the consolations of privacy, pushing men into competitive engagement. As in Andalusia, Algeria, and Truk, among these Brazilian Indians a man is expected to emerge from the shadow of women and children and take an active part in the ritualized dramas of community life.

Because it pushes men into public affairs upon penalty of eternal disgrace, the male image sets up a kind of centripetal force that knits the society together in a way that both sexes can monitor. Again, the penalties for withdrawal from this arena are severe and summary. Gregor notes that men who hang about the women's areas of the village, avoiding the exposed masculine arenas, are reviled as "trash yard men" (ibid.:59), an allusion to the place where garbage is thrown (we will see a parallel to this in the Melanesian "rubbish men" discussed in the next chapter). The uxorious Mehinaku man, the homebody or introvert (like his Melanesian counterpart), "loses part of his claim to masculinity" (1985:93). Referring to one such shifty character nicknamed "Rotten Fish," one of Gregor's informants said, "Look at old 'Rotten Fish.' . . . He is a *real* trash yard man. He never gets up to bathe at dawn like the rest of us, and he sleeps all day in his hammock. . . . When he isn't sleeping he is moping around the trash yard or the back door of his house. He doesn't even know how to play the sacred flutes. He has no friends and goes fishing by himself" (1977:201).

Mehinaku masculinity is rigidly extroverted and sociable—a morality of interaction—and a matter for the severest public evaluation. The Mehinaku call this male sociability a "facing up." Like Bourdieu's Kabyle, a Mehinaku man must "face" his fellows; otherwise he is contemptible, a trash yard man, no better than a child. The Mehinaku have a rich vocabulary of abuse for the villager who "will not 'face' his comrades" (ibid.:200). As among the Kabyle, appearing in public means a readiness to stand up to one's rivals; it symbolizes not only acceptance of the everyday challenges of Mehinaku life but also, at a more general level, man's exterior place in the cosmological scheme of things. Success helps, but active participation in the hurly-burly of village life seems more important.

PSYCHIC DIMENSIONS

Gregor's approach to all this manly "facing," the erotic obsessiveness, the posturing and preening, is a psychoanalytic one. In his keen interpretation of Mehinaku culture, Gregor ascribes the concern for a public face of manhood to a reaction-formation against the ever-present Oedipus complex. He sees Mehinaku manhood ideology as a culturally conditioned defense against castration anxiety; this interpretation follows the standard Freudian view and underlies Gregor's Universal Male. The author argues that these oedipally tormented Indians are anxious about losing their penises: this causes them to overvalue the male organ and its function (1985:131). Thus they strut phallic displays as compensation and in order to reassure themselves that they are intact. Gregor provides a wealth of cultural material—stories and myths, as well as tribal taboos about menstruation—that support his case.

Gregor's argument about the "castration complex" of Mehinaku culture, as he calls it (ibid.:131), is useful for understanding male Indians' individual psychodynamics. I am sure that castration anxiety plays a role here, as it does in most male fantasies. However, it is never clear how such individual fantasies transmute into collective cultural institutions such as a shared mythology, an ethic of "facing," or a morality of generosity as elements of manliness. Gregor has not made this transformation of individual fear into social norm any clearer in his study. More interesting to me is Gregor's passing recognition of the role of regressive instincts in all this. I find this latter emphasis more productive because it takes into account not only endopsychic processes but the practical needs of society—for productive labor and social cohesion—that must be met by such cultural institutions as gender stereotypes and ideology. By taking the role of regression into account, also, we can better grasp the cultural emphases on characterological extroversion, economic energy, and generosity as consensual norms.

Gregor does acknowledge the role of psychic regression as a powerful motive force in Mehinaku male culture. He sees that the primary counterforce working against worldly achievement among the Mehinaku is the retrogressive pull of the man toward dependency and social withdrawal. He refers to the universal desire of men to take "the path back to fusion with the mother and the pleasures of infancy" (ibid.:178), and he sees the relentless demand for a purely masculine image among the Mehinaku, with its stress on sexual aggressivity, productivity, and engagement, as a defense erected partly against this wish. However, although he perceives the importance of this childish wish as a factor in the formation of Mehinaku male ideology, he fails, in my opinion, to ascribe it sufficient causal weight. The reason is that he denies regression the same autonomous ontological status as that given to castration anxiety, which as usual crowds everything else off the analytical stage. Here I must digress briefly to consider Gregor's argument, as it presages my later conclusions.

The first thing to recognize here is that the recessive turning away from adult responsibilities toward reunion with the mother is a different order of psychic magnitude from castration anxiety. This distinction is true in terms of both the psychosexual development of the individual and its cultural implications. As defined by psychoanalysts (e.g., A. Freud 1963; Arlow and Brenner 1963), regression is a pre-oedipal instinct involving anaclitic and nutritional wishes. Castration anxiety develops, according to Freud, at the oedipal stage and is based on a mix of erotic and aggressive instincts. The interpretive weakness in Gregor's work and in that of many others who also attribute manhood values narrowly to the oedipal trauma, is the conflation of castration anxiety and regression as instinctual forces. That is, there is a failure to differentiate between oedipal and pre-oedipal fantasies and their derivatives. These two phenomena are not only ontologically distinct but also, because based on different instinctual wishes, represent problems of different adaptive magnitude to the developing ego. If the unconscious wish that must be defended against is regression toward symbiosis with the mother (which Gregor acknowledges), then, in line with the standard Freudian view, the author perceives this wish as awakening a pre-oedipal feminine identification and thereby—and this is where the reaction develops—giving rise to oedipally-induced fears of castration. That is, to be "at one" with mother means to be "the same" as mother, which means to be female, to have no penis. Thus in Mehinaku society regression has no independent status as a wish or fear but is perceived only as a stimulant to the more important castration dread.

This argument may have merit in specific cases, but as a general explanation it misses the point. A more parsimonious explanation is to consider the primary phenomenon, regression, and its negative relation to masculine role performance as an aspect of economic adaptation. This view gives psychic priority to regression itself as a discrete factor in masculine development (as in all human development, male and female) and holds that regression to a state of primary narcissism is unacceptable in and of itself as a threat to adult functioning. That is, regressive wishes are both causally independent of, and, in aggregate, of greater social importance than developmentally subsequent castration fears. This implies also that the performance ethic of the Mehinaku is not merely a psychic projection of a shared neurosis arising from the oedipal transition with its endopsychic origins, but a response to very real environmental needs—needs that can vary from one society to another. As an example of what I mean, let us take a look at one of the myths that Gregor presents in order to prove his contention about the Mehinaku castration complex (ibid.:178–79). This is the very revealing myth of Tapir Woman.

A MYTH

Gregor provides a number of telling legends and myths. Some of these show that what Mehinaku boys fear is their own wish to

escape the harsh demands of their male role by returning to a
fantasized utopian childhood, a tension-free idyll when all needs
are met and few demands are made. They fear this unconscious
escapist wish because it signals a passive and dependent mode
inappropriate to the requisite risk taking and self-assertiveness
in adult life that leads to social and reproductive success. This
wish to abandon this conflictive maturity spells out to the man,
in Gregor's apt terminology, "the symbiotic union with the
mother and the trauma of separation from her." But here,
Gregor adds, "Our research penetrates a region that the men
must defend. The path back to fusion with the mother and the
pleasures of infancy is symbolic of *regression and emasculation.*
Any lingering temptations to return to this period will be dis-
torted and deflected by the [castration] anxieties it awakens"
(ibid.:178, emphasis added). So in his view, regressive wishes
occur spontaneously in the men but are unconsciously prece-
dent to the more terrifying emasculation fears; once awakened,
these fears cause the compromise solution of reaction-formation
that inspires manhood imagery.

Gregor presents the myth of "Tapir Woman" as confirmation
of his thesis. As recounted in Gregor's book (ibid.:178–79), in
this myth, a child is left alone in his house. Crying out of lone-
liness and fear of abandonment, he is approached by a fabulous
female creature, the Tapir Woman, who comes to comfort him,
saying, "Don't you know me? I am just like your mother. Don't
cry." She then insists that the boy place his arm in her rectum,
and when he reluctantly does this, she absorbs him up to the
shoulder and runs away into the forest with him. Secluded
there, he is happily surfeited on fruits that emerge from her
rectum. His arm, eventually freed, is shrunken, too tiny and
shriveled for further use. Prematurely lost to the mature man's
role, the boy is therefore ruined as a man, for he will never hunt,
fish, farm—or, equally important, wrestle. The point to remember here is that the boy has magically, though voluntarily,
absconded from the rigors of real life in order to luxuriate in
passive orality provided by the mystical motherlike figure, a

goddess of abundance who defecates food. There could be no clearer representation (in displaced form) of the all-flowing breast.

Appreciating the rich oral imagery in the myth, Gregor agrees. According to him, what makes the appeal of the Tapir Woman so irresistible to the little boy is "the fusion with the mother and a return to the passivity and warmth that were until recently the child's everyday privilege" (ibid.:179). In a sense, then, the Mehinaku myth reflects the universal desire to escape a harsh reality by returning to a blissful unity with the mother, what Heinz Kohut has called the pull of "infantile amnesia" (1977:181). It also represents the hidden wish to be "carried off" by her (that is, to be rescued from the terrors of life into a serene primitive unity) while being fed without effort. Here Gregor and I are in full agreement on the unconscious symbolizations of the myth.

But we differ on its secondary implications. Naturally for Gregor, the boy's shriveled arm represents castration, its shrunken state the mutilated penis. Although this interpretation enriches the comprehension of the psychodynamic processes involved, it is not absolutely essential to an understanding of the institutionalized countermythology of a muscular masculinity. The story is a myth, a public manifestation, not just a projection of individual fantasies; as such it also contains a moral message of conformity to tribal work standards, for myths, whatever else they may be, are also guides, or charters for right action. What the Tapir Woman myth warns against is the desire to escape practical everyday responsibilities of social membership, that is, the male role in the social organization of labor, by withdrawing and seeking solace in the embrace of an infantilizing clinging to mother. From this viewpoint, the shriveled arm can just as well symbolize the abandonment of masculine economic function, the shriveling of labor power, as the damaged penis. What has been lost is not only the penis but the man's work potential to society, which it can ill afford to lose. The arm is the functional equivalent to the female organ that produces food.

This substitution of consumptive for productive functions, symbolized by the useless arm, is what is culturally unacceptable and must be countermanded by moral sanction. Cultural forms respond to specific cultural needs, not only to endopsychic ones, and the myth is a collective, not individual, fantasy. Here the demand of society is the familiar one of the masculine image: risk taking and economic productivity. It is childishness and dependency, or rather idleness—what Freud (1930:34) called "the natural human aversion to work"—that the Mehinaku are combating with their manhood mythology, not just castration anxiety.

All this obsession with male powers makes the Mehinaku Indians a case in point in the study of manhood image. Their significance derives not only from the fact that Gregor has provided us with such superb ethnographic data but also because they most clearly demonstrate that manhood is an ambivalent proposition, a cultural construct based on group needs, that overlays and counteracts a hesitant and resisting nature. They show that the manhood pose is the social negation of an antisocial wish to flee the rigors of work-culture. Thus, as Gregor puts it in the book's title, the pleasures of the Mehinaku men are "anxious pleasures," because they are fraught with doubt and shot through with opposing desires. In many ways, the Mehinaku are a classic representation of a pressured manhood because of this tense and dynamic ambivalence, this clash of social need and self-indulgence. To throw more light on them by means of comparison, let us look at some similar manhood imagery in other parts of the world.

✿ ✿ ✿ ✿ ✿ 5

Interlude: Other Men, Other Manhoods

Ah! How the old sagas run through me!
                    —Herman Melville, *Mardi*

Do the Mehinaku, the Trukese, and the Spaniards share a "deep structure of masculinity"
(Tolson 1977:56)? Is Gregor (1985:9) right to
say that there are "universalities in the male
experience"? Perhaps. We have seen an echo
of the masculinity cults of some Mediterranean peoples in far-away Truk, reappearing
in the sexual obsessions of a tribe in Brazil.
The linkage is not simply one of the boastful
male vanity that we call machismo, for not all
these cultures can be called macho. The
Mehinaku are certainly not macho like the
Trukese in the sense of being bellicose or
physically aggressive. This suggests that the
machismo version of manhood is an inten-
sified variant of some underlying phenomenon that occurs more broadly. Having
looked at three specific cultures in some
depth, I want now to adopt a more panoramic
perspective to see how widespread are the
themes we have been considering.

If we travel due west from Brazil halfway
around the world, we come to another arena
where manhood is dramatically put to the
test. This is the island of New Guinea, where
ethnographers have noted for decades the

stress men place on achieving a culturally defined purity of masculinity. It is worth exploring these New Guinea manhood beliefs and practices, some of which are distinctly bizarre from the
Western point of view, especially those of the remote cultures of
the Highlands, for they have been the subject of much anthropological interest and shed much light on the meaning of
manhood as a universal phenomenon.

NEW GUINEA: BIG MEN AND RUBBISH MEN

An area densely populated by neolithic tribes, having been first
contacted by Western civilization only in the 1940s, the high
valleys of central New Guinea retain many aboriginal practices.
A celebrated social fixture in traditional Highland New Guinea
is the figure of the "Big Man," so named in pidgin English, the
lingua franca of the region, because of his bigger-than-life
qualities, his embodiment of the native manly ideal. Crowning
personal charisma with political leadership and a philanthro-
pist's role as a patron to his village or district, the Big Man is the
New Guinea equivalent of the Mehinaku wrestling champion or
the Trukese weekend warrior. For that matter, he resembles any
other self-made male champion, from the Mafia godfather in
urban America, the *uomo di rispetto,* to feudal warlords who dominated by personal power and political savvy, all having clawed
their way to their culture's highest status. The details of their
ascent to the pinnacle of respect differ, of course, but the vener-
ated image of the prodigal New Guinea Big Man is quite similar
to these other paragons of masculine power. The role he plays,
though seemingly self-serving, is the supporting beam of the
neolithic social architecture.

There is a vast literature on the Big Men of New Guinea. The
magnitude of their achievements is impressive and varied, but a
few commonalities stand out. The Highland Big Man is, first, a
charismatic local leader who has achieved, not inherited, a leadership role through dramatic actions of personal derring-do that
prop up his village or tribe. He earns his position of prominence

by a number of practical means, depending upon exigencies of time and place. First, he acts as a leader in war, if warfare is locally a particular concern. If the tribe is threatened, he becomes a military strategist, shielding his group by directing hit-and-run counterattacks to keep the enemy at bay. Like any competent commanding officer, he leads his troops into battle, setting an example by bravely disdaining clouds of arrows and spears. The only difference is that his position is unofficial, without badges or uniforms; but without his "take-charge" management the village would be disorganized and hence vulnerable to deadly sneak attack.

Through this hands-on leadership, the Big Man does something more than fight, fend off enemies, and exemplify a warrior ideal for impressionable boys and aspiring youths: he establishes an artificial social cohesion for the people of his village or territorial unit. This unifying function is necessary because the people who follow him are often of mixed ancestry and diffuse kinship (as is common among Highlands peoples). Weakly tied by bonds of blood, they are drawn together by his protective safety net to form a viable community, establishing a political rather than genealogical unit that otherwise might never gel. Through his example and by the commanding authority of his deeds, he coalesces this community of otherwise unrelated families around his person, counteracting the organic weakness of Highlands genealogy. For example, among the Gururumba (Newman 1965:44), the power of the Big Men derives from their "ability to attract followers outside the circle of their own immediate kinsmen." There is in fact a conscious awareness of this ingathering magnetism among his vassals. Many local people acknowledge this and openly remark that the local Big Man holds the group together almost single-handedly, giving it the strength and unity it needs but would otherwise lack (A. Strathern 1971:190–91).

Beyond these crucial military and sociopolitical functions, the Big Man is also an indispensable economic power, an engine of production, motivating and enriching his followers. In farming and herding, he is the unofficial manager for the village, exhorting his people to produce, to work hard, and to save. In return for their loyalty, he accumulates, stores, and later redistributes great quantities of imperishables and foodstuffs, acting like a primitive banker or capitalist, rationalizing and centralizing production and extending credit. But unlike his Western counterpart, he is expected to return the goods with interest, enriching his trading partners rather than himself. The mark of the authentic Big Man is that he is a large-scale net producer, always giving away "more than he receives" (ibid.:217). To capture Big Man status, he may accumulate food and goods, but only to distribute them later in ceremonies and feasts (Godelier 1986:175). An expert on the New Guinea Highlands, Paula Brown (1979:195), summarizes, "The wealth [of Big Men] is dissipated in distribution at feasts; it cannot be accumulated." The Big Man must be above all a "good manager" (A. Strathern 1971:221), an administrator of goods, enriching his village by amassing capital, cementing exchange networks, diverting group energies away from consumption toward reinvestment. Clearly, he provides the centripetal sources of cohesion and direction that the society needs (ibid.:224–25). All this makes him both charismatic and virile in the eyes of his people (P. Brown 1979:195).

Because the Big Man's promotions are responses to contingent needs of congeries of dependents, these actions, chameleonlike, change over time to suit the circumstances. In one case, A. Strathern (1971), focusing on the Mount Hagen area, has traced the historical shift in Big Man virtues in the past few decades away from warfare, which the Australian colonizers prohibited, toward more peaceful political and economic functions to suit new conditions. As he notes, the Mount Hagen Big Man position is a social function of momentary convenience, a pragmatic process of adaptation rather than an office or position. Thus throughout the island, when warfare declines, as in Mount Hagen, the Big Man achieves his preeminent status through skillful management of production, mustering financial resources, seizing the new opportunities offered by modernization, and redistributing money and other forms of new curren-cy. In this way also, the Big Man operates like a Western invest-ment broker or commodity trader, an innovative, risk-taking entrepreneur, always on the lookout for a killing. Like an Amer-ican capitalist who must "meet tests" of success on the mar-ketplace or perish (Stearns 1979:112), the Big Man manipulates the volatile financial markets of pigs, yams, and shell money and thus facilitates capital accumulation, contributing mightily to the common wealth by seizing fleeting opportunities. To maintain his preeminent status, he must take decisive action, innovate, take substantial risks, and in the end furnish the goods. His mark of success is material profits, always ostentatiously visible, dramatized in heaps and mounds and then given away (P. Wilson 1988:84–85). He hides nothing: his profits are public property, the pride and glory of all his people. Like the Andalu-sians or the Mehinaku, he acts on center stage.

Becoming a Big Man or "Great Man" (Godelier 1986) is a race for distinction that goes only to the swift and the brave. The New Guinea "Alpha male" (a term borrowed with apologies from primate studies) achieves his prominence only in competi-tion with other like-intended men; he prevails over others in fierce contests of wills and perseverance, facing down rivals in endless battles of creativity, oratory, and military prowess (A. Strathern 1971:217). To achieve exalted status, he and his com-petitors thus must work harder than other people and must strive and excel. They must also be innovative, able to improvise in order to augment their village's wealth, power, and tech-nological expertise relative to other communities. The whole society benefits when the goods—consisting of foodstuffs, shell money and other valuables, magical and sacred paraphernalia, and so on—are finally amassed, displayed in massive mounds sometimes weighing several tons (Newman 1965:54), and then freely distributed. As Sahlins (1984:281) puts it, "It is important that not merely his own status, but the standing and perhaps the military security of his people depend upon the big-man's achievements in public distributions." In playing the game of self-aggrandizement, the Big Man creates order from surroundings that are more fluid and chaotic than those of many other primitive societies, thus creating a structured and predictable universe for his constituents.

Some men, as always, fail. There is always the bad example of the unmanly man who falters in these pursuits or who, more often, withdraws from the contest to cower in dark corners. The man who rejects the idealized male role is scorned as inferior and weak, but more damaging is that he is robbed of his masculinity as well as his basic respectability. His main characteristic is his appalling lack of social commitment, measured in inadequate productivity. A poor farmer, this New Guinea reprobate consumes more than he produces; an indifferent or timorous warrior, he cannot be trusted on the battlefield. He takes no risks in food production. A weak orator, he remains silent at village councils, contributing no bright ideas, no improvements. The people call this weakling a nothing, sterile, a worthless thing, useless, a "Rubbish Man," made of trash. They say he is effeminate, "like a woman" (M. Strathern 1981:183). Pathetic and cringing, he is likened to a capricious child.

In Mount Hagen, as in Truk where men think "strong thoughts," the productive Big Men have "strong heads"; the Rubbish Men have "soft" heads like babies. The Rubbish Man is "weak and humble" (A. Strathern 1971:217). He is seen skulking about in the places where women gather, cleaving furtively to his home and hearth. He is passive, asthenic, a parasite. His fellows complain that he "eats" the fat of the land without producing (M. Strathern 1981:183). Sealing his fate is that he is also a failure in a sexual sense. He has few wives and few children. He fails in all the constructive masculine pursuits: he provisions no one, cannot protect his kinsmen from attack, impregnates few women, and contributes little that is new and useful to the economy, religion, or technology. All adult men shrink from being cast in the "effeminate mold of the useless rubbish man" (Herdt 1981:52).

SEXUAL DUTIES

Sex is also important in New Guinea in the evaluation of manhood, because it is part of a man's expected performances. But this is seen, again, in terms of contributions made to a society virtually obsessed with increase and fertility. As among the Trukese and the Mediterranean societies we have looked at, the New Guinea man of respect must spread his seed and multiply. Although these men regard sexual relations with a measure of anxiety like the Mehinaku, for a variety of magical reasons, they are expected to overcome these inhibitions and to reproduce sexually, just as they are exhorted to produce economically and militarily, and to take on a commanding role in trading and oratory. Reproduction is not only a personal pleasure; it is very consciously perceived as a social obligation and a measure of good citizenship. Given the dangers of Highlands life, especially the hovering military threat, the society needs offspring to endure. The society needs more girls to become mothers and to make more babies who will grow up and contribute. It needs more drones to work and to soldier, and especially it needs more Big Men to organize defense and production. The bigger the village, the safer it is militarily: none dare attack a place of many armed men. People are quite aware of this equation, and children are therefore a critical collective resource spelling security and happiness. The stress on reproduction to build up numbers is impressed forcefully upon boys as a civic duty.

For instance, among the Awa tribe (Newman and Boyd 1982:284), the youths are told very seriously of their "responsibility" to engage in sexual intercourse and produce offspring. And among the Sambia, as reported by Herdt, the boys are instructed in their sexual "*duties*." The birth of his first child is an important event for a Sambia man: it is, "de jure, the attainment of manhood" (1982:53). To be "fully masculine" a Sambia man "must not only marry, but father some children" (Herdt 1981:176). Having many children is one of many social functions that constitute the notion of a cultural competence which directly enhances group security. In impregnating his wife, the Sambia man "has proved himself competent" in social functioning (ibid.:176). Not so far away, among the Baruya of the Anga territory, a man gains prestige with each succeeding birth "until he 'truly' becomes a man, that is the father of at least four children" (Godelier 1986:85). The Baruya Big Man is "polygamous, with many wives and children" (ibid.:175). All these masculinizing performances come together in terms of a combined male contribution to stability, security, and collective power. Relying on the evocative magic of such models, images, and sanctions, the clan grows and expands through the exertions of those who respond to its appeal (Meggitt 1967:32).

MEN ARE MADE, NOT BORN

Meeting so many perceived social needs, maleness in New Guinea is a complicated venture, a long, restive journey that not all men can complete. Aside from this notion of fecundity, there are other aspects that need discussion here. Most striking is a powerful belief that masculinity is an artificially induced status, that it is achievable only through testing and careful instruction. Real men do not simply emerge naturally over time like butterflies from boyish cocoons; they must be assiduously coaxed from their juvenescent shells, shaped and nurtured, counseled and prodded into manhood. Among the Ilahita Arapesh, for example, a natural and unaided acquisition of male values and potencies is "presumed to be impossible" (Tuzin 1982:341). Unlike femininity, which comes naturally through biological maturation, the fulfillment of masculinity does not "occur naturally" among the Awa (Newman and Boyd 1982:282–83). In general, throughout the Highlands, men are thought to be incapable of living up to masculine-role expectations without the intervention of cultural artifices. Male gender is "created" rather than "natural" (Keesing 1982:5). Roger Keesing summarizes: "Growth and strength, bravery and manliness are achieved through sequences of isolation and ordeal, instruction and revelation." In New Guinea, "A boy is made into a man" (ibid.:8,9).

PARALLELS?

The idea that manhood must be induced by vigorous intervention should not surprise us. If we ignore the ritual and magical paraphernalia of New Guinea manhood, how close it all is to the standard anxiety-drenched American conception of masculinity! For one thing, in America, too, sexual performance is closely associated with the state of being manly. This insistence on performance, on passing tests, on meeting expectations, hardly needs mention here. As the psychoanalyst Gregory Rochlin remarks (1980:23), "We will recall how early in a boy's development performance is sexually identified as masculine. His penis is a performing organ. It marks a boy for masculinity and associates him with performance." American boys are also tested in this respect, but differently—by gossip and innuendo on the playingfield or locker room rather than by public village mockery. Performance anxiety about sex is as great as among the Mehinaku or Andalusians, for much the same reasons of social status; and both impotence and incompetence are widely feared as negations of manhood and a simultaneous loss of social esteem.

The New Guinea Big Man's stress on hard work and on a competitive and ever-climbing productivity is repeated for the American male in the work place, which becomes a symbolic arena for the acquisition of the masculine image. In America, definitions of masculinity "are bound up with definitions of work" (Tolson 1977:72). Men are driven to greater and greater efforts to succeed in the sense of profitability, getting the job done, amassing the goods, which are displayed not in mounds but are piled up in status symbols and consumer goods. The related theme of testing, of the uncertainty of manhood, is also recurrent in our society. For example, commenting on gender ideas of American culture as expressed in modern fiction, the literary critic Alfred Habegger remarks that masculinity "has an uncertain and ambiguous status. It is something to be acquired through a struggle, a painful initiation, or a long and sometimes humiliating apprenticeship" (1982:199). One wins or loses, but, like the New Guinea Big Man, one must play the game. The worst sin is not honest failure but cowardly withdrawal.

The moral parallels are true of almost all U.S. ethnic subvariants of manhood, not just some hypothetical Anglo-Saxon archetype. In their survey of male imagery in contemporary America, the sociologists Michael Cicone and Diane Ruble conclude that the "common denominator" in all masculine ethnic subcultures is "a kind of go-getting, dynamic attitude about life in general, with the possibility of worldly accomplishment" (1978:11). Aside from this go-getting dynamism, with its heavy emphasis on material success, another pan-American similarity to Melanesia is the belief that the inner resources and determination needed for success are not naturally present but must be inculcated or artificially induced in the boy through a stressful period of indoctrination, or "apprenticeship," as Habegger says. Writing about the American notion of manhood, Stearns notes, "Manhood is a solemn thing. It is not purely natural, for like most of the attributes of a civilized society it has to be taught" (1979:196). (How unnecessary is the word "civilized" here!)

One encounters this anxious notion again and again in modern American fiction, for example. One finds it not only in Hemingway and his followers, but also in the softer autobiographical styles of Frank Conroy, Philip Roth, Geoffrey and Tobias Wolff, and other contemporary male novelists who are always learning (or teaching) about how to be a man and about how hard it is for boys to choose the right road. One finds it also in nineteenth-century romantic writers such as Hawthorne, Whitman, and Emerson, with their concern for the entrepreneurial "man of force" (Leverenz 1989), but it is especially pronounced in the maritime adventures of Herman Melville. More than their contemporary fictional counterparts, Melville's searching, traveling heroes often embody the masculine quest for self-definition and male validation. Recently, critics have argued that Melville's sea stories, both autobiographical and imaginary, reflect an unresolved conflict between a need for manly assertiveness in the specifically vigorous, materialistic American style "and a penchant for passivity and dependence" deeply ingrained in his character (Haberstroh 1980:31). And one can readily see the metaphoric connection between voyaging and rites of passage, a common enough theme in such Western novelists as Conrad and Kipling but also found among many preliterate and ancient societies, as Mary Helms illustrates with a wealth of ethnographic detail in her book *Ulysses' Sail* (1988:88–91).

Though true for the big nautical novels, this theme of ambivalence is especially pronounced in Melville's short story, "Bartleby the Scrivener," set on Wall Street. The hero of this strange, almost surreal fantasy is the passive copywriter Bartleby, a laconic wraith of a man. The story traces his progressing atrophy, in which Bartleby refuses to work or care for himself and gradually wastes away, much to the horror of his stockbroker employer, who narrates the tale with mounting impatience and, finally, gloomy despair. Finally, despite all rational entreaties from his boss, Bartleby dies of starvation curled up in a fetal position in a subterranean place called "The Tombs." When offered opportunities to earn some money and save himself, he always replies, "I prefer not to," and then retreats into passive silence. Although this Dickensian fable has been interpreted most often as a critique of American capitalism (M. Gilmore 1985:132–45), which was in fact most probably Melville's conscious intention, the powerful unconscious theme of regression is in my opinion both more trenchant and more deeply affecting. The Tombs (wombs?) is obviously a metaphor for infantilization, and the story a fantasy of return to the helplessness of infancy and the ultimate passivity, death.

THE MANHOOD QUOTIENT

Although one must be careful not to universalize from these examples, it seems that men worldwide share the same notions, expressed so ambivalently by Melville in his fiction. Recurring continually is a stress on hard work and effective enterprise and a parallel belief that this work ethic must be artificially inculcated in hesitant or passive males who, deep down, like Bartleby, "prefer not" to strive.

Another obvious commonplace uniting the cultures we have been discussing is the association of bigness—as measured in musculature, accomplishments, or numbers of possessions—with masculinity. This linkage of scale and virility is probably universal, attesting to the usefulness of manhood images as inducements to produce quantities of valuable things. Just as the pidgin term "Big Man" inspires an imposing image of true masculinity and a commanding presence, with its intimations of large penis size and physical power, so in our own culture there is "something ineffably masculine about the word 'millionaire,' or even 'the richest man in town'" (David and Brannon 1976:19). The Big Man in any industrial society is also the richest guy on the block, the most successful, the most competent, and he has the most of what society needs or wants. We also call powerful entrepreneurs and politicians "Big Men," because they are big in the sense of power or accomplishment. In many societies, from the preliterate to the postindustrial, wealth or position means creative and manipulative power, and this power signals masculinity; only the details differ. This male bigness may be measured in terms of objects or currency, cash or cattle; it may be judged by the pile of preferred stocks, pretty stones, bureaucratic patronage, or credits on a resume.

Underlying all this is the sense of personal achievement through commanding and assertive action that adds something measurable to society's store. To know a man, to judge him as a man in any of these societies, you have to see him at work at useful jobs; you have to know his energy quotient as a worker, a producer, a builder. Work defines manhood, but not just work as energy spent but as labor that supports life, constructive labor. The sociologist Ferdynand Zweig (1961:79) quotes one of his informants, a blue-collar worker: "A man, to be man, has got to work and earn his living." American poets have voiced similar views. William Carlos Williams has written the following credo: "If you want to know a man, if you find him excellent, why you've got to have something to do together. You've got to work" (*A Voyage to Pagany,* cited in Tolson 1977:47).

EAST AFRICAN BIG MEN

This pragmatic productivity quotient occurs in many different environments. To take a random Third-World example, we can turn briefly to East Africa. There, the Dodoth tribe of northern Uganda furnishes a typical counterpoint to the situations we have just been discussing. These Dodoth people are cattle herders, warriors, and above all famous and feared rustlers. Among them, as reported by Elizabeth Marshall Thomas (1965:39–40), a man must prove his worth as a warrior and a cattle rustler before he can claim manhood and take a wife.

Thomas tells the story of one Dodoth boy who refused to grow up—an African Peter Pan. He ignored his adult masculine responsibilities, including, among other things, perilous cattle raids. So long as he shrank from participating, his fellows treated him as an outcast and questioned his manhood. Finally, unable to stand it any longer, he screwed up his courage and went on a successful cattle raid. After various adventures and mishaps, he finally managed to kill an enemy, an act that enabled him to acquire a fat ox. Full of pride, he immediately slaughtered his prize catch as an offering to the tribe. Before this crowning success, according to Thomas's account (ibid.), he was a mere boy in the eyes of his people; afterward, having procured meat, he became a man in local reckoning and was treated as such. He was permitted to marry and to begin a family. He had produced: his "work" made him a man.

Like the New Guinea Highlanders, these Dodoth also have the institutionalized "Big Man" status to commemorate such achievements. Thomas gives us an account of one such venerable Big Man named Lokorimoe. As a rich and respected Dodoth elder with a large family, Lokorimoe is a typical Dodoth leader. He has killed many enemies and accumulated many head of fine cattle. He is rich in worldly goods, strong, and generous. People say that before he achieved these laurels he was "nothing," not a man at all, a useless thing. "A man," say the Dodoth, is "a man with cattle" (ibid.:146). Lokorimoe, they say admiringly, is a man among men, a true man: he is generous with his wealth. Dodoth manhood, in a familiar theme in East Africa, rests on two accomplishments, both involving risk and danger and both contributing to the welfare of the group: cattle raiding and war (ibid.:147). But success here is not enough: a real man is not only brave but, like Lokorimoe, also wealthy and generous—a veritable human cornucopia. Thomas gives us another example of Dodoth masculine values in action in a revealing story involving two men, Lapore and Remi, who have an argument over a cattle raid. Lapore is a proven warrior and accomplished rustler; Remi is a poor and cowardly ne'er-do-well who, although physically fit, has never performed up to expectations. One day, tired of his subordinate status, the disreputable Remi decides to organize a cattle raiding party to be led by himself. Boasting loudly of his plans, he induces other men to follow him into the bush. But when he has lined up a number of prospective raiders who accept his proposal, he gets cold feet at the last minute and backs down, abandoning his fellows in the lurch. This is too much for Lapore, who has been watching all this with mounting suspicion. Indignantly confronting the poseur, he accuses him of both cowardice and incompetence. But his most telling insult is to question Remi's manhood. He says to him, "You think yourself a man, but it is not so" (ibid.). Unable to counter this line of attack, the unmanned Remi slinks off to lick his wounds in private. A real man never hesitates to pursue wealth and glory.

MANHOOD AND CREATIVITY

To be sure, there are contexts other than rustling and violence in which manhood is linked to enterprise. This linkage, with its resultant practical effects, is a common theme in Western literature; the theme of solving collective problems figures in most mythologies of the world as the basis of the myth of the culture hero (J. Campbell 1968). But it is not only among workers or primitives that such ideas rule gender attitudes and ideals. Among scholars, literary critics, and poets, this connection between heroic resourcefulness and manhood is also often celebrated, if only in hypothetical terms. For example, there is a venerable literary tradition that identifies masculinity with the act of artistic creation, the process that forges beauty from an unyielding raw material. Among those following this view, a definition of masculinity is bound up with purposive construction. Manhood is seen as the conjoining of disparate elements into an ordered whole, the imposition of form upon chaos (Schwenger 1984:8)—a kind of aesthetic confabulation obviously the counterpart to motherhood. In the emphasis on effective ends, there is a certain inescapable resemblance here between the masculinity of the thinker, who adds beauty or knowledge to his society, and the masculinity of the worker or peasant, measured in cruder material enterprise. No one has said it better than the nineteenth-century British essayist and aesthete, Walter Pater. Masculinity in art, according to Pater (1910:280–81), has to do with "tenacity of intuition and of consequent purpose, the spirit of construction as opposed to what is literally incoherent or ready to fall to pieces." A contemporary of Pater, the poet Gerard Manley Hopkins (1935:133), writes something similar: "Masterly execution," he muses, "is a kind of male gift, and especially marks off men from women." Feminist critic Judith Fetterly calls this the masculine myth of the "executive will" (1978:155)

MANHOOD AND THE HUNT

Naturally the raw materials of this male creativity differ from place to place, but the special quality that these writers describe as tenacity of purpose or masterful execution, this executive will, differs little as a matter of formulary self-definition from the masterful activity of New Guinea or Dodoth Big Men. In many primitive societies, where there is no writing and where people live more on the margin of existence, this tenacity of purpose, the hard-edged constructiveness that Pater speaks of, centers not only on war and material accumulation, as in New Guinea or Africa, but upon subsistence activities, especially the hunt. At the primitive level, but not only at that level, hunting is the primary means of extracting value from nature by literally transforming wild animals into food. Because it is dangerous and risky, and because it supplies needed protein, hunting is the provisioning function par excellence. It is a necessary condition of subsistence that falls upon the shoulders of men, who are anatomically better suited to it than women and who, unburdened by pregnancy and nursing, have the necessary mobility (Quinn 1977:187). Too often in modern Western eyes hunting has been looked at as something destructive or cruel, as basically aggressive or atavistic. On the contrary, from the hunter's point of view, and as seen by his society, hunting is both constructive and generous. In fact, it is even perceived as a kind of male nurturing, because it uses the raw materials provided by nature to furnish food; it is an act of ingenuity and giving as well as a statement of caring to those who are fed. Hunting provides more than food alone; it also furnishes tools and clothing as well as critical ritual and religious materials, thereby feeding both body and spirit.

For example, among the Sambia of New Guinea the hunt is a "social necessity" for many reasons. It provides the Sambia not only with their sole ready supply of meat (Herdt 1981:138), but also with feathers and skins needed for ritual and aesthetic purposes. Because it is so important an enterprise, the hunt provides a "personal perspective for achieving and measuring masculinity" (ibid.). Hunting is usually dangerous and always a challenge; it must be done, and, as Herdt says about the Sambia (ibid.:140), there is always an exacting standard of masculine prowess in this.

It is not only in violent societies like the Sambia that hunting prowess is a measure of manhood. For example, there are the utterly nonviolent Mbuti Pygmy of the Congo region, who have been described by Colin Turnbull (1981). Among these peaceable Pygmies, boys must learn the requisite masculine skills, especially hunting of big game, such as elephants. Hunting supplies the tribe not only with needed nutrients but also with such indispensable materials of life as skins and bones, and with ritual paraphernalia. Any man who falls short in hunting has his manhood questioned and is put into the androgynous category of "clown" (C. Turnbull 1981:207). Similarly, there are the intensely studied !Kung Bushmen of the Kalahari desert in southwest Africa. Like the Mbuti, these gentle foragers are often held up by anthropologists as an exemplar of social harmony. Men and women are equal in most things, and men exercise no invidious powers over their wives. Yet the Mbuti too have an image of an elusive manhood, and here too it connects directly with male prowess in securing food, clothing, and magical objects for the group. Among the Bushmen studied by the Marshall-Thomas family, for example, hunting skill is linked to male sexual power (L. Marshall 1976:270). A boy cannot be considered a man, nor is he permitted to marry, until he has successfully made his first kill of an antelope. Elizabeth Marshall Thomas tells how boys in their late teens are initiated "into manhood, having shot their first buck" (1959:170).

In a more recent study of the Bushmen, Richard Lee (1979: 235) confirms this equating of skill with the bow and skill with the penis. The symbolic unity of masculine economic and procreative functions is expressed comically in jokes: "The bow . . . is a bawdy metaphor for the penis. When a man jokingly says *mi kwara n!au* ("I have no bow"), he implies he is at a loss sexually" (ibid.:206). Among the Bushmen, as elsewhere, this masculinity is ambivalent and fragile; it can be lost. It has to be defended by taboos. For example, if a man steps over the detritus of birth after his wife has a baby, he loses his masculinity, simultaneously being stripped of his power to hunt

(Thomas 1959:161). The connection between hunting and manhood is not just a confirmation of violent tendencies or an outlet for aggression. Rather, as Ernestine Friedl has shown (1975:12–32), it is a contribution to society of both indispensable economic and spiritual value. It is a creative, even tender, activity, a triumph of utility in the service of others—truly a kind of indirect nourishing or nurturing. Above all, it is a cultural transformation: the appropriation, through work, of value from an unyielding nature. As Stearns remarks (1979:111–12), "Manhood was at first bolstered by analogies between work and the hunt."

The metaphor of the hunt as an initiation into manhood is of course also a common theme in the literatures of the modern Western cultures. One has only to think of Hemingway's story, "The Short Happy Life of Francis Macomber," where the hero gains his manhood on an African safari when he stands up to a charging lion. His triumph is too much for his castrating wife, who promptly shoots him in an apparent accident. There is also Faulkner's "The Old People," where the boy Quentin is given the task of killing a buck deer, "whose blood will initiate him into manhood" (Schwenger 1984:97); and one could mention such novels as James Dickey's *Deliverance*, Norman Mailer's *Why Are We in Vietnam*, and Robert F. Stone's *Blood Sport*, all of which return to the same archetypical male theme. The same idea finds celluloid echo in Cimino's *The Deer Hunter* and countless others. Among such recreational hunters, too, hunting is a metaphor for manhood because it demonstrates a tenacity of purpose that supposedly reflects the character traits needed for male success in a tough competitive world.

Similarly, the identification of the hunt with masculine sexual maturity, textured in images of mastery over nature, is equally common both in Western folklore and in literature. One classic example is the hunt scene in William Golding's *Lord of the Flies*, in which the castaway English boys kill a wild sow while experiencing their first erotic sensations and intimations of manhood. Led by the aggressive Jack and his henchman, Roger, this first kill is both a rite of passage and, metaphorically speaking, a recreation of man's original conquest of nature—a double coming of age: "Jack was on top of the sow, stabbing downward with his knife. Roger found a lodgment for his point and began to push till he was leaning with his whole weight. The spear moved forward inch by inch and the terrified squealing became a high-pitched scream. Then Jack found the throat and hot blood spouted over his hands. The sow collapsed under them and they were heavy and fulfilled upon her" (Golding 1964:125). The implications are obviously erotic, although the "fulfillment" the boys experience could also be interpreted as the successful overcoming of inhibitions against killing. The boys have shown that they are effective (though for Golding's purposes, merciless) killers. They have established dominion over nature; they have bent the animal world to their will and have furnished meat for the hungry castaways.

Golding's purpose is specifically to equate the "primitive" with the Western by arguing universal themes and impulses. In doing so, he takes some artistic license, but what he describes in psychological terms as an act of initiation is concretely reflected in many rites among hunting peoples, both primitive and civilized. As Northrop Frye writes (1976:104), "The hunt is normally an image of the masculine erotic, a movement of pursuit and linear thrust, in which there are sexual overtones to the object being hunted." In the hunting theme, all the variables of manhood—economy, skill, hardiness, sexuality—come together most directly and dramatically both in symbols and in the fact of putting meat on the table. Again, I think the aggressive or atavistic theme has been exaggerated in all this. Equally important is the procreative urge; skill and nurturing play a motivating role as much as blood lust does.

WOMAN AS PROVIDER

Throughout this book, I have been emphasizing man's breadwinning role as a measure of his manhood. But this admittedly overlooks the female contribution to the household economy.

What of women who also provide for their families? Recent studies have shown that women's contribution to food procurement (not just processing, cooking, or serving) has been overlooked or unjustly minimized in the anthropological and sociological literature. Women are providers of food, too, sometimes as much or more so than men. For example, a recent book edited by Frances Dahlberg (1981) entitled *Woman the Gatherer* shows that even in hunting societies women who collect wild plants may provide as much or more food in weight than their menfolk. Although they do not hunt by themselves, they may assist men in hunting by holding nets, setting traps, or beating the bush to flush out game. Worldwide, it has been calculated that women contribute about 30 to 40 percent to subsistence in all kinds of societies, from the most primitive to modern civilizations (Sanday 1973:1690).

But do women ever hunt by themselves? Do they hunt big game? Do they thereby assume the same risks as men? Only one empirical case has been reported in which women actually do kill large game by themselves. The case is that of the Agta, a Negrito people of northeastern Luzon, the Philippines (Estioko-Griffin and Griffin 1981). This case has been offered as evidence that hunting can just as well be a female occupation as a male one. For the light it throws on the above discussion, the Agta case bears looking into.

Closer inspection of the evidence presented shows that Agta female hunting has been somewhat exaggerated. The authors of the study note that most native women hunt full-time only in "extreme circumstances," and those that hunt on a day-to-day basis are laughed at by neighboring peoples of both sexes (ibid.:128). In addition, Agta women do not hunt when either pregnant or nursing, so that the general emphasis still remains on hunting as a male role. Hunting, the Agta say, is a "'sort of' male activity" (ibid.:132–33), something loosely associated with men, and something that men are better at doing.

Further, one must point out the unusual subsistence adaptation of the Agta. These people collect virtually no vegetables, because they prefer to trade meat to their farming neighbors for cultivated crops. This is a relatively recent development, which has eliminated the traditional female gathering role and which may explain the anomalous female hunting (ibid.:124). Finally, the authors of the Agta study admit that they were in the field too briefly to advance quantitatively based generalizations on female hunting (ibid.:129). The Agta are only a "sort of" exception to the rule of masculine hunting—a very tenuous one.

Although women rarely hunt dangerous game, they do take part in primary food procurement: they gather, help farm, collect firewood, and may even assist in herding. Significantly, the degree to which women contribute directly to the food quest in any given society seems to correlate with the degree to which manhood is emphasized—a finding that seems to support my argument here. In her cross-cultural survey of economic activities, Peggy Sanday (1973) notes that the smallest female contribution occurs in the Mediterranean region, which as we have seen is the home of machismo; and the highest feminine contribution occurs in West Africa, where, as Robert LeVine has pointed out (1979:313), there is very little interest in conventional masculinity (with some exceptions: see chapter 8 below). However, some anthropologists have questioned Sanday's conclusions about the extent of female subsistence activities because her data were drawn from a relatively small sample of world cultures. For example, in the case of foragers, Carol Ember (1978:441), using *all* the cases in George Murdock's *Ethnographic Atlas* (1967), finds that men contribute much more to primary subsistence than do women in such societies. Her statistics show that men predominate in 83 percent of the cases, whereas women predominate in only 8 percent, the remainder being ambiguous. Martin Whyte (1978), also using the *Atlas,* finds that men contribute most, if not all, primary foods in two-thirds of societies of all types.

I do not think, however, that the sexual division of labor and its cultural consequences are profitably addressed from this quantitative standpoint. Obviously, women are providers too, and their work is equally important. Rather, it is the huge qualitative difference in sex assignments that matters. Men are always given the tasks of procuring animal protein, fending off predators, and fighting wars. Like warfare, hunting involves not only danger but also risk—to both body and reputation—because hunting is a contest of wills in which there is always a winner and a loser. The man tries to kill an animal much more mobile than he; his quarry uses all its cunning and strength to escape, and it may be bigger and stronger than the hunter. It is this challenging, combative, winner-take-all aspect of the male role that demands the kinds of toughness and autonomy that need special motivation. Women's contributions are equally important in their own way and may demand extreme patience and dexterity, but they do not often involve personal risk, a struggle with nature, or the killing of dangerous foes. Roots and berries do not fight back and do not run away. Childbirth is painful and a test of stamina, but it is not a contest a woman can "lose" by running away.

In addition, the hunting and fishing that men do often involve distant journeys over rough or dangerous terrain, as, for example, among the Mehinaku and Trukese. Women perform most activities close to the home, where they can be protected by men and where they can work with children in tow (J. Brown 1970:1074). Because male tasks so often involve contests and bloodletting rather than gentleness and patience, and because of their consequent win-or-lose nature, these tasks are often harshly evaluated as to performance. If women fail to collect vegetables, people may go hungry for a short period. But if men retreat in terror on the battlefield, or if they stop hunting, the tribe may well face destruction. Even in sex and procreation, the man must "perform" in the same sense. Men must initiate courtship and must penetrate and impregnate the females. In a physiological sense, only the man runs the risk of a humiliating "failure" in the sex act, just as he does in his economic and military roles.

Beyond this, men have always been solely responsible for military defense—a fact that must not be underestimated. Although some women, like the Agta, may hunt, there is no society I am aware of in which women are principally, or even occasionally, the warriors. Even in Israel, only the men are sent into combat to fight and to die. Contrary to many myths about man's natural proclivity to fight wars, most of these men do not make good soldiers. Most men have to be inspired to fight; if that fails, they have to be forced at gunpoint by their commanding officers. Numerous studies have shown that the average soldier is extremely timorous in battlefield situations and that he "regresses" and reacts "passively" under enemy fire (Bednarik 1970:134). Obviously, as it often includes a military obligation, the male role often requires certain kinds of discipline or indoctrination to put reluctant youths in the proper frame of mind.

This defensive (and potentially lethal) role goes beyond warfare to include protection against the destructive forces of nature: fighting wild animals, controlling fire, neutralizing natural catastrophes, building shelter, and so on. Because men are endowed with greater upper body strength than women, and because men do not give birth or nurse, it is logical as well as efficient that they be used in this expendable manner by the group, as Friedl has convincingly argued (1975). Simply stated: for biological reasons "a population can survive the loss of men more easily than that of women" (ibid.:135). It is, in fact, the accepting of this very expendability that often constitutes the measure of manhood, a circumstance that may help explain the constant emphasis on risk taking as evidence of manliness. If one considers the hazards thus inherent in the male role in both provisioning and protecting, it becomes clear that in most societies men face qualitatively different risks than women; such differences exist both in the way danger is negotiated and in the implication of risk-taking behavior for the person's reputation.

Again, one must not exaggerate sexual differences. All human beings experience dangers: women face severe risks in childbirth, and they also have to measure up to stringent and sometimes punitive community standards. More to the point, women face the unpredictable danger of sexual abuse or even of rape with all its terrors and humiliations. Yet, unlike all-male contests such as war or sports, rape is rarely conceived of as a noble contest in which a women is expected to prove her fighting abilities. Few societies actively encourage women to seek out potential rapists in order to prove their bravery in physical combat. Rather, most societies regard rape as a crime or, in some cases, as a punishment for a moral transgression to which women are expected meekly to submit. In the former instance, to run away from a rapist carries no social opprobrium and is in fact a generally approved strategy. An intended rape victim's womanhood will rarely be questioned in any case, although she may be unfairly criticized for other reasons. Again, I do not wish to suggest that women have it easier than men, but rather that their performances are judged by different standards and that these inspire different gender ideals. The main difference seems to be that men are expected to seek out and confront danger as a means of showing valor, while women are most often expected to avoid such situations. I think it is safe to add to this that men are no more "naturally" brave than women are and that their risk-seeking response is counterphobic and culturally—rather than biologically—conditioned. This difference in role is important and explains much about manhood cults and images.

But now it is time to return to our extended case studies. In the next two chapters, we look at tribal societies in which manhood is marked by chronological stages and rituals. Our first case is that of the Samburu, an East African people; after considering them, plus a few other ritualized examples for comparative purposes, we move back to New Guinea for an in-depth look at the Sambia of the eastern Highlands.

❋ ❋ ❋ ❋ ❋ 6

Markers to Manhood: Samburu

> It has always been the prime function of
> mythology and rite to supply the symbols
> that carry the human spirit forward, in
> counteraction to those other constant
> human fantasies that tend to tie it back.
> —Joseph Campbell, *The Hero
> with a Thousand Faces*

Living in different continents, pursuing different goals, the Trukese brawlers, the Mehinaku wrestlers, the American he-men, and the Spanish macho-men have little in common other than their passionate concern for demonstrating manhood. But they are alike in one other way: they all navigate a pathway to manliness that is without clear signposts. To attain their goal they inch forward by trial and error, following sometimes vague injunctions laid down by their cultural script. Along the way, they must avoid pitfalls and temptations that tie them back, in Campbell's terms above, to childhood.

Their voyage to manhood, then, resembles what Erik Erikson in his *Childhood and Society* (1950) referred to as epigenetic stages of psychosocial development. By this he meant step-by-step sequences of growth which, when transversed, confer upon the individual simultaneously an ego-identity, or sense of self,

123

and a cultural identity appropriate to his or her time and place. As Erikson showed by comparing a variety of cultures, each society provides its own unique materials and rewards by which incremental steps are encouraged. The process itself remains similar with the same end, but the details of the passage differ widely.

Many traditional societies are highly structured in the way they acknowledge adulthood for both sexes, providing rigid chronological watersheds as, for example, ceremonies or invest-ments, complete with magical incantations and sacred parapher-nalia. Others, more changeful, such as Western industrial so-cieties, are loosely structured with little public recognition of progress and certainly no magic. Some, as Erikson showed for modern America, offer a bewildering range of options for men at every stage of life, creating problems of diffuseness and ambi-guity—a "dilemma" (Rochlin 1980; Kamarovsky 1976) or a "crisis of masculinity" (Habegger 1982)—that men must resolve in their own way to reach their culture's goal. The result, as in contemporary America, can often be a "makeshift masculinity" (Raphael 1988).

A number of primitive societies provide collective rites of passage that usher youths through sequential stages to an un-equivocal manhood. Such rites "dramatize" (Young 1965) the masculine transition through a clear-cut process of ritual inves-titure complete with emblems and culminating in the public conferral of an adult status that equals manhood. The basic framework for interpreting these male rituals of initiation was provided long ago by Arnold van Gennep in his classic *The Rites of Passage* (1960), first published in 1908. The underlying theme of such passage rites, according to van Gennep, is a change in status and identity: the boy "dies" and is "reborn" a man, each stage accompanied by appropriate symbolization. For van Gennep, rites of passage represent the death of childhood. Van Gennep claimed that this death-rebirth theme is played out in three stages: separation, transition, and incorporation. During the first stage, the boy severs relations with childhood, often literally, by renouncing the mother or being forcibly taken away from her. In the transition stage, he is sent away to a new place in the bush or is otherwise isolated where he remains in limbo, a "liminal" (or transitional) status when he is neither boy nor man but something in-between. Finally, he emerges a "man," through the vigorous exit ceremonies such as those we will examine here.

Such prolonged and collective rites of passage are found mainly in primitive (or preliterate) societies. Peasants and urban peoples rarely celebrate adulthood for either sex through elaborate or sacred ritualization, usually opting for tacit recognitions of individual growth. As we have seen, the Mediterranean and Middle Eastern peoples, in particular, are generally left to their own devices, as are modern Americans and most other Westerners. An exception is the Jews (if the Jews indeed can be so classified), who present an interesting case in point of ritual dramatization. Let me consider them for a moment as we turn toward the issue of ritualized manhood.

As is well known, the Bar Mitzvah ceremony among the Jews confers an official manhood status, usually at age thirteen. A centerpiece of religious and ethnic identity, it is both a chronological marker and a ritual of initiation, dramatized publicly. The ceremony is individual, rather than collective, but often the entire congregation participates, adding a community flavor. Because Jewish culture in the United States has a familiar, close-to-home quality, the Bar Mitzvah has not been the subject of much sociological interest here, especially since, in modern secular Jewish-American culture, the rite resembles nothing more profound than an exercise in extravagant partying. Still, observation of the rite can tell us much about the nature of the masculine transition under advanced, monotheistic, literate conditions, because underlying everything is the traditional involvement with the acquisition of male powers.

One feature of the Bar Mitzvah often forgotten in the modern vulgarization of the ceremony is that it entails, among other things, a specific test of the initiate's mettle. The youth must memorize and publicly recite important passages from the

Torah, in Hebrew, in the presence of both the congregation and a ritual specialist, or rabbi, who has instructed him and who certifies his performance. The initiate can either pass or fail in this; the whole procedure depends upon his public performance. This examination element is present even in the watered-down Reform ceremony in which circuslike entertainments overshadow the serious religious purpose. But how comes this arcane recital to be a test of cultural competence? Can this memorization and recitation of sacred texts be compared to the physical testing of the other peoples we have discussed?

On the surface there is a tenuous similarity to the strong thought of the Trukese weekend pugilists, which also implies a competence in male "thinking," and certainly there is an element of risk in the public exposure. Yet the deeper homologies are obscured by the surface variability of expression, its doctrinal rather than physical outcome. The similarity lies in a form of testing that measures cultural fitness and prepares the individual for making contributions to specific, and historically valid, group goals.

The test for the Jewish boy is one of memory and comprehension, the successful mastery of sacred texts; but the abilities being measured are clearly intellectual skills of a particular sort, especially scholarly potential. For example, in my own experience—typical of secular suburban culture in the northeastern United States—the process amounted to a purely academic performance, rather like taking an examination in school, or so it seemed to me. This performance constituted, in this milieu, a critical arena of personal achievement with all its attendant anxieties and possibilities of both public humiliation and triumph. During the memorization and recital, the boy is, as van Gennep argued, in a limbo or transitional status; afterward, if successful, he reemerges a "man" and childhood is dead, a victim again of manly competence.

Stereotypically, the Jewish people are not associated with the phallic posturing of the more warlike peoples we have discussed above. Their avenue of success has always been intellectual, to live by one's wits. Viewed in this light, we can see that the Jewish youth achieves a transition to a culturally constituted manhood in a way that serves to measure publicly those skills by which the group itself excels and by which it survives and prospers. This "ethnic niche" approach (Barth 1969) to male ritual lets us see manhood imagery in the light of a broader theory of economic adaptation of the group within a wider context of social relations. Not all challenges are physical and not all success can be measured against an external opponent.

Yet, despite their lack of a warlike tradition, the Jews do have a manhood concept that shares certain features with that of more bellicose peoples. Even secular, assimilated Jewish-American culture, one of the few in which women virtually dominate men, has a notion of manhood. A wife who is satisfied with her husband will say that he is a "Mensch," which in both Yiddish and its parent tongue, German, means a real man; and her mother, the ultimate judge of manly virtue, might even agree. Being a Mensch means being competent, dependable, economically secure, and most of all helpful and considerate to dependents. In modern middle-class Jewish culture, the Mensch is a take-charge kind of personality, a firm, dependable pillar of support. He has fathered presentable children, provided economic support for his family, and given his wife what she needs (or, rather, wants).

The opposite of the Mensch is the bungler, the failure who lets others take advantage of him. He is alternately called, in all the richness of Yiddish, a schlemiel (jerk), a schnook (dope), a nudnik (nincompoop), a schmendrick (nitwit), a schnorrer (toady), or most commonly a schmuck ("prick," but literally a useless bauble, used to mean bumbling or incompetent). All these synonyms (and there are many others: putz, nebbish, schmo, schmeggegie) convey the sense of masculine inferiority or disgrace measured in degrees of inadequacy and comic ineptitude in culturally-assigned jobs and tasks. The schlemiel or the schmuck is a failure in the Jewish tradition of what a man should be (one rarely hears these terms used to describe women). He is the subject of endless ridicule. He has let his family down by being incompetent. He represents the Yiddish equivalent of the Mehinaku trash yard man or the New Guinea rubbish man: the antihero, the nonman. He has failed the test of manhood.

But to return to the question of more exotic rituals of passage, in this and the following chapter we will look closely at two very different societies that award manhood through ritual testing of male competence: the pastoralist Samburu of East Africa and the horticultural Sambia of Highland New Guinea. Neither could be confused with suburban Jews. First the Samburu.

A STRUCTURED ASCENSION TO MANHOOD

The British anthropologist Paul Spencer (1965, 1973) has studied the East African Samburu tribe for many years, beginning in the 1950s. The following account is drawn mainly from his classic monograph, *The Samburu* (1965), and from a worthy companion study, *Nomads in Alliance* (1973). The Samburu are a black Nilotic pastoral people who live in an upland plateau between Lake Rudolf and the Uaso Ngiro river in northern Kenya. They were colonized like many of their neighboring tribes by the British at the turn of the century but not so severely treated or forcibly acculturated as some other tribes. In language and culture, they are very similar to the more famous and colorful Masai (or Maasai), to whom they are historically related (we will take a peek at the Masai later), and to a host of neighboring East African cattle pastoralists such as the Rendille, Jie, Turkana, and Nuer, among many others.

Like these other pastoral tribes, the Samburu still live mainly off their herds of cattle, sheep, goats, plus a few donkeys, as their ancestors did, using everything but the squeal. It is upon the value of cattle in particular that the emphasis is squarely placed in traditional Samburu culture, as it is among the Dodoth of Uganda, whom we met earlier, at times almost to the exclusion of small stock. Possession of cattle here is the mark of a man of substance, a big man. A man who has cattle is important, they say. "He can have many wives and many sons to look after his herds" (Spencer 1965:3). Cattle represent both the principal source of nourishment and the main trade item; they are the central cultural value—aside from wives and children. It should therefore come as no surprise that their manhood imagery revolves around competence in dealing with herds, as it did among the Dodoth.

In the Samburu culture, cattle represent liquid wealth—an all-purpose currency for trading and for thus acquiring other good things. The Samburu are as obsessed with this cattle wealth as the Jews are with learning, the Trukese with fighting and accumulating consumer goods, and the Mehinaku with fishing and wrestling. The most deeply held ideal among them is the notion that each man should have his own herd and ultimately be able to manage it independently and see to its increase. The key term in this equation is *independent,* meaning both economic and social freedom: no debts, no lords, no masters. But aside from possession, a man must also be in full, uncompromised control of his stock; he must be viewed as an autonomous entrepreneur of herds, exercising administrative control, without even a whiff of dependency about him. The Samburu are insistent upon this point, regarding independent husbandry as the very basis of adult male status.

Accumulated wealth in the form of meat, managed and augmented through careful and unencumbered stock-breeding, allows a man to marry often in this polygynous society and to achieve the coveted status of "worthy man" by adding wives, wealth, and children to his lineage. A man rich in cattle is a worthy elder and "a man of respect," but only if he is also "generous to the point of self denial" (ibid.:26). That is, Samburu men accumulate herds so that, bursting with pride, they can give them away, engaging in a "battle" of generosity in the tribal competition to distribute food to the people (ibid.). To manage this greedy generosity, a man must be free to trade and breed cattle and to slaughter on his own initiative.

In the past, before the British came in the early years of this

century, the Samburu, like the fierce Masai, were courageous
warriors as well as stockmen, but warfare has virtually ceased
since the arrival of the Pax Britannica. One of the main goals of
East African warfare and raiding formerly was to capture cattle,
and the Samburu warriors ranged far and wide, battling and
raiding the powerful Masai and the tough Boran (to whom they
are also distantly related) in order to build up their herds. In
return, they were raided and preyed upon by their equally opportunistic neighbors. Accordingly, the principal way for a Samburu youth to garner approval was to travel far and wide in
order to kill people of other tribes and to steal their stock for
prestige, "without any political justification" (ibid.:125). In turn,
they were attacked by others, so every Samburu man was expected to be a brave warrior. The survival of the tribe depended
upon it.

It appears, then, from Spencer's description that warfare had
an overt economic as well as prestige motivation. When all this
abruptly ceased after the imposition of peace by the British, the
Samburu were not to be denied, and they continued to engage in
small-scale skirmishing with the purpose not so much of killing
but of rustling cattle, as did their neighbors. Because cattle rustling is the easiest and most expeditious means of acquiring stock
and of increasing herd size in a short time, it remains a critical
coefficient of male social value. Manhood thus retains a military
quality, and all "worthy" men are expected to engage in successful marauding, for otherwise they cannot be rich and cannot
sponsor the festivals and feasts that nourish and enrich the tribe.
So previously, while the youths engaged in warfare "with a definite role to play in the survival of the tribe" (ibid.:149), today, with
the tribe's survival no longer at stake, the main context for the
display of courage and manly virtue is in the accumulation of
stock through raiding, an economic end of lavish gifting in feasts
and rituals, in which personal courage provides the means of
expression. Especially for young men (called *moran*, an important
term we will return to shortly), who have little other opportunity
to amass animals for breeder stock, raiding and rustling represent the principal means of achieving manhood and all its social

rewards: respect, honor, wives, children. The only way to win a wife is by showing one's potential as a herdsman to potential parents-in-law.

In some respects the Samburu, like the Ethiopian Amhara, have a set of fiercely held gender ideals that closely resemble those of the Mediterranean peoples we met earlier. Aside from personal autonomy and force, they, too, have strong notions of masculine "honor" (*nkanyit*) and a corollary ideal of "prestige" (Samburu term not given). These notions are related, but not identical. Honor is tied up with meeting expectations as a member of a corporate group defined by genealogy or affinity— whether lineage, clan, club, or age-set—and thereby protecting the group's collective reputation. Prestige is tied up with matters of personal status within any particular social group (ibid.:107), therefore containing an element of intragroup rivalry. As Spencer describes it, questions of degrees of masculine honor imply satisfying tribal ideals, not necessarily leading to intra-tribal competition (ibid.:107–10). However, both notions relate strongly to displays of physical courage, and both imply a touchy male vanity that will tolerate no slights. Both notions also imply a fierce defense of the social unit of which one is a member. Honor is clearly male reputation measured by degrees of control over and protection of units of collective identity—no different structurally from the Mediterranean variants we have seen.

These traditional male values, despite modernization and government suppression, remain vibrant. They strongly resemble the main components in the discussion of Mediterranean honor by Jane Schneider (1971) and Julian Pitt-Rivers (1965, 1977), among others. Spencer says the following: "Today, honour and prestige are still treasured values of the *moran* [youth], and account for much of their behavior. A moran who has been slighted in some way—perhaps he has been taunted or his mistress has been seduced—is expected to retaliate against the offender, and hence it is his *honour* which is involved. But when he exceeds these expectations in some way, asserting himself more than is necessary, it becomes also a matter of personal prestige" (1965:111).

Strong stress on personal prestige and group honor is a social value we would expect from a society with a proud military tradition and an acephalous, segmentary political organization. But the Samburu, like the Andalusians and many other less militaristic peoples, round out this corporate "honor" with other associated male values that relate directly to notions of cultural competence and sexual prowess. The composite image of the worthy man includes a heavy emphasis on economic self-sufficiency and productivity. Material self-denial and an associated "giver" status are elevated to moral paramountcy. The ideal among the Samburu is that a man "should aim at increasing his herd and the size of the family he founds until he can form a homestead in its own right" (ibid.:12). In other words, he is expected to reproduce the homestead, the basic kinship unit of the tribe, by the sweat of his brow and to make it grow and prosper so that it becomes more than self-sufficient, to be fruitful and multiply, as in Jehovah's exhortation to the Israelites. A man must produce both cattle and children in equal measure, protecting them both from predators and interlopers, and he must expend his social energies in economic reinvestment rather than personal consumption that might deplete his family's precious patrimony. The Samburu man is always under public pressure to measure up in this regard. But his worthiness comes not only from accumulating but also from lavish gifting during feasts. This donor function looms larger in Samburu male imagery than sexual valor.

An institutionalized competition of tribal generosity spurs men to try to best each other in a kind of potlatching of meat. At every feast, each man tries to give the most and take the least. "At most feasts, for instance, younger men would insist on giving their seniors the best pieces of meat, and affines would be treated in a similar way. Even among age mates, whose equality was beyond question, there was a continual battle of politeness in which the man who seemed to eat the least and encourage his neighbors to eat the most was the moral victor, the truly worthy man" (ibid.:26). A selfish man, an "eater" of his own herds, is described as *laroi*—a term used among the Samburu for small, paltry things, undersized or fragile objects, and for tools that do not work effectively, like a leaky water bucket or a Land Rover that keeps breaking down. The *laroi* man, then, is childlike (undersized), mean, deficient, wasteful, inefficient (ibid.:27). He takes more than he gives. Like the trash yard man, the rubbish man, the schlemiel, he is despised on this account, and this dislike can amount to an "unvoiced curse bringing with it disaster" upon his useless person (ibid.:28). Conversely, the Samburu sense of masculinity is a kind of moral invisible hand that guides the activities of self-respecting individuals toward the collective end of capital accumulation. The goal is to become a tribal patron, creating dependencies in others, involving oneself in battles of generosity with other men in which everyone indirectly benefits (Spencer 1973:39–41). In this equation, subordination to another man is considered by the Samburu "an ineradicable stain upon personal honour" (1965:108–09).

AGE-SETS

What makes the Samburu famous in the ethnographic literature is their system of age-sets and colorful attendant rituals by which the male life cycle is advanced and celebrated. In this, they are similar to their related East African tribes, but because of Spencer's superb documentation they serve as an exemplar of the ritualized masculine transition common to all. Samburu males must pass through a complicated series of age-sets and age-grades by which their growing maturity and responsibility as men in the light of these tribal values are publicly acknowledged. Basically, there are three main age-grades, which are subdivided into a number of chronological age-sets. These main groupings, the age-grades, are those of, first, boy; then *moran*, or adolescent/young adult (Spencer gives moran as both singular and plural); and finally elder.

A celebrated feature of East African cattle societies, the special status of moran is a long, drawn-out transitional period of testing; it is the one with which I am most concerned here. Previously adapted toward preparing boys for a stoic warrior's life, and today for success in rustling, moranhood begins at about age fourteen or fifteen and lasts for about twelve years, divided into numerous age-sets. It is initiated by a circumcision procedure described below, which begins the separation stage.

After passing the test of circumcision, the initiates are spatially isolated as a group, being removed from the confines of the village to a preselected place in the bush where they will live for the next decade or so, perfecting their skills and functions as elders. In addition, during moranhood there are a number of subsidiary rituals and tests that each youth must perform. The most important of these are the arrow ceremony, the naming ceremony, and, finally, the bull ceremony, all involving tests of skill, endurance, or competence. The bull ceremony involves the boy's first sacrifice of his own ox and the distribution of its meat. This represents the exit ceremony of moranhood, eventually ushering the young man into full status as *lee,* or worthy man (ibid.:108), corresponding to van Gennep's incorporation stage. But no moran may marry or father children until he kills his first ox, so everything, again, revolves around the moran's ability to acquire and provide meat. Reflecting this, the ritualization of manhood culminates in a very specific act of tribal generosity indicating a future of successful industry. Rather than describing all the minor details of the age-grade series, which the reader may find clearly elaborated in Spencer's classic studies (1965, 1973), I will only point out the main features of this transitional period as they relate to the question of the meaning of manhood.

MORANHOOD

The first test for the boys entering moranhood is that of the traumatic circumcision procedure. A trial of bravery and stoicism, the operation is intensely painful, and no anesthetics are used; nor is anything done to lessen the anticipatory terror of the initiate, suggesting that the purpose is specifically one of testing. Each youth, placed on view before his male relatives and prospective in-laws, must remain motionless and silent during the cutting, which may last four minutes or more. Even an involuntary twitch would be interpreted as a sign of fear. The word used for such a minor movement is *a-kwet,* literally "to run," which Spencer glosses as "to flinch" (1965:103). If the boy makes the slightest movement or sound, there is a collective gasp of shock and dismay; he is forever shamed as a coward and will be excluded from joining his age-set in the march toward adult status. No other initiate would want to form an age-mate relationship with a boy who "runs," for this boy will bear a stigma of inferiority for the rest of his life. Besides being cruelly ostracized himself (1973:89), he brings ruin upon his entire lineage forever. In the Samburu proverb, all of his people must publicly "eat their respect" (1965:104) because one of their boys has run.

This use of an oral metaphor to express collective shame is of comparative interest here, reminding one not only of the New Guinea Rubbish Man, whose main fault is to "eat" the land without producing, but also of the role of oral or "hunger" imagery and of similar physical tropes in the construction of masculine identity that others have noted elsewhere (see Brandes 1980; Herzfeld 1985a). The Samburu metaphor conjures a frequent image that relates prestige to the function of giving others food to eat, in this case, of provisioning with cattle. Instead of providing the stuff of respect—the meat of worthiness for others to eat, that is, to admire—the shamed lineage members are forced to swallow (and to choke on) their pride. In producing a boy who has "run," they become consumers rather than donors of a value symbolically likened to meat: the substance of honor. The entire lineage suffers from this inversion of valences.

The food references continue, made concrete in associated moran proscriptions on meat and milk, both primary foods. During the early stages of the moranhood, the young novice must ritually pass by his own mother's hut for the last time. At this dramatic and stylized juncture, he swears publicly before her and before all those assembled that he will no longer eat any meat "seen by any married woman" (Spencer 1965:87), that is, a woman of his mother's social status. Such meat is henceforth *menong'*, despised food. Furthermore, the boy swears to refrain from drinking milk from any source inside the village settlement, and he also forswears drinking milk altogether if it has been produced by certain categories of people related to the women he may later marry. This self-denial is important because milk, either alone or mixed with cow's blood, is a major source of food for the Samburu. A much loved delicacy in all its forms, it is naturally hard to resist. Giving it up is a real sacrifice. Doing so demonstrates a maturity of resolve that amounts to a symbolic disavowal of dependency.

These frustrating food taboos are of major cultural significance to the Samburu; they see such abstemiousness as "a determining criterion of moranhood" (ibid.:87). Although this is missed by Spencer, whose interests lie elsewhere, essentially what the young initiates are communicating through these oral renunciations is the symbolic forswearing of the nourishing of mothers and potential affines. It is an act of self-denial by which the boy enacts a personal transformation from receiver to giver of sustenance. The milk prohibitions communicate two linked declarations: first, the boy renounces all food dependency on his own mother; second, he renounces the juvenescent wish to seek substitute oral gratification among affines and older women, people whom he must later support through his own economic activities. This double abnegation of maternal nurturing reenacts both ritually and psychodynamically the trauma of weaning, for it conveys a public confirmation that he has renounced the breast voluntarily in favor of delayed gratifications of work-culture. All women will henceforth be treated as receivers rather than givers of food; the boy will no longer need mothering.

Aside from food and ritual taboos, the main ideal of moranhood has to do with acquiring cattle, which, as we have seen, is the main source of tribal wealth. Much of moranhood is spent in learning how to manage a herd and how to procure cattle, as this skill will enable a moran to create and sustain a new homestead. The boys learn husbandry early: they are led out to their isolated bush settlements by elders, who exhort them, "Go to your cattle camps . . . to your herds . . . so that you may become rich elders" (1965:141). For the impecunious youths, this entails mainly raiding and stealing, which in turn demand raw courage and steely fortitude. As Spencer notes, stock theft, preferably from some other tribe, remains an ideal of moranhood today, "and many are tempted to try it" (ibid.:141). Rustlers may be captured, beaten, jailed, or even killed, but, if successful, rustling bestows manhood on the young moran. This naturally makes him attractive to the girls, who find such exploits manly. The girls are "enthralled with the notion that moran should be manly in every way (ibid.:118).

SEXUAL MAGNETISM

In this confluence of the erotic and economic masculinity, there is something truly universal—which prompts a brief digression on male courtship styles. The way the Samburu moran impress their objects of desire by running risks in foreign lands seems to conform to a virtually global strategy of courting. It reminds me very much, for example, not only of the Trukese, but also of certain peripatetic heroes of Western myth and literature who win the girl by heroic deeds that advance fundamental group interests. A classic example is the figure of Shakespeare's most virile hero, Othello.

In the tragedy, which is very much concerned with male honor and its sexual component, the Moorish captain steals the desirable Desdemona away from a host of lesser suitors. But he does not win her by good looks or physical charm alone. Moreover, he is considerably older than she is—an "old black ram," as his critics say, not very beautiful to look at. Rather, the love magic he uses is the splendid history of his own military escapades told in loving but modest detail. Right at the beginning of the action, after their elopement, Othello appears before the Duke of Venice to explain himself and to answer charges, having been accused publicly by lesser men, Iago and Brabantio among them, of having used witchcraft to seduce Desdemona. How else, they ask, could this crude warrior have succeeded where more likely men have failed? So he must have "Abus'd her delicate youth with drugs or minerals" (act I, scene i.).

Always forthright and honorable, Othello states the unvarnished truth: that Desdemona heard from his own lips in her father's house of his many exploits in foreign lands and of the risks and dangers he had experienced in defending the realm. Hearing of these "hairbreadth scapes i' the imminent deadly breach," she has fallen in love with this fearless adventurer, wishing that "heaven had made her such a man." Othello continues, "She lov'd me for the dangers I had pass'd; / And I lov'd her that she did pity them. / This only is the witchcraft I have us'd" (I. iii). His simple explanation is convincing, restoring his honor and winning over his listeners. His bravery in service to the realm has made him irresistible, hence masculine. In Elizabethan England, as among the Samburu, this romantic appeal of "passing danger" in defense of basic values is something that everyone would easily have understood as the mythic confabulation of manhood.

As a collective representation, masculinity often forges an iron shield of protectiveness on the smithy of honor and courage; sexual magnetism follows, as though virility were itself a matter of braving danger to succor those one loves. The connection between virility and civic-mindedness comes out clearly and dramatically in Spencer's discussion of courtship and sexuality among the Samburu. Let us return to these East African Othellos.

The context for this heroic theme is the Samburu tribal dances. Fabulous entertainments bringing youths and maidens together in their finery, these are main times for sexual dalliance. During these exuberant affairs, in which all the young people participate eagerly as a preliminary to trysting, the nubile girls, standing on the sidelines, sing lilting songs that taunt those moran who have never been on a stock raid. In their finery they chant their lyrics, making galling insinuations of cowardice. Moved by the beauty and challenge of the girls, the boys are whipped into a frenzy of desire. Driven to try their hand at rustling without delay, they impulsively take up the challenge. Spencer observes: "That the taunts of the girls help to maintain this ideal and induce the moran to steal may be judged from this description by one moran. 'You are standing there in the dance, and a girl starts to sing. She raises her chin high and you see her throat. And then you want to go and steal some cattle for yourself. You start to shiver. You leave the dance and stride into the night, afraid of nothing and only conscious of the fact that you are going to steal a cow'" (1965:127).

Aroused by the girl's taunts, the youthful swain decides he must make his mark to impress her. Ostentatiously "afraid of nothing," he strides out of the settlement into the dark night of danger to prove himself by filching cattle-wealth. His objective, consciously stated, is to pass dangers in order to gain the laurels that win a woman. How like Othello and his deeds of "disastrous chances / Of moving accidents by flood and field . . . the battles, sieges, fortunes" (I. iii.). The link between cattle rustling and sexual conquest is linguistically recognized in the Samburu language, as also in colloquial Swahili, for, interestingly, the word *a-purr* ("to steal") can also mean "to seduce" when applied to a woman (ibid.:148).

In the passage just quoted, the fleeting mention of "shivering" merits a note as well. A traditional muscular discharge of tension among the East African warriors preparatory to battle in precontact days, this shivering forms part of the manly code of the modern Samburu cattle rustler. Like their neighbors, the Masai, the Samburu moran do a "shaking" or palpitating in which they say they are "angry" and about to perform noteworthy deeds of bravery. The body movements indicate a total lack of fear, a contempt of bodily danger, a willingness to expend their blood—their lives if necessary. According to Spencer's ac-

count (ibid.:264), the Samburu regard this muscular phenomenon as a sign of "manliness, an indication of the assertive
qualities expected of the moran." So when the men "shiver" they
are again publicly communicating their courage in the face of
death, their commitment to be men, to meet the demands made
upon them by their culture in which they are no more or less in
social terms than the sum of their achievements. The palpitations are a signal of intent, like drinking or self-scarification
among the Trukese.

The conjunction of moral and gender images shows that the
requisite character traits of the moran—assertiveness, productivity, fearlessness—serve as proofs not only of Samburu manhood but also of worthiness and rectitude more inclusively, and,
one may also say, of practical utility. The code of the moran
creates at the same time respectability and gender-identity,
which are again equated in manly images; so the ritual cycle that
makes men from boys is a kind of structural transformation by
which children are changed into adults, narcissistic passivity is
changed into selfless agency, and the raw protoplasm of nature
is changed into finished culture. In this respect, the moran's
code, effected through ritual performances, resembles the heroic self-defining code created by such twentieth-century Western
novelists as Hemingway as a means of establishing moral order
from the disillusionment and cynicism that followed the Great
War. And in its mythic power to confabulate a male identity
through the appropriation and ordering of value from the natural world the moran's code also resembles Walter Pater's criterion of the artistic act of masculine self-creation.

There could be no purer exponents of grace under pressure
than these virile Africans. But what of the youths who fail the
test of manliness? Like the Trukese reprobates who are told to
take the breast like a baby, these black African youths are accused of a failure to grow—that is, they are accused of the worst
sin, of backsliding. Spencer notes that any failure of the moran's
code of behavior is met with immediate accusations not so much
of deviance or immorality as of "immaturity," of "behaving like

a child" (1965:87), which is worse. This type of criticism bites deeply enough to force the necessary reforms, since the accusation of retrogression is the most humiliating of taunts. Like the mockery of the pretty girls who during the tribal dances show their throats and demand a cow in return for their affections, the charge of being childish strikes a mortal blow to the progress of the moran toward the status of manhood, the goal of his ten-year apprenticeship.

A PARALLEL: THE MASAI

As I mentioned before, the Samburu experience is repeated among a host of other East African cattle-herding tribes. A colorful parallel is the Masai, sometimes held up as the apotheosis of the East African cattle-warrior complex. Let us take a brief comparative look at their ideas of masculinity. Here I use data provided by a female anthropologist, Melissa Llewelyn-Davies (1981), to avoid male bias; in addition I use data from the autobiography of a Masai man, Tepilit Ole Saitoti (1986), to avoid ethnocentrism—charges that might be made, though not substantiated I think, about Spencer.

The Masai, living in the hills of the Kenya-Tanzania border, have the same age-set institution and moran transition as the Samburu. Among these famous warriors, also, the qualities of masculinity are created by passage through this critical threshold, which they call "the door to manhood" (Saitoti 1986:56). For the Masai, manhood is a status that does not come naturally, but rather is an elaborated idea symbolically constructed as a series of tests and confirmations during the moran period, which lasts for approximately the same length of time as among the Samburu (Llewelyn-Davies 1981:352). Paramount in this formative period is the demonstration of physical courage, which is the sine qua non of the Masai warrior. Physical courage, however, is needed not only against human enemies but also against the destructive forces of nature, especially wild animals and predators such as lions, rhinos, and elephants, which are particularly active in Masailand. Whenever there is danger, the moran mobilize to meet it head on:

> Moran are, first of all, warriors. In the event of an attack upon a village, all able-bodied men present will attempt to defend it. But the responsibilities of moran in this regard are greater than those of others. . . . They are always the first to be called upon for the execution of dangerous tasks such as dealing with the wild animals that sometimes harass people and livestock; indeed lion hunts are an important and highly ritualized feature of moranhood. . . . Thus moran are associated with death and killing of enemies, both human and animal. (Ibid.:345)

As guardians of their people, the Masai moran therefore must be very brave. They live unaided in the forests; they hunt lions, scare away rhinos, and they face death on raids. The message comes across early: mothers constantly exhort their small sons to be brave "like moran" (ibid.:349). Induction into moranhood begins only when the Masai boy has shown indications of the necessary qualities. In his autobiography, Tepilit Ole Saitoti (1986) writes of how he nagged his father to let him be initiated into manhood, only to be told to wait. His cautious father was looking for signs of readiness in the boy. Finally, one dark night Tepilit bravely confronted and killed a huge lioness that had attacked his family's cattle and threatened the children. After this, his father relented: "Two months after I had killed the lioness, my father summoned all of us together. In the presence of all his children he said, 'We are going to initiate Tepilit into manhood. He has proven before all of us that he can now save children and cattle'" (ibid.:65).

During their apprenticeship, the boys undergo the same painful circumcision as the Samburu. The initiate must not so much as blink an eye. Shortly before his initiation, the apprehensive Tepilit is told, "You must not budge; don't move a muscle or even blink. You can face only one direction until the operation is completed. The slightest movement on your part will mean you are a coward, incompetent and unworthy to be a Masai man" (ibid.:66). Although Masai girls are also circumcised (excision of the clitoris and the labia minora), bravery during the operation is not an important matter for them. No lasting stigma attaches to the many who do cry out or even try to escape. Girls are not expected to be brave; their self-control is "of little public significance," as the feminist Llewelyn-Davies writes (1981:351). Tepilit again: "It is common to see a woman crying and kicking during circumcision. Warriors are usually summoned to help hold her down" (1986:69).

The Masai conception of masculinity has much to do with physical courage, but it encompasses much more. Llewelyn-Davies in fact argues that Masai manhood is firmly based not only on the warrior ethic but also on the idea of economic independence, and that Masai manhood is grounded in property accumulation (1981:331). A moran must not only learn the art of war but must also learn to be an autonomous herdsman and to create disposable wealth. His masculine potential is based as much on the accrual of wealth and its control and distribution as it is upon military prowess. She argues that moranhood must be seen as a process by which "propertyless boys" become "men" by gaining rights to property (*in jus*) and by giving this property away, creating rights over dependents (*in rem*). In contrast, women are permanently and inherently "dependent" (ibid.). It is this contrast that defines both gender statuses. This notion of maleness as dominance over property and persons is tied to a generalized stress on reproductive success and fertility. The aspiration of all men is conceptualized as being "the indefinite increase, not merely of his herds and flocks, but of the number of his human dependents" (ibid.:334–35).

Given the stress on prolific procreation, there is a macho sexual element here. Sexual competence is important to the Masai male image. A man must be aggressive in courtship and potent in sex. Tepilit tells the story of his friend, a young moran warrior, who boldly approaches a much older woman:

> He put a bold move on her. At first the woman could not believe his intention, or rather was amazed by his courage. The name of the warrior was Ngengeiya, or Drizzle.

"Drizzle, what do you want?"

"To make love to you."

"I am your mother's age."

"It's either her or you."

This remark took the woman by surprise. She had underestimated the saying, "There is no such thing as a young warrior." When you are a warrior, you are expected to perform bravely in any situation. Your age and size are immaterial.

"You mean you could really love me like a grown-up man?"

"Try me woman."

He moved in on her. Soon the woman started moaning with excitement, calling out his name. "Honey Drizzle, Honey Drizzle, you *are* a man." In a breathy, stammering voice, she said, "A real man."

A real man is brave in all risky situations. Like the audacious Honey Drizzle, he performs under pressure.

As among the Samburu, a generalized emphasis on procreativity is ritually formalized during the stage of life when a moran is expected to start procuring food. A high point of the boy's moranhood is the sacrifice of his first ox. The major portion of the meat is then given to the boy's mother, an act that is described as a thank-you to her for having reared and fed him as a boy. This ritual feeding of his mother symbolizes the boy's status reversal from consumer to provider of meat and thus indicates a responsible adult manhood. The tests of moranhood are thus "crucially important to masculine identity" (Llewelyn-Davies 1981:352). As the central concept upon which the tribe's prosperity rests, however, moranhood embodies even more to the Masai: "Moranhood thus embodies more than an abstract ideal of masculinity. It also displays Masai culture at its most brilliant; it is crucial to the image of the culture as Masai represent it to themselves and to the outside world" (ibid.:354). For the Masai, as for the Samburu, the idea of manhood contains also the idea of the tribe, an idea grounded in a moral courage based on commitment to collective goals. Their construction of manhood encompasses not only physical strength or bravery but also a moral beauty construed as selfless devotion to national identity. It embodies the central understanding that the man is only the sum of what he has achieved and that what he has achieved is nothing more or less than what he leaves behind.

Rites of Manhood: Sambia

Femininity unfolds naturally, whereas
masculinity must be achieved; and here is
where the male ritual cult steps in.
—Gilbert Herdt, *Rituals of Manhood*

With their rituals and their honor, the Samburu are closely related in both culture and
blood to their neighbors, and their practices
are common over a wide area. The same may
be said of the Sambia of New Guinea, whose
customs concerning gender are fairly representative of neighbors in the adjacent Highlands, although some have been forced to
abandon them because of white interference
or, more lately, Papuan government pressure.

The Sambia are an exceptionally well re-
searched people within the relatively large
Melanesia literature, thanks to the untiring
efforts of anthropologist Gilbert Herdt, who
has been reporting on them since the late
1970s in fascinating and voluminous detail.
They are of unusual interest to anthropologists because of the intensity and, to Western
eyes, perversity, of their masculine rites of
passage. These include acts of homosexual
fellatio, as well as the more usual bloodletting
and hazing. Given its oddity, this ritual homosexuality makes them an important test case
for our study of manhood images. How does

this homosexual passage fit in with the hyper-heterosexuality that we have seen before in manhood codes?

We have already met the Sambia in passing in chapter 5. They are a people obsessed with masculinity, which they regard as highly problematic, a quandary and a penance. Like other Highlanders, they are firmly convinced that manhood is an artificially induced state that must be forcibly foisted onto hesitant young boys by ritual means. Like the Samburu, they subject their boys to a painful induction into manhood through sequenced rites of transition. These rituals have been minutely described by Herdt in two engrossing publications (1981, 1982). What makes the Sambia special, even unique, is their phase of ritual homosexuality in which the youngsters are forced to perform fellatio on grown men, not for pleasure, but in order to ingest their semen. This then supposedly provides them with the substance or "seed" of a growing masculinity. As one of Herdt's informants, Tali, a Sambia ritual expert, instructs, "If a boy doesn't 'eat' semen, he remains small and weak" (Herdt 1981:1). This homosexual phase, however, like the alcoholic violence of the Trukese, is only temporary; it is later superseded by an adult life of "full heterosexuality" (ibid.:3), including marriage, procreation, and all the more usual masculine virtues. The homosexuality, therefore, is a passageway to "masculinization" (ibid.:205), but it is this seemingly contradictory relation of means and ends that makes the Sambia case so interesting and important.

THE CULTURAL CONTEXT

Unlike the Samburu, the Trukese, and the Mehinaku, who are plains or lowland peoples, the Sambia are at home in the steep mountains of the remote eastern New Guinea Highlands, today part of the new nation of Papua New Guinea. Proud of their high aeries, the Sambia like to say that their home is the nest of the high-ranging eagle, which they admire for its independence and power—qualities they cherish in men.

Their mountainous environment is one of breathtaking beauty and topographical drama. Herdt (ibid.:21–22) describes Sambia country as a land of lush panoramas, deeply vegetated valleys, and vertiginous precipices, often veiled in thick mists. It is also a land of "horrendous isolation," with unending precipitation and gloomy cloud cover that assert a melancholy influence upon the inhabitants at certain times of year, as they themselves declare. The Sambia are accustomed to living perched among high mountains and steep cliffs upon which they terrace their gardens. Great peaks surround and bulk over their settlements, creating a sense of both majesty and enclosure. Grandest of all is Mount Guinea (11,000 feet), in whose colossal shadow lies the village Herdt studied. The people who call themselves Sambia are relatively small in numbers, amounting in total to only about two thousand in the 1970s. This population is dispersed in various contiguous settlements along the mountain walls, constrained in its upward movement by ecological considerations that limit native horticultural practices. The Sambia are avid gardeners, relying mainly on the typical Highland staple, the sweet potato, and a few other herbaceous crops that flourish only at certain altitudes. In addition, the Sambia raise pigs and are practiced hunters, taking various forms of meat. Formerly, they were also brave warriors, fighting and raiding their neighbors, playing endless games of combat in both sneak attacks and pitched battles. It was an important way for a man to show courage and to build up his reputation. All this was stamped out by the colonial Australian government, but Sambia men still lovingly relate myths that associate their very existence to fissioning in the past as a result of tribal clashes.

One such myth tells of a great violent battle in which the aboriginal inhabitants of Sambia territory were vanquished. This defeat was followed by a cannibalistic feast of victims and subsequent immigration of the present population into what is now the Sambia heartland (Herdt 1981:23). The Sambia are veritable children of war and conquest; for them, the warrior was the archetypical hero upon whose feats their very existence as an independent people was predicated. This lasting heritage forms a living part of their image of manhood today and is enshrined in the tribal consciousness.

Also important to the image of manhood is competence in hunting, "that most masculine pursuit" in Sambia cultural reckoning (ibid.:83). Their hunting is not particularly risky in a physical sense because their prey is mainly small game, but it is risky in terms of status, because men are expected to be successful hunters and are ridiculed if they fail. Only men hunt; women are not allowed to participate. Hunting is of special value to the Sambia, not just as a source of needed protein in an area where domesticated pigs—the main meat of the Highlands— are few, but for ceremonial reasons. The rich ritual life of the Sambia is inextricably linked to the use of feral possum and forest birds, which provide skins and feathers for necessary decorations. Other animals provide equally vital ritual products. Unlike some other regions in the Highlands, for example, the Sambia "*must hunt* to acquire marsupials" (Herdt 1982:88) for the meat to celebrate marriages, funerals, and especially male initiations. These animals have attained an almost mythological importance in Sambia cosmology. Hence expertise in hunting, like war, is considered essential for demonstrating manliness, not only to acquire food itself, but also to sponsor feasts and ceremonies in which food is exchanged. Thus each killing "becomes a special triumph" for young men on their way to establishing their masculine credentials by public beneficence and display (ibid.:141).

Adult male status depends upon a few other criteria. As among the Samburu, an incompetent hunter may be denied the privilege of marrying; yet marriage is expected of all men, as is fatherhood, for reasons we have already discussed in chapter 5. Children are considered the most valuable resource and are eagerly desired by everyone, partly because of the belief that numbers mean safety. As in other societies, success in hunting leads not only to social prestige but also to sexual success. In this polygynous society, as in others, a good hunter can acquire many wives and mistresses; a poor hunter is scorned by women and potential affines. The similarity of Sambia hunting, as a moral obligation, to cattle raiding among the Samburu or fishing among the Mehinaku is immediately evident. In all cases, this culturally defined competence in resource management leads directly to reproductive success. Indeed, a poor hunter may lose not only his social standing but also his wife, who can legitimately leave him for another man who is a better hunter (ibid.:83). Thus, for all these reasons, men perform their manly functions as a route to social success in general, and, as Herdt says, "They must be that way" (ibid.:203). They must be manly because "warfare demands it, hunting requires it, women expect it. This is the Sambia view: it is the consuming impetus of masculine ritual" (ibid.).

SAMBIA GENDER IDEALS

Responding to such exigencies, the Sambia have two pivotal beliefs about the way men should be. First, drawing upon the glorious mythology of a warrior past and a hunting present, they espouse an ideal of masculinity based on an aggression model linked to bravery and stamina. Sambia men spin such idioms into "a particular conception of manhood" (ibid.:16) extolling toughness, imperviousness to danger and pain, decisive action, physical strength, and risk taking. These are the exact opposites of what they envision as ideal female traits. The embodiment of this ideal is the wartime fight leader, who serves as a model to all other men. The fight leader is, in every sense, strong, aggressive, and virile—the purest form of maleness. "So Sambia are consequently preoccupied with a warrior's concept of masculinity" (ibid.). Suffice it to say that this convergence of inspirational images and the warrior ideal, converted partially today into aggressive snaring of game, was of existential value to the group as a whole, since their very survival depended upon military prowess and killing. Unlike in some other places in Melanesia, warfare was no game for the Sambia. A man, and, by extension, his village, had to demonstrate his fitness in battle "or face destruction" (ibid.:18).

Herdt recognizes the obvious similarities to other preindustrial warrior societies in the Western tradition. He digresses momentarily to discuss resemblances between the Sambia and the ancient Spartans, who, like other Greeks of the time, also practiced a "manly" homosexuality while on the battlefield (cf. Vanggaard 1972). In both cases, the warrior ethic not only permitted but encouraged temporary homosexual relations between soldiers and boys. Such relations were not seen as effeminate either by the men or their society but in precisely the opposite terms, as masculine and as conducive to warrior resolve (more on this later).

One must point out, though, that in the cases of both Sparta and Sambialand, the soldier was always in the active role in the sex act, that is, the penetrator. The soldier's lover or partner was always a youth of inferior status who acted out the passive "feminine" role. The catamite, or male lover, in the ancient world, for example, was usually a youthful slave who was sodomized by an adult in a superior status (Veyne 1985:32). Similarly, the neophyte or initiate in contemporary New Guinea is a prepubescent boy, not yet considered a "man," so that the homoerotic act involved is, from a Sambia perspective, not truly homosexual at all, if by that term we mean consenting adults. Indeed, among the Sambia, adult homosexual relations are unheard of. Because of this and because of their ritualized and transient nature, "homosexual" may in fact not be the most accurate term to use in describing Sambia practices. As the fellatio is a means to an end rather than an end in itself, ritualized masculinization may be a more accurate (and less ethnocentric) term.

The other important Sambia belief about what constitutes manhood concerns its physiological or ontological status. Like other peoples already discussed, the Sambia believe that male maturation is not the result of innate biological development, which they believe does not occur in men. It must therefore be forced or initiated through the intervention of cultural artifices. In this way, masculinity is different as a status from femininity, which unfolds through biological maturation, a product of inherent physiological processes. In this respect, men are "weaker" than women, because they need outside help to develop; hence the elaborate rituals by which maleness comes about.

This belief is given very detailed exposition in Sambia ethnoscience. The Sambia actually have a kind of double standard in their concept of sexual development. As Herdt notes (1982:54), femininity is thought to be an inherent development in a girl's continuous association with her mother. Masculinity, on the other hand, is not an intrinsic result of maleness; "it is an achievement distinct from the mere endowment of male genitals" (ibid.). In short, while girls develop womanhood naturally because they retain ties to their mothers, boys have to be "grown" into men by cultural means: "masculinity must be achieved" (ibid.:55). All this makes one wonder if the Sambia have been reading the neo-Freudians (cf. Stoller and Herdt 1982).

However, their dualistic view of sexual maturation derives from Sambia notions of physiology, not from scholarly textbooks. The Sambia believe that women have a special internal organ, called *tingu,* present from birth, that slowly matures them naturally. Although boys have the same organ at birth, they are constitutionally inferior in this regard: their tingu is weak and inactive and requires semen to grow (Herdt 1981:167–72). The Sambia believe that masculinity is achieved only through ritual "insemination," which triggers the process, and through step-by-step guidance by elders thereafter; hence the importance of their male initiation rites, with which Herdt's book is principally occupied. The key to all this, as we shall see, is to get the boy away from the baneful influence of his mother so that his tingu may be stimulated to grow and implement the masculinization process. Closeness to the mother prevents this, pulling the boy back to a sexually indeterminate infantilism.

Though extreme for the New Guinea Highlands, Sambia beliefs about gender differences are not unique. In fact, such ideas are quite common in the Highlands; they represent an extreme version of a widespread and passionate insistence on the artificiality of maleness, which in some nearby societies attains the status of a kind of obsession. For example, among the Etoro, Onabasulu, and Kaluli tribes, described by Raymond Kelly (1974:16), there is a shared belief that "boys do not become physically mature as a result of natural processes." These peoples, like the Sambia, believe that "growth and attainment of physiological maturation is contingent upon the cultural process of initiation" (ibid; see also Schieffelin 1982:162). All these people go to extreme lengths to ensure male development.

Likewise, among the nearby Gururumba tribe, boys do not mature into men naturally but must be "made" into men by ritual activation (Newman and Boyd 1982:283–84). In all these cases above, the rituals of manhood include homosexual fellatio. Other Highlands tribes, for example the Mountain Ok, have the same beliefs about the frailty of manhood but without the ritualized homoeroticism (Barth 1987). Still others have retained the beliefs but have given up the fellatio rites because of the outrage of white Australian administrators. In all cases, these beliefs are intensely held and are the source of unrelenting anxiety.

Comparative studies of the Highlands material have shown the universality of this belief in the organic weakness of masculinity. For example, in his comprehensive survey of New Guinea male cults, Roger Keesing starts out by saying that their most distinctive feature is an emphasis on male gender as a created "rather than a natural" consequence of maturation (1982:5). He adds that everywhere in the region, growth and physical strength, bravery and manliness, are achieved through artificial means usually involving "sequences of isolation and ordeal, instruction and revelation" (ibid.:8). Almost everywhere in aboriginal New Guinea, he concludes, a boy must be "made into a man" through an abundant elaboration of ritual means (ibid.:9). Even where such beliefs are not stressed, as among the Mountain Ok (Barth 1987), boys' initiations are richly infused with growth magic to assure maturation. In all cases, boys must undergo tribulations that test their commitment to male ideals and propel them toward manhood, which is otherwise inconceivable.

SAMBIA RITUALS

All this brings us back to the question of the ritual fellatio—the standout feature of Sambia male initiation. As noted, the boys need to ingest semen, the kernel of masculinity, in order to stimulate their bodies to "masculinize." Such homeopathic beliefs may seem bizarre to some of us, considering the Western equation of a "healthy" heterosexuality with masculinity. But aside from the method of expression, I do not think this concept of masculinization should shock us too much. There are underlying similarities in motivation across cultural boundaries, if not in the actual practice.

Moreover, as we know from acquaintance with the ancient Greeks (Dover 1978), sexual inversion per se is not universally linked to a lack of masculinity in all the major Western traditions, nor is pederasty always a sign of effeminacy. Greek and Roman texts are full of homosexuality in action, and "lovers of boys were just as numerous as lovers of women" in classical antiquity (Veyne 1985:28). These Greek and Roman homosexuals did not necessarily give up their claim to masculinity. So long as this homosexuality conformed to current images of the "male" (active) role in sex play, it was entirely compatible with, in fact, supportive of, a fully masculine image in the society at large. Indeed, the Spartans, like other Greeks of the time, thought that such men made better soldiers because they had their lovers with them on the battlefield to prevent them from becoming lonely and depressed. In his study of Greek homosexuality, Kenneth Dover (1978:106) explores the issue at length and concludes that the "abandonment of masculinity" occurred in ancient Greece only if an adult man accepted the passive or receptive role in the sex act, because then he surrendered the male prerogative of control or dominance. The same was true of the Romans, who believed that "to be active was to be male, whatever the sex of the compliant partner" (Veyne 1985:29). Plutarch, in his *Dialogues on Love*, remarks, "Those who enjoy playing the passive role we treat as the lowest of the low, and we have not the slightest degree of respect or affection for them" (cited ibid.:103n.). This attitude is also found in modern Greek culture, although its provenience is unclear. For example, Peter Loizos notes (1975:286) that many Cypriot Greeks distinguish between the *poushtis,* a man who takes a "passive" or womanlike role in sex, and his homosexual active partner. The poushtis, or *poustis,* as he is called on the mainland (J. K. Campbell 1964:216), is strongly denigrated, but the active participant may suffer no rebuke because he plays the male role.

Placing the Greek case in its wider European context, Dover in fact sees this tolerance of transient homosexuality as a fairly common notion in the preindustrial warrior societies throughout Western Europe, including the northern countries. He notes that in medieval Scandinavia, for instance, a respectable manhood was fully compatible with homosexuality so long as a man retained the active role in the encounter: "In the old Norse epics the allegation 'X uses Y as his wife' is an intolerable insult to Y but casts no adverse reflection on the morals of X" (Dover 1978:105). This kind of manly love was also common among the Japanese samurai and was equally condoned, for much the same reasons. In Japan, as Ian Buruma notes (1984:127–31), for many centuries—and recently, as in the case of the novelist Yukio Mishima—homosexuality was not only tolerated but was actually encouraged as a purer form of love. In Japan, "as in Sparta or Prussia . . . gay lovers make good soldiers, or so it was hoped" (ibid.:128). Indeed, some of the German militarists in the 1920s and 1930s entertained similar ideas, especially members of the proto-fascist Freikorps, as Klaus Theweleit shows in his book *Male Fantasies* (1987), a study of masculinism in German culture.

To return to New Guinea: what distinguishes the Sambia from all these warlike civilizations is the formal ritualization of the passage to manhood, not its erotic content. Like the Samburu moranhood, the Sambia ritual transition lasts many years and incorporates countless ceremonies. Confined to boys, these rites of passage start at age seven or ten and last for the next ten to fifteen years. There are six intermittent initiations, constituted and conceptualized as two distinct cultural systems consecutively enacted. The first three stages are collectively performed for groups of boys over a period of a few months; the final three stages constitute a second phase that is individual-centered and not associated with the participation of larger units. The events of male initiation begin with the most important single event in the male life cycle: the physical separation of boys from their mothers. This is a dramatic rupture that signals the first step in the masculinizing process; it coincides with the construction by the elders of an all-male cult house where the boys spend much of their time as initiates. There then follow numerous symbolic and psychological rites of transition and induction.

As in other parts of New Guinea, the boys are formally removed from the vicinity of mothers (the "separation" stage in van Gennep's scheme) and taken to an all-male place in the bush. There they are subjected to numerous tests and brutal hazing, some of which involve either physical beating or painful bloodletting. The most lurid of these is the famous nosebleeding, in which the boys cause a flow of blood from their nostrils. (Formerly they also forced stout bamboo canes down into the esophagus, causing both bleeding and painful vomiting, but this practice has been abandoned.) Herdt describes the nosebleeding (1981:224) as the single most painful ritual act and probably close to an authentic physical and psychological trauma. The method is simple: stiff, sharp grasses are thrust up the nostrils until the blood flows copiously. The grown men, having "terrorized" the boys into submission to this self-torture, greet the flow of blood with a collective war cry (ibid.:225). As they will have to do on the battlefield later, the boys have shown fortitude and have learned to disdain the shedding of their own blood.

This dramatic event, with its military trappings (the war cry), is followed by various other rites of both ingestion and egestion and by ritual flogging with ceremonial objects. The boys are also flailed violently with sticks, switches, or bristly objects until their skin is "opened up" and the blood flows (ibid.:222). No efforts are made to mitigate the initiates' terror or pain, and in fact overcoming such agonies seems to be the point. Herdt notes that the rites teach the boys to ignore the flow of their own blood and to show a stoic resolve. These experiences "explicitly" prepare them for the life of manly endurance that awaits them (ibid.:226–27). Much the same occurs in other parts of the Highlands (cf. Read 1965; Newman and Boyd 1982; Keesing 1982), where boys are likewise toughened up by physical beatings. For example, Fitz John Poole (1982) speaks frequently of the shocking violence of male rites among the Bimin-Kuskusmin, describing the fear and terrorization of the boys, the testing, pressure, and trauma. One ethnographer (Tuzin 1982:325), overwhelmed by the bloodcurdling events he witnessed among the Ilahita Arapesh, has spoken of the male rites as "cruel, brutal, and sadistic," terms tempered by avowals of awareness of the value judgments involved.

On the other hand, the rite of homosexual fellatio, the culmination of the initiation, involves no physical pain and demands only submission. Interestingly, Herdt describes the Sambia as being too "prudish" to do this publicly. Rather it is done in private between individuals usually under the cover of darkness. The boys are forced repeatedly to suck on the penises and swallow the semen of the older men; the ingested semen passes down into the inactive "semen organ," where it is absorbed and accumulated. As noted above, repeated inseminations "create a pool of maleness" (Herdt 1981:236). Sambia believe that the semen actually strengthens the boy's bones and builds muscles; eventually, with enough semen ingested, the boy begins puberty, signaled by the arrival of facial hair. (Remember the symbolic importance of the mustache among some Mediterranean peoples, discussed in chapter 2).

INTERPRETATIONS

Among anthropologists and psychologists, the New Guinea male cults, with all these dramatic oddities, have excited much interest, as one might expect. Both the bloodletting and the homosexual fellatio have been interpreted in a number of ways, from both sociological and psychological perspectives. For example, the nosebleeding has been attributed both to womb envy and to castration anxiety (see Lidz and Lidz 1977 for a review of these debates). But it is clear from Herdt's descriptions and from the data compiled by numerous other New Guinea specialists that what is going on is really an effort, quite consciously avowed by the people themselves, to separate the boys from their mothers and thereby to terminate childhood. By breaking this primordial bond, the Sambia rites of manhood expunge from the boys all longings for passivity or dependency, instigating in them an angry self-autonomy in accordance with the political and economic exigencies of the Highlands. The rites have a collective, rather than an individual, function: they create an instrumental character structure adapted to a life of warfare and killing. The violence of the proceedings corresponds to the perceived absoluteness of the rupture with the past.

To illustrate this thesis, first let us take a look at the nosebleeding; then we will address the question of the fellatio ritual. One of the rather facile psychoanalytic interpretations of the ritual bleeding (and of ritual vomiting caused by cane-swallowing) is that such egestive ritual represents male imitation of female menstruation (cf. Bettelheim 1955). At some level, this may of course be part of what is going on, but if we listen to the people themselves, another more sociologically convincing explanation is at hand. The point of the nosebleeding of initiates among the Sambia is quite clear. The Sambia themselves say that it is for the express purposes of, first, preparing the boy for the rigors of the soldier's life; and second, to rid the boy's body of maternal influences—a purgative that is preparatory to maturing. The point of the bleeding is specifically to remove the mother's blood and milk and other "polluting" feminine influences from the boy's body, because these maternal influences inhibit masculinization and therefore adult role performance. As Herdt puts it (1981:225), "Like cane-swallowing, bloodletting is a necessarily painful way of getting rid of inner maternal influences." To illustrate, Herdt draws upon native rhetoric, the elders' exhortation to the initiates as the rites are finishing. The elders lecture: "You novices have been with your mothers. They have said 'bad words' to you. Their talk has entered your noses and prevented you from growing big. Your skins are no good. Now you can grow and look nice; we have helped you to do this" (ibid.:226).

The same emphasis on distancing from mother and renunciation of her stunting, effeminizing nurture occurs in the case of the ritual vomiting. In all of the New Guinea examples, the object is explicitly not to simulate menstruation or to imitate women but to remove maternal substances from the boy's body and to enact an independence from the mother as the locus of sustenance: the vomiting is said to rid the boy of any of the mother's womb blood swallowed while he was in her womb and of any dangerous menstrual blood he had inadvertently ingested "with the food his mother prepared for him" (Lidz and Lidz 1977:20).

The avowed objective in this is not to mimic women or their functions, to imitate menstruation or childbirth, but quite the contrary, to reject the mother, to root her out of the boy's body by washing away her milk and blood, to wean him psychologically from her, to set the boy on the road to independence. "Boys must be traumatically separated—wiped clean of their female contaminants—so that their masculinity may develop" (Herdt 1982:55). This process is therefore not mainly one of imitation, or even symbolic sex-reversal, but rather of masculine status transition. It is not so much a question of establishing self-identity as male, although it is that, too, but one of instilling autonomy as a keystone of the male character, inducing an agential mode, by overcoming what Bettelheim called the "pregenital fixations" of an unreconstructed childhood (1955:124–26). The other native peoples of the Highlands, not only the Sambia, are quite clear on the purpose of their rites. For example, the Siane people say of their nosebleeding, "His mother's blood is being washed away" (Salisbury 1965:62). The Ilahita Arapesh say that the purpose of such male initiations is to "rid the male child's body of the polluting influences of his mother's milk." They continue, "Without this . . . there is no guarantee that future growth will lead him toward competent manhood" (Tuzin 1980:37). In their stimulating discussion of New Guinea rituals, the psychoanalysts Lidz and Lidz agree (1977:29). They argue that the rites of expurgation in New Guinea serve "to separate the boys from their mothers."

Curiously, a similar idiom of weaning provides a thread of unity with the homosexual fellatio rites. What is striking about Herdt's account of this is the strong association, even equivalency, in Sambia culture between mother's milk and semen. "Semen is the substance closest to breast milk," the Sambia vouchsafe (Herdt 1981:235). They themselves argue that semen is a "man's milk" (ibid.:186–87), and fellatio insemination is often "likened to maternal breast-feeding" (ibid.:234). Among themselves, initiates refer to semen as *neimi aamoonaalyi,* "our breast milk," and the boy's actual consumption of semen is likened to *monjapi'u,* "feeding by a mother of her infant" (ibid.:235). Similarly, the penis is likened by the Sambia to the breast as a creative organ, and both are symbolized by pandanus tree roots, which, when cut, yield a milky white sap. Herdt regards this identification as a form of "focal projection," a process of symbolization by which a part of a larger cathected object stands synecdochically for externalizing subjective images or fantasies and their relations.

One may clearly surmise from this that the fellatio is again a form of psychic reinforcement of weaning from mother into autonomous maleness and a symbolic enforcement in cultural idiom of maternal separation and masculine self-creation—a homeopathic substitution of phallic for oral cathexis. As Herdt notes in passing (1981:235), fellatio and imbibing of semen replaces dependency on mother's milk, as the consumption of pandanus roots replaces suckling at mother's breast. Milk has a dual symbolic significance: aside from its procreative meaning, it takes on the secondary meaning of boy's nutritional dependence upon his mother. Thus we may conclude, along with Herdt, that the Sambia rituals are not specifically about castration or female imitation but are about "maternal separation" (ibid.:279).

Herdt explains further this felt need to separate from mother in Sambia culture. He proposes a sociopsychological explanation, which I find interesting but, as it gilds the lily, supererogatory. He argues convincingly that the need for this forced separation stems from the protracted dependence of Sambia boys on their mothers and their late weaning. As elsewhere, boys cling to their mothers, but Sambia boys continue to sleep in close proximity to their mothers until well after the toddler stage. Children remain strongly attached to their mothers even after postpartum taboos, while men avoid children for fear of appearing "unmanly" (ibid.:213), so that young boys are effectively brought up in a world of older women. Breast milk remains the baby's "key source" of food and strength well into the second and sometimes third year of life (ibid.:214). Herdt notes that when in crisis, many boys even at age five will run to suckle at their mother's breast. In many cases, then, the mother's care becomes stultifying, turning into a stranglehold and inhibiting the boy's transition to an autonomous condition associated with masculinity. The men cannot help noticing how the child is "too dependent" on the mother and her breast (ibid.:213–14). Apparently, the aggregate response is to wean the boys on their own penises.

All of this seems very much in support of the famous argument of John Whiting and his co-workers (1958) to the effect that harsh or bloody rites correlate with protracted infant-mother symbiosis. However, although it sounds plausible in this case, this connection is not very convincing as a general rule. Similar rites occur in various societies with widely differing forms of childrearing—for example among the Samburu—and it seems more likely that the regressive tendencies that the Sambia are fighting with their rituals are universal ones and are not culture-specific. What seems to vary is their intensity, or degree, which of course correlates with degrees of harshness or competitiveness of the adult male role. Nor is the late intimacy of Sambia boys and mothers all that unusual; late weaning occurs in many societies in which there are no such rites and in which masculinity is down-played, for example among the gentle Semai of Malaysia (see chapter 9). Although some psychological anthropologists have tried to do so, it is not possible to correlate ritual practices per se with forms of early child care with any certitude.

In sum, despite other differences, one may perceive striking underlying similarities between the Samburu and Sambia rituals of manhood that support a hypothesis about masculinity ideals being an instrumental response to group needs. The social con-ferral of manhood occurs only when the individual completes prescribed tasks of renunciation and renewal that contribute to the group's security and prosperity. What the voyager toward manhood gains is both a social good and a social identity—as well as the affections and attentions of women.

OTHER RITES, OTHER MANHOODS: THE GISU

Until very recently, the Sambia and the Samburu were warrior and raiding societies, living and dying by the spear. With war-fare and battlefield glory fresh in their memory, their manhood requirements clearly reflect a residual militaristic adaptation. But such similarities as they share in male ideology recur else-where in many other kinds of society where male rites are elabo-rated but where warfare and raiding are little practiced or un-known. The connection between militarism and masculinism (cf. Divale and Harris 1978; Theweleit 1987)—strongly and admit-tedly present in both these cases—is only partial cross-culturally. Let me try to illustrate the last statement by reference to another African society, the Gisu of eastern Uganda, as reported by Jean La Fontaine (1986) and Suzette Heald (1982).

Living not far from the Samburu, the Gisu are a predominantly agricultural people. Like their East African neighbors, they also practice herding and trading for their livelihood. Although they were warriors in the distant past, they gave up fighting for good in the early part of this century under the Pax Britannica (Heald 1982:17); nor do they engage in cattle raids or other forms of organized violence. In fact, the Gisu dislike displays of anger or temper in men and, demanding self-control and civility from both sexes, have a concept of manhood based on ideals of "creative energy" that implies not so much physical power as resourcefulness—what we would call "strength of purpose" (ibid.:18). Obviously the past experience of warfare may exert some lingering influence on their view of manhood, but it is no longer a primary consideration.

Among these relatively peaceful farmers, boys are subjected to rites of transition to manhood, less violent perhaps, but as stressful as those of the Sambia and Samburu. These rites include a similarly painful bloodletting that the Gisu consider a kind of "rebirth" of the boy into the world of masculine maturity. In the words of La Fontaine (1986:119), the Gisu boys must "conquer fear" and learn "self-control" during their initiation before they can be accounted men. Including various fertility rites in which the adolescents are rubbed with yeast and other substances, the centerpiece of the initiation is the circumcision ceremony. Called *imbalu,* this rite is explicitly designed as an ordeal, requiring "the greatest fortitude under extreme pain" (Heald 1982:17).

Like the Samburu boys, the Gisu initiate must stand perfectly still, without the slightest movement, while first his foreskin is ripped open and then the subcutaneous flesh is slowly stripped from around the glans penis. The degree of pain is never underplayed before or after the ceremony, and the elders describe it to their charges as "fierce," "bitter," and "terrifying." It happens to the boys when they are between the ages of eighteen and twenty-five. Any show of cowardice before or afterward, even the slightest hesitation or an involuntary twitch during the cutting, carries the penalty not only of individual disgrace but also the potential for the entire destruction of his patriline. If a boy falters or runs away, he is said to have "cursed his kin" (ibid.:17). No efforts are made to mitigate the boy's anxieties prior to the operation or to lessen his agony during it. The whole point is indeed to make "tough" and "fierce" men by extirpating the boyish fear of pain (ibid.:26).

Like the Samburu and the Sambia, the peaceful Gisu admire "independence and competitiveness" in men (La Fontaine 1986:122). This is based not on war but on the realities of tribal life in which resources are scarce and technology primitive. The boys are entering an adult world of "free competition with other men" in which they must support a homestead by pitting their skill and prowess against other like-minded men (Heald 1982:23). This competitiveness is reflected not so much in the killing of enemies or marauding for cattle, as among the Sambia and Samburu, but, as among the Mehinaku, in material productivity. The qualities of creativity and perseverance are demanded of novices. Ritual exhortations stress the values of responsibility, thrift, fortitude, and hard work, and they always include the command "Beget sons" (La Fontaine 1986:125). The male rites are therefore public expressions of male commitment to procreative civic goals that require a man to produce the goods and services that support the growing lineage (Heald 1982:26). their ascension to manhood is therefore a public test of these indispensable civic virtues. In their rites of passage, the elements of testing, publicity, and performance are paramount. As La Fontaine notes (1986:124), "It is important to convey the very public, very critical, evaluation of performance in the ordeal."

After their circumcision, the Gisu boys are isolated away from the village and are forbidden contact with older women. They must learn to fend for themselves in the bush. Finally, when the period of initiation is over, the boys are ceremoniously approached by the circumcisor and given the tools that symbolize their future work: fire, a hoe, a knife, a drinking tube, and other utensils of adult life. The emphasis throughout is on self-sufficiency in the work role.

Although not directed at war and killing, the Gisu initiation ceremonies, like those of the Samburu and Sambia, also revolve around the linked themes of dependence and independence. Their objective is to instill manly strength, "which is responsible and independent" (ibid.:125). Ties to mother must be broken while self-reliance is instilled and labor power maximized. The Gisu believe that the ordeal of circumcision awakens a "fierceness" in the boy that makes him an independent actor afraid of nothing, for he has already experienced the worst pain life has to offer. In short, Gisu male initiation is a parallel pathway to an elusive manhood seen as a commitment to group goals, being "thus overtly concerned with the testing and embracing of male powers" (ibid.:119). Again, the content of the rites seems less important than their effect: the maximization of productivity in all areas of male life.

BEYOND CIRCUMCISION: THE MENDE PORO INITIATION

Although circumcision is common in East Africa, not all African male initiation rites center on it. This operation plays no part, for example, in the rituals of the Mende people of Sierra Leone in West Africa (Little 1967). The Mende are an agricultural people. Like the Gisu, they gave up warfare under the British in the early part of the present century. Among the Mende, a boy must be inducted into the Poro Society before he can be accounted a man and take a wife. Although lacking circumcision, the Poro initiation is an equally strenuous and harsh test of endurance. The Mende believe that the Poro spirit must "swallow" the boy before he can be reborn a man. To ensure this metamorphosis, the boy must be scarified upon his back, the marks representing the teeth of the hungry spirit. With his peers, the novice is taken to a place in the bush where the elders await to enact the Poro ritual.

Each boy is seized in turn by a number of the older men. He is stripped naked, his clothes being kept aside to staunch the flow of blood to come. Then the initiate is hurled roughly to the ground and thrown on his stomach; the elders make the appropriate marks upon his back either with a hook that scores the skin or with a blunt razor. If the boy shows any fear or tries to escape during this brutal session, he is temporarily incapacitated by the elders, who push his head into a hole in the dirt that has already been dug for this purpose.

After this ordeal, the boys are sent into the bush for an extended apprenticeship in survival. There, without the benefit of adult supervision, they are expected to bear hardships and dangers without complaint and to "grow accustomed to it" (ibid.:120). They are allowed no modern equipment (like the Aegean sponge divers discussed in chapter 1), and all their material requirements, including food, must be provided by themselves. No crying is allowed under pain of corporal punishment. During this time the boys must learn to become "proficient in the particular craft they choose" (ibid.:121). The Mende rite of passage, Little notes (ibid.:120), is both symbolic and practical: it inculcates the boy with the deeper implications as well as the rules "of the part he has to play as a man. It aims at teaching him self-discipline, and to rely on himself."

CUI BONO?

The Sambia, the Gisu, and the Mende boys become men by passing exacting tests of performance in war, economic pursuits, and procreativity: civic goals all. But what of the argument of some feminist critics that manhood rituals, with their androcentric celebration of male powers, are really mystifications to justify the oppression of women (Rubin 1975; Ortner 1974; Godelier 1985)? Is the purpose of such rites and their associated beliefs to buttress male dominance and to denigrate women? Do boys suffer so they may later inflict suffering on women? This line of argument has some merit. Male rites and cults occur most commonly in patriarchal societies where the sexes are strongly differentiated and ranked. These rites often lend a certain mystique to men that makes them "superior" to women, or they enhance male unity, which in turn can bolster this sense of superiority. Although one must be cautious in applying single-feature traits to whole societies, one may justifiably consider the Gisu, Samburu, Mende, and Sambia as androcentric societies in the sense that men exercise political control monopolistically. But sex domination cannot be the sole purpose or effect of such rituals and beliefs. It is important to note that such stressful male rites are not always associated with conditions of male dominance and gender opposition or hierarchy, but always with fecundity, service to kin, or collective defense. More significantly, they also occur in many societies where men are physically gentle and where the sexes exist in relative equality.

For example, take the secular assimilated American Jews that we discussed earlier. In this physically gentle culture, women tend to dominate men in daily life and in family organization. Yet even here, under conditions of relative sexual equality, there exist both masculine initiations and moral injunctions about manhood that are based on similar proofs and evaluations. As we have seen, the Jewish Mensch is a man who assists and protects his women rather than dominates them. He is a gentle soul and a supportive husband and father. Likewise, the Mehinaku he-man is one who provides for and satisfies his wife, not one who beats her. Similarly, Spanish hombría is based on service to wife and family, not domination. Male dominance may be present in some of these cases as an epiphenomenon of male ideology or initiations, and it may be part of the explanation of the ceremonies, but I do not think it can be considered the only or even the most significant consequence of such masculine rituals and ideology.

For another example of this nonsexist aspect of male imagery, we can return momentarily to the "harmless people," the !Kung Bushmen of Botswana (Thomas 1959). They represent a supposed ideal of sexual equality that feminists such as Eleanor Leacock (1978) have offered as a model for the West. Yet the !Kung boys are also subjected to tests by which they officially become men. Aside from having to kill an adult antelope, they must undergo a severe form of hazing, called the *Choma*. Like the other rites we have looked at, this Bushman example involves the usual separation of boys from their mothers, a "liminal" period of status ambiguity, and a "rebirth" into the world of men, in van Gennep's typology. It includes hardships that prepare boys for the dangerous tasks that await them as hunters. What happens is quite similar to the other male ordeals above, although no human blood is shed and no pain inflicted gratuitously. Nevertheless, grueling tests of masculine stamina are involved. A brief description of the Choma will illustrate.

The !Kung adolescents are isolated from women for a few weeks between the ages of fifteen and twenty. They are forced to fend for themselves in the bush, where they will later hunt game. Marjorie Shostak, who has studied the !Kung for many years, explains: "During this intense and rigorous ritual the initiates experience hunger, cold, thirst, and the extreme fatigue that comes from continuous dancing" (1981:239). The ritual takes place over a period of six weeks and is considered a sacred time. The boys may not appeal to their mothers and are not assisted by their fathers, for they must learn to fend for themselves. During this sacred time, they are also literally forced to study and to learn their environment: its flora, fauna, and topography. After they prove their ability in survival by using their knowledge to kill an antelope, the boys are considered men; they may marry and begin a family. Henceforth they are expected to be providers rather than consumers of meat.

The Bushman passage to manhood is more gentle than elsewhere, perhaps, but it is still a test of cultural competence, resembling that of the Samburu and Sambia in both means and ends. The gentle, egalitarian, nonsexist Bushmen boys must suffer extremes of deprivation and fatigue; they must learn to cope, to master themselves and their environment, before they can become men. This rite of passage does not seem fully consistent therefore with the argument that male initiations are uniformly or even primarily concerned with inculcating male dominance. *Cui bono?* Who benefits? Everyone.

Action and Ambiguity:
East and South Asia

The road to manhood is a hard one.
    —Ian Buruma, *Behind the Mask*

The idea that manhood is a triumph over the impulse to run from danger can be found in some cultures not normally associated with the hypermasculine bravado we have seen above. Although the subject has not been explored at any length–because of a lack of interest rather than of ethnographic clues, I think—there are some arresting, if faint, echoes in the populous civilizations of Asia. These traces are especially suggestive in China, India, and Japan, societies not known either for rugged individualism or for sexual boastfulness. Asian ideas about manhood are worth exploring for the many nuances and contrasts they add to the composite image we have at this point. We begin with China, a society that has been studied intensely, but only recently from the standpoint of gender. We then turn briefly to India, and finally to Japan.

REAL MEN IN CHINA

One bit of information about Chinese attitudes comes from a recent study of the Chinatown in Oakland, California. After

169

looking at this transplanted case, we will consider data gathered in mainland China by cultural anthropologists. The source for the Chinese-American material is a doctoral dissertation by Rita Chou (1987) on health and medical practices among the elderly.

In the Oakland Chinatown, municipal health workers are frustrated by their inability to convince the men of the community, especially the less acculturated elderly men, to seek medical attention. Chou describes how these old, culturally conservative men refuse indignantly, as a matter of honor, to visit the clinic. They would actually prefer to die or to suffer silently, she reports, rather than avail themselves of the services of the health workers who seek them out. Asserting their right to remain in control of their lives, they resort to often ineffective traditional curing practices over which they exert control, or they dispense with assistance altogether, with predictable results. Distressed by their plight, Chou sought answers to their reluctance.

The reason they give is familiar. To seek medical attention, they insist, is to appear helpless or dependent. "Men don't need help," they say, "only women do," adding parenthetically that help-seeking is all right for little children. To run to others is incompatible with their image of masculinity (ibid.:176). Chou does not give us more information on this self-image or its historical provenience, but it is clear that a critical ingredient is to avoid dependency. Is this notion traceable to Old World antecedents?

Many Westerners regard traditional Chinese culture, with its strong emphasis on filial loyalty, as less concerned with masculinity issues than their own. Some scholars in fact argued that many Chinese traditions, especially religion and art, contain an androgynous quality (cf. Ames 1981). Although this may be true, if we look closely we can see that a concern for manliness does exist alongside such traditions, especially, as Chou shows, among the rural people who constitute the bulk of immigrants to the United States. This concern is often manifested more subtly than in the macho societies, precisely because of Chinese cultural proscriptions of individualism and indecorous display.

It certainly does not seem to include a readiness to respond violently to challenge. But manhood as a special category of achievement, complete with its own linguistic label, is still a subject of considerable public interest and a matter of comment for young men and women especially. In fact, we can trace the Oakland Chinese-American anxiety about maleness back to its roots on the Asian mainland.

For example, the investigative team of Emily Honig, historian, and Gail Hershatter, anthropologist (1988) recently carried out a detailed survey of gender ideas and ideals in the People's Republic. They found that the following characteristics are still held up as the ideals of the male image—despite government lip service to sexual equality. The ideal man, according to their informants, must display "courage, self-confidence," and other attributes of what the people refer to as "'manly temperament' (*nanzihan qizhi*)" (ibid.:101). This term, cited frequently by informants and discussed informally, is loosely described as having to do with moral bravery and initiative in the work place. A "real man" is disciplined and independent, especially of women. He must be helpful and respectful to old people, especially to his parents and older siblings. He is never a complainer, a clinger, or a toady.

Articulating such attitudes, one young woman said that she would firmly reject any man as a suitor who acted dependent or who neglected his work role in pursuing her. This informant, a typical unmarried farm worker, said, "If a man is only capable of prostrating himself at a woman's feet, he is not worthy of my love" (ibid.:110). Other women surveyed concurred, indicating equal contempt for the immature or dependent males who were not, in their words, real men. These ideas seem to be prevalent in urban areas as well. They are found, for example, among industrial workers in the big cities. One female anthropologist, Margery Wolf (1985), conducted field research on gender ideals and stereotypes in the People's Republic in the early 1980s. She found traditional views of gender differences firmly entrenched in Beijing. Interviewing factory workers there on why men and

not women still occupied positions of leadership in Chinese industry, she heard the following responses. One male worker
replied that men are better workers because they are more independent and have "more energy." This man's superior elaborated: "Men don't need other people's help to do their jobs, but
women do." An avowed feminist, Wolf was disappointed to find
that most women "shared this attitude" (ibid.:71–73). Both men
and women told her that a real man was expected to work hard
to support his family, while this was less important for a woman.
"A good wife takes full responsibility for the house and the
children so that her husband is free to work," the women insisted (ibid.:73).

MANLY TEMPERAMENT

These attitudes stressing hard work are to be found also in the
popular press. In addition to their interviews on sex roles and
attitudes, Honig and Hershatter (1988) also conducted a comprehensive review of Chinese popular literature published in
the past twenty years. They found a certain thread of male imagery running throughout. In one case, the author of a tract on
etiquette described the "real man" as possessing three special
traits. The first of these was firmness or decisiveness, which was
said to be needed more by men than by women because men still
played the main role in work. The second quality was strength—
both physical and mental. This was again said to be more important in men than women. The third was devotion to work, which
was described as the most distinguishing quality of the real man
and something much less needed by women, whose devotions
were said to be more properly directed toward childrearing. In
all the popular writings on male-female relations, "manly temperament" and its correlate, "real man," were mentioned again
and again. Although vaguely defined throughout, manly temperament "excited a great deal of social attention among both
sexes, even giving rise to a magazine called *Real Man* (Nanzihan)
exclusively devoted to its elaboration. Just as women were told to

make themselves pretty for marriage, men were instructed to 'act like men'" (ibid.:110). The authors are at pains, moreover, to show that such beliefs are venerable ones, not merely implanted since 1949. In fact, because they harken back to the prerevolutionary past, these ideals are not wholly compatible with Communist doctrines. Yet they have survived almost without modification.

PSYCHOSOMATIC MANIFESTATIONS: KORO

Some of this concern about "manly temperament" in Chinese culture, and the associated anxiety about backsliding, is manifested psychosomatically in the famous culture-bound syndrome called *koro*. This condition is known to many oriental psychiatrists and to psychological anthropologists the world over. A male disorder, koro consists of a number of debilitating symptoms, including acute anxiety, palpitations, precordial discomfort, trembling, and intimations of impending death. The most flamboyant symptom, however, is the belief that the penis is either shriveling or retracting into the belly. With all its florid symptoms, koro resolves to an overriding fear that manhood is taking flight. It is worth a digression.

Climaxing in southern and eastern China, koro is extremely widespread in its geographical distribution. As well as occurring in most of mainland China, it is also found in Taiwan and throughout southeast Asia, including the islands. It is very common in Indonesia, where it attacks both locals and Chinese immigrants. Cases have been reported as far afield as Thailand and India. Interestingly, the disease is not dying out with modernization; in fact, the opposite is true. Severe epidemics of koro have been reported recently in both Hainan in southern China (Tseng et al. 1987) and in the province of Assam in northern India (Dutta et al. 1982).

Psychiatric studies of the disease have shown that koro tends to afflict certain categories of men. The usual victim is a young or adolescent man of a weak or dependent personality who is anxious about his ability to live up to the stringent standards of performance his culture sets for him. P. M. Yap, a Chinese psychiatrist who has studied the disease, says, "The syndrome is usually to be found among young men of poor education and immature, dependent personality who lack confidence in their own virility" (1965:49). Yap describes some of the cases he observed in Hong Kong as follows (ibid.:44).

One victim was a young man, aged about twenty-two. He was the subject of much malicious teasing by girls his age because of his unusual shyness with them. This maladjusted individual retreated from the outside world and insisted upon following his mother about all day after he was taken ill, causing her "much exasperation," although she was otherwise a concerned mother. Another afflicted man apparently suffered from agoraphobia (fear of public places), because he "never left the house without asking his father's permission." A third victim, somewhat older, about thirty-two, had always been highly dependent upon his mother. He was the only surviving boy in the family, the others having died in infancy. Whenever he felt insecure or threatened, he would seek urgent help from his mother, following her about and demanding attention like a child. Fearful of the world outside his house, he refused to seek employment and became a severe burden on his family. Another case was that of a young man, age unspecified, who was pathologically fearful of marriage, but who had been forced into matrimony by his parents. On his wedding night, he became panic-stricken and confused, complaining of koro. He remained unable to consummate his marriage for years afterwards. Anxious and withdrawn, he was also a poor provider.

Other studies have found this connection between an immature, dependent personality and the koro symptomatology, expressed in specifically economic terms. For example, another Chinese psychiatrist, Hsien Rin (1963, 1965), found that the Taiwanese cases he studied occurred among young men who had difficulty making successful psychosocial adjustments to adult life; that is, they were narcissistic personalities and unable to take up the challenge of supporting their new families. Experiencing daunting "economic difficulties" (1965:11) and unable to cope or otherwise incapable of worldly success, they preferred retreating into themselves. Then, like Melville's fictional Bartleby, they proceeded to lose their jobs and to withdraw from an increasingly frightening reality into a self-absorbed fantasy life. Later this regressive withdrawal is symbolically manifested in the conversion symptom of the withdrawn penis and psychotic fears of dissolution. In sum, koro is a male hysteria that reflects underlying pressures for "achieving masculinity" (ibid.) in China mainly, but also throughout southeastern Asian culture.

INDIA: POINT AND COUNTERPOINT

Let us follow the path of koro to the Indian subcontinent. Here we encounter some new themes interwoven with the more familiar ones. The colorful cultural tapestry we find in India is partly a reflection of that nation's intricate mosaic of subcultures and religions, its regional and ethnic diversity, probably more varied than anywhere else in the world. But is richness is also due to the almost unbelievable complexity of Hinduism, with its protean mythology in which everything is at once itself and its opposite.

In some parts of South Asia one finds a warrior tradition (*kshatravirya*) very much like those we have seen elsewhere, similarly imbued with notions of manly courage and prowess. But it is in the northern parts of the subcontinent in particular that such ideals abound. This is especially true of the tribal areas heavily influenced by the Mogul conquerors: Pakistan, the Punjab, Kashmir, Uttar Pradhesh, West Bengal, and Bangladesh. In these places, there are strong male codes of courage and achievement that have much in common with the Mediterranean and Middle Eastern variants. These values are summarized by the oft-heard word *izzat*. Izzat is an Arabic and Persian term for which "honor" is the usual English gloss. Not so important in southern India or

Sri Lanka, this northern concept crops up as a final, irreducible moral justification for aggressive male behavior and is said to distinguish men from women more than any other quality.

The culture of izzat is most pronounced in certain Indian communities and castes—again mainly in the north but distributed throughout the subcontinent—that emphasize "manliness in its *machismo* elaboration" and that keep their women in seclusion (*purdah*) (Kakar 1981:134). The prime example of such "macho" Indians is the fierce Rajputs, a proud caste of landowners and businessmen. Formerly, the Rajputs were warriors by profession whose job it was within the Hindu canon to defend the elite Brahmans, who are barred by caste proscriptions from bearing arms or killing. Like their most famous exemplar, the fierce Gurkhas of Nepal, the Rajputs have maintained the stress on a rugged, courageous manliness of action. This image constitutes one of the many strands of "right action," or *dharma,* that in sum make up the Hindu tradition. But the concern for a masculine image is found among many ethnic groups and castes—be they Hindu, Muslim, or Sikh—who are not warriors by profession. For most of the men of north and central India, regardless of religion or caste, the notion of honor conveys a salient theme in gender identity and represents the most highly cherished purposes of a man's existence.

Among the Hindu Pirzada of Delhi, according to Patricia Jeffery (1979:99–100), honor is the central concern of a man's life, a code of behavior that he learns at his father's knee. The Pirzada man, to be honorable and thus manly, must be courageous, generous, and able to protect and support his family by taking risks and working hard. For the Muslim Pakhtun of northern Pakistan, their code of masculine honor "is everything" (Lindholm 1982:189).

Among these fierce Pakistani Pakhtun, the code of manly honor is a motivation and justification for acts of aggression, revenge, and self-assertiveness in general. It has a strongly, almost obsessively, competitive connotation that often leads to feuding and violence. The reason for this is simple: a Pakhtun man must be tough and courageous to survive in a very contentious environment. Learning to cope with the harsh realities of life forms the basis of the Pakhtun boy's upbringing:

> The Pakhtun man is accustomed to a lack of affection, hardened by a harsh physical environment, and prepared for a life of struggle, betrayal and cruelty. To survive, he must strive to subdue his fellows, who all have the same desire. . . . A proverb clearly expresses the philosophy behind raising a male child: "The eye of the dove is lovely, my son, but the sky is made for the hawk. So cover your dovelike eyes and grow claws." What the Pakhtun man must present to the world is the hawk, the bird of prey. What he must conceal is the dove, the sensitive victim. The egocentricity of the Pakhtun is a fragile facade, hiding the insecurity that is its opposite and its dynamic.

This sense of a beleaguered honor, threatened both by enemies and by inner weakness, does not always relate to aggression, but it always has to do with forceful actions that counteract the inward insecurity to which Lindholm alludes: honor in the sense of a "covering" for potential sources of shame. It is also bound up with the central civic values that men must aspire to in order to win over a public opinion that despises weakness and passivity as effete. As David Mandelbaum remarks in his recent survey of the ethnography of north India (1988:20), izzat refers to a complex bundle of proprieties that encourage a man to steel himself in order to carry out the group's definition of the masculine role. For the Sikh Jats of the Punjab, for example (Pettigrew 1975), the concept of izzat is a philosophy of life that reflects their paramount concern for male power, in which a man's duty is to be stalwart in defense of his family. Above all, the Sikh Jat man must never give in to threats that might diminish his family's position; if threatened he must "at least threaten back" (ibid.:59).

In this Sikh society, a man's first duty is to take risks in the service of the family. Among the Jats living in the state capital of Chandigarh, for example, courage and the "willingness to take risks" were the major values of the male and of manliness (ibid.).

The penalty for failure in this regard is summary and severe: if the reputation of a relative is compromised or lost through the unchallenged action of an outsider, "so also is the family's entire public position" (ibid.:58–59). Equally important to a man's image among the Sikh Jats is gift-giving, the continual and showy distribution of consumer goods and food. This is a masculine prerogative and another important means of accruing izzat. Gift-giving is especially esteemed in a man when gifts are made generously, judiciously, and publicly. His public philanthropy must be lavish and unstinting to earn a Jat man claim to izzat.

Moving south into central India, we encounter parallels. Among the Muslim villagers in the Lucknow area of central India (Bhatty 1975:32), male honor is achieved by a number of different kinds of forceful actions. Such actions include matchless piety, the accrual of material wealth, success in various kinds of male competitions, winning out over one's rivals, the retention of followers and dependents, and especially the generous distribution of gifts. This emphasis on generosity is paramount not only among the Muslims of Lucknow and Sikh Jats but also in the manly image among all castes and sects in north and central India. In general, according to Mandelbaum (1988:24), lavish gift-giving is an important means of promoting izzat throughout the region, especially when gifts are made without apparent thought of return and when they enrich the group and extend its power.

ANOTHER IMAGE: ANDROGYNY IN HINDU MYTHOLOGY

In many ways these male virtues of courage, generosity, and defense of family are a carry-over from the adjacent Middle Eastern culture area. In turn, these Middle Eastern sexual ideals resemble the Mediterranean emphasis on honor and shame (Peristiany 1965). This convergence of values seems to indicate a shared complex extending geographically from Portugal to Bangladesh, which for some historians possibly reflects an Indo-European archetype (Wyatt-Brown 1982:xiii). But whereas virile ideals of honor create a monochromatic male image in most of these areas, an irreducible core, one may say, of masculinity that is complementary and opposed to femininity, they are only one part of a much more polychromatic portrait in India—a culture in which every coin has three sides. In Hindu mythology there is a contrasting theme that reflects the obverse to "pure" manliness. I refer to a powerful theme of sexual ambiguity and role ambivalence. Numerous observers have commented on this indeterminacy of Hindu gender ideas.

The Sanskritist Wendy Doniger O'Flaherty, for example, has written a number of books on the subject. In *Women, Androgynes, and Other Mythical Beasts* (1980), she shows that Indian mythology and iconography are replete with images of androgynous gods and creatures, and that hermaphrodites and sexual transformations are routine in Hindu traditions. According to the Indian psychoanalyst Sudhir Kakar (1981:110), Hindu cosmology, despite the Rajput warrior tradition, is feminine to an "extent rarely found" in other civilizations. Kakar notes that most village gods worshipped in local cults are feminine, and the most powerful Hindu gods are portrayed as female—for example, Lakshmi, Savasvati, Paarvati, Kali, and Gauri. (For more on feminine deities and their psychological implications, see Roland 1988:266–68.)

Using Freudian concepts in their analyses of this sexual ambiguity, Kakar, O'Flaherty, and Roland are in basic agreement about its meaning and psychic origin: all three see it as an expression of unresolved sex-identity conflicts in Indian men. They interpret this inner turmoil over male identity as resulting from the unusual strength of attachments to mother in the culture. Like their predecessor, the Anglo-Indian psychoanalyst G. Morris Carstairs (1958), whose clinical work they often cite, they regard these maternal identifications as a focal point and defining feature of Indian male personality. According to all four observers, there is in fact a powerful unconscious theme in Indian culture of specifically masculine sex reversal in which Indian men voluntarily relinquish their phallic identity (Kakar and Ross 1987:99) in order to return to the unity with the "good mother," a universal motif in which there are both oedipal (incestual) and preoedipal (regressive) elements. (For some Indian points of view, see Roy 1975; Nandy 1980.) Most psychoanalytic observers argue that preoedipal fixations in Indian culture and personality outweigh castration fears: "From clinical work, men's sexual anxiety seems related more to their unconscious fear of a symbiotic, sensual envelopment by powerful women of childhood than from oedipal castration anxiety" (Roland 1988:262).

O'Flaherty (1980:100–05) carries this observation into her fascinating analysis of the Vedic tradition. She sees an explicitly regressive tendency in the Hindu treatment of masculinity, repeated in various guises in literature and pictorial art and decoration. For example, she identifies an iconographic motif in the sacred texts of what she calls the "child as consort." This refers to numerous images of copulation, bonding, or symbiosis, in which a relatively smaller male figure is reduced to the state of a helpless infant totally dominated by the engulfing female figure. She interprets the latter as the universal mother-figure and the motif itself as a regressive male fantasy of maternal supplication. This psychology of infantilizing the male, she adds, occurs in many myths and legends in the Hindu canon and is manifest also in a less obvious way in the Indian belief that the husband is reborn in his own son (ibid.:105).

As another example of this psychosexual regressiveness, she refers to the widespread worship of the demon-goddess, Kali (ibid.:110). In this cult, which is very common throughout India, the rapacious multilimbed goddess must be appealed to in an attitude of complete acquiescence and humility, that is, like a child. Only through this absolute male submission does the goddess lose her demonic characteristics and become kind and gentle—like a good and generous mother. Previously, Carstairs portrayed this Kali worship as pure male regression: "one has surrendered one's manhood and become a helpless infant once again" (1958:159). Recently Sudhir Kakar and a collaborator, John Mundar Ross (1987), have attempted to place the Indian material within a broader context of universal psychic fantasies. Comparing Indian to Western folklore and literature, they argue that such expressions of submission or reversal reflect, in typically Indian terms, the universal male desire to restore the idyllic unity with the "good mother," which is simply another legacy, they state, of the universal "prehistoric experience with our mothers" (ibid.:99). In any case, it is clear that the abandonment-of-masculinity theme in Hindu mythology, as well as reflecting universal regressive fantasies, also paradoxically implies a distinctive model of pure manhood: if something can be renounced in this fashion, it first has to exist as a conceptual category; its negation is a dialectical process of creation and denial.

In a purely anatomical sense, this "puerile identification" with the mother in the sacred texts (Kakar 1981:102) can be seen even more explicitly in tales of sexual reversal, for example, in some tales from the *Mahabharata*. To give just one instance among many, there is the story of King Bhangaswana, who undergoes a sexual transformation. After being changed into a woman by the goddess Indra, he expresses the desire to remain in that state rather than being restored to his prior masculinity. Rejecting Indra's offer to be transformed back into a man, he argues that womanhood is both more pleasant and more erotically satisfying than manhood, which is hard. There are also vibrant transvestite traditions in local village Hindu rituals (Spratt 1966), in which men dress up as women and experience temporary "possession" by female goddesses or demons—much like the Moroccan tradition of female *jinn* possession, although voluntary in the Indian case. In the Dhed community in Gujurat, the men are periodically possessed by the spirit of the goddess Durga and are allowed to act in an obscenely juvenile way (Kakar 1981:102). Legends about Indian culture heroes who have succeeded in transcending manhood and feminizing themselves are quite common. To give one striking example, there is the fifteenth-century saint Narsi Mehta, who writes, "I took the hand of that lover of *gopis* [Krishna] in loving converse. . . . I forgot all else. Even my manhood left me. I began to sing and dance like a woman. . . . At such times I experienced moments of incomparable sweetness and joy" (cited in Alston 1980:24–25).

VIRILITY ANXIETY

As a state of being separate from femininity, manhood therefore has its own debatable status in Hindu culture but seems to reflect an unusual degree of psychological and cultural ambivalence. There is clearly both a stress on a virility that is difficult to cultivate and to sustain, something both exalted and anxiety-ridden; and there is also its converse: a retreat to a childlike state that finds elaborate, if ambiguous, expression in myth and art. As in China, some of this tension manifests itself in psychosomatic conditions. There is in fact a great deal of concern about virility among many men in India, Sri Lanka, and Bangladesh— as much or more than in China. As we have seen, koro occurs in epidemic proportions in parts of northern India. In addition, many Indian men have been described as obsessively worried about their sexual capability, a theme that Carstairs (1958:167) and others (Edwards 1983) have referred to as an identifiable culture-bound psychiatric syndrome: "virility anxiety." This heightened fear of impotence occurs throughout the subcontinent and is said to be distinctively Indian (O'Flaherty 1980:108–09). In some cases, men adopt special diets to fight impotence and bolster performance. Often these involve both magical potions and the ingestion, in homeopathic fashion, of semenlike fluids such as milk or egg whites, or even (shades of the Sambia!) semen itself (ibid.:51). Fear of virility loss has given rise to more than the usual panoply of cures and treatments for impotence— real or imagined—in both India and Sri Lanka (ibid.; Obeyesekere 1976:214).

THE MASCULINIZING IMPULSE

Weighing all this contradictory data, one may conclude that manhood in India, at least among southern Hindus, is a complicated proposition, reflecting the all-embracing inclusiveness of

Hindu logic. Given their polymorphous expressions, ideas of gender seem changeful and self-contradictory, rather like the protean Hindu deities themselves. Yet the thematic dualism of Hindu imagery reflects an underlying concern for masculinity that is expressed dialectically rather than, as in some other societies, being reduced into ossified, single-sided codes. The internal sex-identity conflicts that other cultures resolve by repression are given untrammeled freedom of expression in India, to be worked out by many alternative solutions involving shifting identifications and representations. In southern India, especially, the androgynous themes indicate anxieties we have encountered elsewhere, but they are portrayed there in labile images rather than as immutable verities. Interestingly, this contradictory quality has been noted, often disapprovingly, by Indian intellectuals and political leaders, who for their own reasons wish to stress the more "masculine" side of the Indian character. This disparagement seems to have both practical and religious implications relating to Indian national crises. Let us take a brief look at some examples.

Some modern Indian leaders have exalted masculinity as a form of national character-building in the struggle for independence. One example of this is found in the work of the great Bengali writer Bankim Chandra Chatterji, a virile proponent of Indian independence who wrote in the early part of this century. Commenting on the influence of the Vedic myths, this modernist (he was Bengal's first novelist) expressed disgust at the sexually indeterminate and regressive themes in the sacred texts, especially the *Gitagovinda*. His complaint was that these works had no "manly feelings," that they were "effeminate" and thus a decadent influence on Indian youth. Arguing for a masculine self-image as a first step toward modern nationhood, Chatterji believed such traditions contributed to the submissive personality that was holding India down. Such statements apparently met with general approval in nationalist circles, where Chatterji's ideas won wide acclaim (cited in Kakar and Ross 1987:98).

Chatterji's appeal for manliness as a political ideal is reflected even more strongly in the charismatic figure of the sage Vivekananda, a turn-of-the-century holy man and activist. The founder of the Ramakrishna order of monks, this swami attracted a mass following in British India, foreshadowing Gandhi as a national leader. Vivekananda (real name Narendranath) was born in 1863 into a Bengali family of the Kayastha community. A contradictory man himself, he was both an impassioned adherent of the traditional Hinduism and a crusader for modernization and Hindu revitalization. An activist holy man, an introspective poet, as well as a fiery orator, his objective was to rehabilitate selected elements of the ancient Hindu traditions by making them more relevant to problems of contemporary Indian society. He was therefore a reformer and a traditionalist at the same time—much like Mahatma Gandhi, whose passive resistance campaign also reflects the rich and stark contrasts within Hindu thought.

On the one hand, Vivekananda was a confirmed yogi and spiritual advisor in the ancient sage-guru tradition. As such, he exhorted his fellows to adhere to the otherworldly preoccupations prescribed by their dharma. Yet, dismayed at India's decline into helpless colonial status, he was also a convinced believer in the efficacy of practical action, a devotee of social change, and a dedicated advocate of scientific and technological enlightenment. He and his monks were among the first holy men to go out into the Indian countryside and engage in mundane improvement activities such as building schools, wells, and hospitals and assisting relief operations during famines and epidemics (Kakar 1981:161).

Like Chatterji, this activist monk also preached that the androgynous themes in the old texts were enervating, dissolute, and effeminate. But, appreciating the inclusive quality of Hindu pantheism, he also found support in the same texts for his revisionist beliefs. Seizing upon the submerged masculine side of the Vedic teachings, he used them to inspire his countrymen with self-pride and a burning desire for independence. "Who cares for your *bhakti* and *mukti* (devotion and piety)," he would retort indignantly to his fellow Hindu monks when they chided him on his activist ideas. "Who cares what your scriptures say? I will go into a thousand hells cheerfully if I can arouse my countrymen, immersed in darkness, to stand on their own feet and be *men* inspired with the spirit of Karma yoga" (Vivekananda 1953:128).

Constantly trying to arouse his charges to action, he lectured them: "No more weeping, but stand on your feet and be men. It is a man-making religion I want. It is man-making theories that we want. I want the strength, manhood, *kshatravirya* or the virility of a warrior" (Vivekananda 1970:3.224). And later still: "O Thou Mother of the Universe, vouchsafe manliness unto me— Make me a man!" (ibid.:4.143). Meditating on his career in his later life, he exclaimed that "the older I grow, the more everything seems to me to lie in manliness. This is my new gospel" (1953:151). Some of the growing militancy of this new gospel, of course, had to do with the deepening shadow of the Indian independence movement, a purely political event, but it is clear from our discussion of izzat, above, that such themes were already firmly entrenched as one of the many supporting pillars of Indian life and that Vivekananda's gospel was also a revitalization of such dormant cultural themes.

As Kakar notes (1981:174–76), Vivekananda admired the British for their strength and energy, for knowing "what should be the glory of a man" (the guru's words). Perhaps he was speaking specifically of the Oxbridge public-school elite that John Chandos has written about (1984), with their "serviceable" manhood. But his obsession with manliness did not come from a vulgar aping of Western ways. It was strongly grounded, at least in Vivekananda's mind, in certain traditions well established in the ageless Hindu myths that, as we have seen, are full of androgynous forms, and so represented a selection from the great arc of indigenous possibilities. It was a selective revival of old traditions he wanted, *kshatravirya*, the virility of the Hindu warrior, not a revolutionary or imported ethic. This manliness was already part of Hindu culture; the guru was simply adapting it to the needs of the moment—a clear example of the usefulness

of sexual ideology in nationalist movements such as we saw in
the case of the American South.

Vivekananda's followers understood this. For the young men
who represented the guru's constituency, this call to manliness
was (as it still is for many) an irresistible appeal because it imbued the search for national identity with the glories of the past
and with the justifying imprimatur of sacredness. The thrust of
this kind of masculinizing campaign, Kakar argues (ibid.:175),
touches a deep current of "potential militancy and aggressive
activity in Indian society." Here the desire for independence has
both a psychological and national relevance.

These masculinizing efforts are especially interesting because
they underline the pragmatic and political uses of such manly
doctrines. Here in the teachings of the Indian sage we see an
example of culture being renegotiated and remade to meet the
practical needs of political crises. Perhaps what we see in the
exhortations of Chatterji and Vivekananda is manhood in the
making: the recombination of indigenous elements into a cult of
manliness in response to the practical exigencies of the moment,
the "invention of tradition" (Hobsbawm and Ranger 1983), or,
in this case, its reinvention.

MANHOOD IN JAPANESE CULTURE

India, then, is complicated, its gender imagery protean and
polychromatic, its manhood ideals a matter of debate. It is not
surprising that populous, ethnically diverse civilizations such as
India and China should display many alternative notions of
manhood (as well as of womanhood) because of the great variety
of social roles, religions, and subcultures. In addition, as in India, historical and political vicissitudes may also complicate the
picture by evoking manly images conducive to nationalist or
anticolonial struggles. Finally, because these ancient civilizations
are so hierarchically organized, their people, especially in the
lower socioeconomic strata, may adhere to rigid norms of deference, cooperation, and self-effacement that soften or even su-
persede virile norms promoting individualism.

What about relatively homogeneous Japan—one of the few non-Western nations to avoid the colonial encounter? With little of the subcultural diversity of India (or China for that matter), Japan is an interesting case in point when it comes to the relationship of nationalism, self-image, and manhood. The Japanese have a notion of manhood that has something in common with Western ideals; yet it also has some of the polymorphous flexibility of Indian culture. Add to this the insular stamp of putative "specialness" or "uniqueness" that characterizes the way the Japanese envision their society and culture (Smith 1983:110) and the unique (for Asia) experience of industrial expansionism and of militarism in the 1930s and 1940s, with its samurai antecedents. Unfortunately, this rich lode has not been deeply mined. The equally important subject of womanhood in Japan has received a great amount of attention recently (Lebra 1985; Lebra and Lebra 1986; Smith and Wiswell 1982), but Japanese manhood has been largely ignored by scholars.

As far as I know, the only work specifically on this subject of man's gender ideals in Japan is Ian Buruma's *Behind the Mask* (1984), an entertaining treatise on Japanese sexual mores and cultural heroes. Basing his ideas mainly on popular culture—films, pulp literature, plays, and so on—Buruma argues that achieving a culturally defined manhood status is a developmental struggle in Japan as in the West, but that Japanese culture provides at least two traditional alternative pathways. He calls these the "hard" (*koha*) and the "soft" (*nanpa*) schools. The first is expressed in heroic or aggressive action, often warlike, and is recognizable as a variation of "machismo" (Buruma's term). The other involves more placid but always "useful" pursuits, or perhaps more accurately stated, the selfless industriousness and moral conformity that Westerners today associate with the Japanese "salary-man" mystique that has brought Japan to the zenith of economic power. Both schools, however, reflect the underlying emphasis in Japanese culture on devotion to duty, discipline, collective goals, diligence, and tenacity as primary male virtues. Buruma sees this dichotomy as a reflection of the inherent tension in Japanese society between the stress on individual performance and the opposing tendency toward conformity to group ideals and self-effacement.

If Buruma is correct, manhood in Japan, as in the West, is an achieved state, a cultural artifice, but with some unique characteristics reflecting the stress in Japanese culture on reconciling public and private interests. Thus, the road to manhood, via the hard or soft route, "is a hard one" he says (1984:136). For the Japanese youth, the quest for manhood is as "traumatic" as anywhere else and is subject to similar tests and proofs along the way. The test of manhood, not to mention the infinite variety of grails, is an endless source of myth and drama in Japanese culture. The main requirements for passing "The Test," according to Buruma's reading of Japanese culture, are "blind perseverance and victory of mind over body" (ibid.). Let us look at what Buruma has to say about the "hard" tradition and its blend of personal achievement and conformity; we will then look at other manifestations. Incidentally, none of the following should be accepted uncritically: for comparative purposes I will refer to other, perhaps more scholarly, works as we proceed in order to place Buruma's musings in perspective.

BUSHIDO ANTECEDENTS

To understand the image of manliness in Japanese culture, we have to start with the ancient warrior tradition of the country's feudal past. The unflinching, virile hero who performs great deeds against all odds is a venerable cultural model in Japan. It takes its origin from the famous samurai code, or *bushido,* the warrior's way. The main qualities of bushido are not simply self-serving heroism or gratuitous personal self-aggrandizement; rather, they are blind loyalty to lord and family and "deeds of outstanding merit" in such service, even to the death (Bellah 1985:97). Although the samurai caste itself died out during Japan's industrialization, its central value system of unquestioned loyalty to constituted authority did not disappear entirely but lived on in a modernized bureaucratic form. It was taken over by

Japan's growing bourgeoisie as a generalized code of conduct useful in nation-building and administration. It was gradually universalized to all other classes in Japan, rather like the Protestant Ethic in Western Europe, so that the entire country was more or less "bushido-ized" by the late Tokugawa period (1600–1868): "Basically the ethic of a warrior class, under the influence of Confucianism and Buddhism, became sufficiently generalized so that it could become the ethic of an entire people" (ibid.:183).

By 1900, this samurai code, with its insistence upon blind, selfless devotion and meritorious service, had become part of the national spirit of Japan, its military aspect taking precedence in the 1930s and put to rest only after the defeat in 1945. Bushido, however, is not a narrow military code but, above all, a moral code governing behavior and attitudes, of which military service is only perhaps the most pure and noble expression. Remaining today is the emphasis on "self-abnegating performance" in the service of collective or national goals (ibid.:14), on "surmounting yourself" for the good of the collectivity (Morris 1975:315), ideals now directed at group economic success rather than war. In this moral system, with its single-minded pursuit of collective goals, selfishness is the greatest vice, and the self-serving man, as well as appearing insincere (the greatest sin in Japanese eyes, with a much stronger negative connotation than in English), is also regarded as corrupt and "effete" (Buruma 1984:161). With its stress on personal performance as an obligation of group membership, bushido (and its modern work-ethic reincarnation) is definitely a code of male honor, with elements of masculine self-control and service found in many other cultures. As such, it is linked to a complementary female behavioral code of "shame" emphasizing sexual modesty and the standard domestic virtues. As a guide to right action, Japanese gender ideals bear certain functional resemblances to some Mediterranean moral counterparts, with their emphasis on honor and shame, although there are important differences having to do, especially, with the governance of sexuality (Asano-Tamanoi

1987). Being a man in Japan, as in Andalusia (but in heightened form), implies doing your duty to others, as defined by this code, and honoring your social obligations despite all odds and regardless of personal cost. Ivan Morris has written a fascinating book, *The Nobility of Failure* (1975), describing the intense valuation in Japanese thought of the doomed hero who fights on to the bitter end to implement group goals. Such heroes personify the Japanese ideals not only of virtue but also of masculinity.

As Morris gives us many useful examples of this heroic ideal so dear to Japanese self-image, we can borrow one from his book before returning to what Buruma says on contemporary popular culture. Our case example is the warrior and leader Yoshitsune Minamoto. A charismatic figure of the Kamakura period (1185–1333), Minamoto was a small, physically unimposing man who defeated bigger and stronger opponents because of his unshakable "sincerity" (selfless devotion to cause, the national obsession). He was a famous strategist and soldier who helped unite portions of the islands under the relatively enlightened rule of his clan, momentarily bringing justice and order to a fratricidal, anarchic countryside. A brilliant general and prodigy of administrative ability, Minamoto won battle after battle until finally brought down, as legend has it, not by superior forces but by the treachery of effete manipulators. Despite his delicate appearance, Minamoto is revered today as a national cultural hero because of, among other attributes, his "powerful masculinity," as Morris puts it (ibid.:74). Minamoto showed this quality both by a number of heroic accomplishments—his military prowess and his risk taking both on the battlefield and in his military stratagems—and also by his generosity and kindness to followers and his "active amorous life" (ibid.:73–74).

Warriors such as Minamoto gave rise to a virile Big Man tradition in Japan with powerful nationalistic overtones. Over the centuries of Japan's development into a nation-state, this heroic tradition became part of a national consensus of self-identity in the image of a physically small man's defiance of overpowering odds. Some of the heroic and activist qualities identified as part of this culture-hero mythology have been incorporated into Japanese notions of how men should be today, naturally on a greatly reduced scale. These qualities were given new life during the militarist period of Japanese expansion, with its samurai overtones and spectacular exploits. But after Japan's defeat in 1945, the bushido aspects were transformed and redirected toward economic ends; they were not, however, eliminated as moral ideals. Let us turn to some specific and often fascinating examples from modern Japanese popular culture.

JAPANESE MACHO MEN: SOME BACKGROUND

As we have seen in the case of Minamoto, the modern Japanese "macho man" has a venerable national pedigree. Let us backtrack briefly once again, this time to the transitional Tokugawa period, a time when modern Japan was just beginning to emerge from its dormant feudal past. During early Tokugawa times, as Japan urbanized, the government attempted to control the expanding cities by appointing neighborhood political chiefs, rather like village headmen or ward leaders. These local bosses commanded by personal charisma and patronage as well as by their swords. They therefore had to inspire enough awe in the populations they controlled to keep order. Knowing this, the Tokugawa government often chose these headmen from occupations known for bravery and endurance, such as firemen or builders; often they were samurai fallen on hard times and in need of work. Such leaders therefore already had an established reputation for derring-do and for "fierce independence" (Buruma 1984:167–68). As local heroes and models, they represented a swashbuckling style that became ingrained in Japanese culture as the *Hard School* of manhood: "hard, stoical, manly, and macho" (ibid.:149). In the popular imagination these local macho men, called *kyokyaku* (ibid.:168), became legendary figures, acquiring a (partially undeserved) Robin Hood reputation for protecting the poor, succoring the weak, and punishing evil.

Later, the social role of these myth-inspiring local bosses

changed somewhat. Toward the end of the Tokugawa era, as Japanese society became increasingly unstable and corrupt, many of them began to support their rule through gambling, crime, and extortion, eventually becoming indistinguishable from ordinary gangsters, or *yakuza* (the Japanese Mafia). Like the famous *ronin,* or unemployed samurai of the same period, some of these outsiders lost their roots in the cities and towns, becoming wanderers and drifters—rather like the lonesome cowboy hero of Wild West lore. Despite this slide from grace, the Robin Hood image endured in the popular imagination (which perhaps needed such figures in a period of social flux). Gradually this tradition gave rise to the myth of the itinerant crusader, a Japanese knight errant who, obeying a strict code of honor based on samurai prototypes, came to the aid of the poor and the weak in crises, mysteriously materializing and then disappearing just as magically once the noble deeds were done and the villains dispatched. The great exploits of such popular heroes became irresistible subjects for plays, poetry, and popular literature, and, today, especially films. A good example, familiar to Western audiences, is Akira Kurosawa's 1960 picture *Yojimbo.* In this film, the popular movie actor Toshiro Mifune plays a wandering ronin who single-handedly restores order and justice in a local civil war. The archetypical plot of the wandering hero is similar to that of the *Seven Samurai* (also Kurosawa) and is repeated in countless Hollywood epics.

The same motif, with its haunting echoes of Western tough-guy traditions, finds further expression in other films by this acknowledged master of Japanese cinema. Let us take as an example the hero of Kurosawa's very first film, *Sanshiro Sugata* (1943). Like his later pictures *Ikiru, High and Low, Redbeard,* and his masterpiece, *Ran* (based on *King Lear,* with the three daughters changed into sons), this first effort is about the spiritual initiation of a boy into manhood, about "The Test." Like so many other Japanese youths depicted in popular fiction and films, the eponymous hero undergoes an initiation into the martial arts—in this case judo—as a metaphor for the transition to adulthood. This callow adolescent joins a master who lives in a temple. Being naturally gifted, Sanshiro soon becomes an invincible fighter. But something is missing in the boy's character, and his master is not satisfied with the young man's progress. Sanshiro's ascendancy has perhaps been too easy; he has not suffered and overcome defeat: he has not faced death. Perceiving that something is lacking in his training, he confronts the master, who simply but mysteriously orders his pupil to "die!" The young man's response is a classic example of the Japanese version of a boy's "initiation into manhood" (Buruma 1984:141–42). "Without blinking Sugata jumps into the pond behind the temple, where he spends the entire night staring at the moon, hanging onto a wooden post for dear life. It is his initiation. At dawn his spiritual crisis comes to an end: he has seen the ultimate truth in the beauty of nature. Wildly excited he jumps out of the pond to tell his master the good news. He is on his way to becoming a man."

The martial-arts hero is a good example of the *koha,* or hard school, in which the individual triumphs over a set course of obstacles to emerge both tough and wise—a true man in the Japanese fashion. The typical characteristics of the koha hero are stoicism and a purity of motive that is almost naive ("sincerity" again). He always has a fierce temper that flares up in the face of injustice, and, above all, he shows perseverance unto death. The koha hero is concerned about his manhood; like the Western cowboy hero he "has to prove his manhood over and over again in fights" (ibid.:143). With its echoes of bushido, this kid of manly spirit has been assimilated into the Japanese national self-image as a defining feature and as the moral basis of a patriotic stereotype: the smaller, though more sincere, hero conquers much bigger (foreign) foes. This hard school is a heroic ideal not often achieved.

Buruma further illustrates his thesis with reference to popular literature. One example he gives is a popular boys' comic book called "I Am a Kamikaze." These comic magazines are immensely popular among Japanese boys and men, more so than their equivalents in the United States. Nearly all such magazines are filled with melodramatic stories featuring the exploits of swaggering samurai, adventurers, or sportsmen (Schodt 1983:87), all of their adventures "solid macho stuff" (Taylor 1983:188). Words such as *shunen* ("tenacity") and *otoko-rashisa* ("manliness") regularly issue from the heroes' bellowing mouths (Schodt 1983:80). Standard fare for adolescents, one of these comic books features a young hero called Shinko Yamato. The name has symbolic significance: Yamato is the classical name for the Japanese nation, an ancient term often used jingoistically, as in *Yamato no tamashii*, "the spirit of Japan" (ibid.:143). The comic strip supplies a patriotic message rather like the "G.I. Joe" or "Terry and the Pirates" equivalents in the United States.

The story is about how young Shinko learns to be a man through his father's teachings. The young man has all the requisite qualities of the hard Japanese hero: he is small in stature, but his fierce dedication makes up for his size (the indomitable Japanese spirit again). He has youthful integrity and idealism. He is painfully sincere. He is short-tempered and stoic to a fault, pure in his emotions, and single-minded in his cause. However, and this is the crux of the matter, Shinko himself is not a suicide pilot, for he was born after the war. His father was. Oddly, (and this explains the old man's obsessive behavior) the father did not die: to his everlasting disgrace he crashed his plane without getting himself killed. To make up for this humiliation, he has decided to make the perfect man out of his young son.

The story then goes on at length about Shinko's education into manhood. To set the stage, his father keeps repeating this message: "Once a Japanese man decides to do something, he carries it out to the bitter end, at all costs." The boy is then subjected to various tests. His father pounds him over the head with bamboo swords to toughen him up; he throws him off a speeding truck; he ties him to a pier during a howling blizzard. Tough little Shinko survives all these trials. His main test of prowess, however, involves his battles with the local school bully, Wada, who is the son of a big gangster boss. Unhappily, Wada is much bigger and stronger than Shinko, who loses every fight. Yet having fully absorbed his father's message—as well as the blows of his rival—he perseveres like a true samurai. Eventually, in a climactic final confrontation, the smaller boy defeats his tormentor in a duel with bamboo swords. Having learned the true path to manhood, he does not kill his cruel and cynical opponent but lets him escape to rue his ways. Once he has proven himself a man and thus verified the Japanese way, there is no point in killing. Shinko magnanimously shows his enemy (and his impressionable young readers) "the Way to true manhood" (ibid.:145). (For more on macho Japanese comic-book culture see Schodt 1983.)

KAMIKAZE HEROES

The reverence for tenacity and sacrifice reaches its apogee in the figure of the real suicide pilot—the kamikaze—the ostensible subject of the comic strip above. Because this brief phenomenon (the concept was only implemented after 1944) seems so unaccountable to Westerners, it has been the subject of some study about motivation. In his book on Japanese heroism, Ivan Morris (1975) has shown, by examining written accounts, letters, and diaries, how the motives of the suicide pilots and submariners coincided with some of the more extreme Japanese ideas, also derived from bushido antecedents, concerning loyalty or "obligation" (*on*) to authority figures and parents. This concept taught that life was a web of inescapable mutual obligations. The entire purpose of a man's life was to repay the debts he had accumulated to parents, who had raised him to manhood, and to the collectivity, personified by the Emperor, which had nourished him. Indeed, life was deemed worthless and dishonorable unless devoted utterly to service to these significant others. The ultimate price was therefore a great honor, and the doomed pilots were "joyful" at having the chance to fulfill these obligations in so dramatic and final a way. Interestingly, there was little expectation of a reward in an afterlife; most of the pilots, as they say in their letters, were agnostics or even "atheist," as one of them wrote (ibid.:318). What they achieved in death was post-humous honor, not a paradise of battlefield martyrs as in some fanatical Muslim sects.

Aside from whatever psychological adjustments may have been going on, part of the strange joy that seized the doomed young men in their last hours was also a response to what was considered the ultimate test of their manhood. This, as we have seen it exemplified above, is morally inseparable from social role, from duty to society, and therefore from patriotism. For example, one young pilot named Isao Matsuo, of the Hero's Special Attack Unit, wrote home in 1945 of the great honor of being chosen to die. It gave him, he announced, the opportunity "to die like a man!" A young sailor who volunteered to die was asked by his commanding officer why he had done so. His answer was simply, "A man must do what he can for his country." Exclaiming on their luck in being chosen for the ultimate sacrifice, one young volunteer said to a fellow suicide, "How fortunate . . . that you were born a boy! A woman could have no adventure such as this" (Morris 1975:319–20). Such sentiments remind one of Japanese celluloid heroes who, when faced with overwhelming foreign enemies, go off to certain doom crying, "Let us be like men, let us die like men" (Buruma 1984:187): a Japanese tradition that is not perhaps too different from Western ideals about manly courage, at least in certain circles.

OTHER ROUTES TO MANHOOD

The self-abnegating hard way represents one theme in Japanese culture. There is a softer way (*nanpa*). This is epitomized by, among other examples, the famous Japanese film hero "Tora-San." The Tora-San film genre is about a wandering do-gooder with a pacifist bent. With an audience only in Japan, these films are among the most well-attended shows in the islands. In contemporary Japan, the single most popular film hero is Torajiro Kuruma, who is known in his films as Tora-San. He is arguably the most beloved character in the history of the Japanese cinema. Since beginning in 1939, his films have all revolved around the same archetypical theme: the noble, gentle adventurer helps the weak, solves problems, and upholds all the family virtues associated with "essential goodness" (Buruma 1984:210). Not overtly bellicose or violent, but sweet-natured and above all sincere in his firm support for traditional values, Tora-San represents a classic father-figure of the retiring, lovable sort—teaching adoring boys a manliness of inner strength. Many of the Tora-San films are specifically about the difficulties of a responsible manhood of duty, honor, and honesty. This quality is portrayed in film after film as a process of acquiring the salient virtues of sincerity, selfless devotion to cause, and perseverance in a hard world. The title of Tora-San's first film was *It's Hard to Be a Man* (ibid.:210). Established early, this theme is elaborated continually.

Nanpa emphasizes the other Japanese icon, duty (*giri*) and social responsibility, especially filial loyalty, rather than blood and thunder. For the average middle-class Japanese today, it is the way of the salary-man or the technocrat, a mode of "pulling your own weight," but this has always been a parallel theme in the Japanese scheme of things. Yet even here, for those who reject the samurai's fierceness in favor of avuncular teaching or white-collar diligence, there is a similar emphasis on tenacity and on practical expediency within the constraints set by group needs. For example, Robert Bellah (1985) and George DeVos (1973), in their classic studies of Japanese culture, have noted that goal-attainment has always been the central focus in Japanese society and that the thrust of Japanese culture and social arrangements has been to reconcile the emphasis on individual achievement with collective goals.

Efficiency and activism are very important in the soft school of Japanese manhood. No accomplishment counts for much unless it is expressed in a socially productive way. Even learning and erudition are seen as means to an end in Japanese culture, rather than as valuable in their own right. Bellah writes of this (1985:16):

"The merely erudite man is not worthy of respect. Rather learning should eventuate in practice." The worthy Japanese man is one who accepts the challenge that drives him "from the safety of his study into the hurly-burly of the outside world" (Morris 1975:216). Whether he chooses the battlefield or the office or wanders about the countryside doing good like Tora-San, the Japanese man is an engaged group player; the male role is "ethically activist," whatever the profession (Bellah 1985:98). The good man, the sincere man, shows "a blind devotion to direct action and an infinite capacity for hardship and pain" (Buruma 1984:139).

The male role is therefore based on a familiar praxis of engagement and activism, but with strong nationalistic overtones. It demands socially meaningful performances, always with group goals in mind. Indeed, Earl Kinmonth, in his book *The Self-Made Man in Meiji Japanese Thought* (1981), has contrasted turn-of the-century Japanese ideas of entrepreneurship with Western ones. He has shown that the stress on worldly success that seized Japan during its period of industrialization between 1868 and 1914 did not extend to an endorsement of self-aggrandizement, as was common in the West. Rather Japanese culture, although equally demanding of study and hard work, also insisted that individual performance always be directed at higher collective ends, at "state or social purposes" (ibid.:234). Wealth and honor were perceived as collective, not individual, goals, and the emphasis was on creativity rather than simply on success, narrowly defined as accumulated wealth (ibid.:16). The Japanese idea of male achievement was summarized in the early Meiji period (as it may be today) by the typical exhortation found in magazines and journals: "Every time a youth opens his mouth, it is time to insist upon enterprise." But the goals then, as now, were decidedly collective ones: "wealthy country and strong army" (ibid.:111).

Enterprise in service to family, company, and nation is manly; shirking is effete: a specifically Japanese way of conceptualizing the contours of a man's moral life. The male role in Japanese society seems to rest, more than in many places, on a rarefied sense of duty—whatever social referent that may take at a given time: family, nation, Emperor, or business firm (Buruma 1984:162). "To live like a man" (ibid.:181) is to follow the path of duty through hardship and sacrifice and beyond. A real man does his job to the bitter end, as the failed comic-book kamikaze tells his son. Acceptance of social fate "is what separates the men from the boys in Japan" (ibid.:184).

ETHNOGRAPHIC EVIDENCE

Yet, as I said, it may be a mistake to generalize from Buruma and from the popular expressions on which he relies. As Buruma is not a trained anthropologist, his work could be guilty of ethnocentrism or male bias, and we have to remain on guard against such distortions. Perhaps this is also true of the other authors cited above. I am not able to judge their impartiality, but Buruma's book has been criticized by some Japanese scholars (Kondo 1984) for overstressing the bizarre and exotic in Japanese society and for extrapolating too much from pulp fiction and movies, which after all appeal to certain (though large) segments of society. Yet recent works by respected scholars, mainly women, reveal some interesting parallels and make me less skeptical about his findings.

For example, in her study of Japanese childrearing practices, the female fieldworker Joy Hendry surveyed people on the character traits that Japanese people wished to instill in their children (1986:93). The "list of aspirations" for boys that she painstakingly collected stressed "courage, steadfastness, resoluteness, responsibility, and manliness," all the qualities touted in the films and movies that Buruma cites. In her interesting study of Japanese gender attitudes, the anthropologist Sonya Salamon found a strongly developed "stereotype of maleness" in Japanese thinking that stressed an active role in economic and sexual relations, resourcefulness, and especially personal independence (1986:134). Autonomy and strength of character are very important to this masculine image. "One is not a man" in Japanese culture, she notes (ibid.), unless one "is free," that is, able to act independently and thus meet challenges (here defined as those of career). And in her survey of women's attitudes, the anthropologist Takie Lebra, herself Japanese, found that the prospective brides she interviewed stressed familiar qualities of masculinity as desirable in husbands. Most young women said they would shun weaklings who acted dependent or irresolute. These weaklings were not considered real men. What the women all wanted was a "manly man" (1985:137), an ideal expressed in phraseology hauntingly reminiscent of Buruma's musings above.

Finally, as we have seen in the case of the feudal hero Yoshit-sune Minamoto, with his "active amorous life," sexual assert-iveness is also important in establishing masculine credentials in Japan. Let me illustrate this, again, by reference to ethnographic participant-observation. When the American anthropologist John Embree was about to leave Suye Mura, a village he had studied in Japan during the 1930s, the villagers made one collec-tive request of him. They insisted that before he leave Japan he sleep with one of the local women. Somewhat put off by his reticence during his stay, the village people said that this was his last chance to "show that you are a man" (Smith and Wiswell 1982:66). Embree politely demurred, with everlasting damage to his reputation. In Japan, the road to manhood is indeed a hard one.

Exceptions:
Tahiti and Semai

Every man is the son of his actions.
                              —Cervantes, *Don Quixote*

Whether "hard" or "soft," manhood has to be
validated, vindicated, and defended in many
societies. Even when equivocal, as in Hindu
culture, manhood is experienced as a problematic status—a labile boundary that can be
traversed in either direction. With all its attendant anxieties, however, the manly threshold is not universal as a cultural category.
There are some societies where the concept is
either insignificant or absent. These virtually
androgynous cultures raise questions about
the universal "need" for masculinity in male
development, and in my opinion they suggest
that cultural variables may outweigh nature
in the masculinity puzzle.

We already have some famous examples of
such sexually indeterminate cultures in Margaret Mead's *Sex and Temperament in Three
Primitive Societies* (1935). Championing an extreme cultural determinism in this book,
Mead tries to show the limitless plasticity of
gender roles and images by describing three
societies where sex roles are utterly unlike
those of the Western model. Though appreciating the colorful palette used in the ensuing descriptions, I prefer not to use her data

here because her work has aroused controversy as to accuracy (Freeman 1983). Rather than involving myself in this debate, I will use two examples, the people of Tahiti in French Polynesia and the Semai of Malaysia, who have been described in less controversial monographs. Here I rely mainly on Robert Levy's fine work on the Tahitians (1971, 1973) and Robert Dentan's (1979) exemplary monograph on the Semai of Malaya. First, the Tahitians.

TAHITI: CROSSOVERS

Tahiti is one of the Society Islands, formerly a part of French Polynesia. Today almost synonymous with the phrase "tropical paradise," Tahiti was first contacted in the middle of the eighteenth century by, among other Western explorers, Captain Cook. From the very first European visits, Tahitian culture, especially its treatment of sex roles, has piqued Western curiosity because of its casualness. Most visitors have remarked upon the unusual and—by Western standards—bizarre lack of sexual differentiation and role playing on the island. For example, one of the first Westerners to write about native sexual mores, the sailor John Forster (1778:421–22), noted that Tahitian women had a remarkably high status and were permitted to do almost everything that the men did. There were women chiefs with effective political power; some women dominated and even beat their husbands; any woman could participate in men's sports, sometimes even wrestling against male opponents; and in general women went about conversing "freely with everybody without restriction." Forster went on to contrast this state of affairs with the other islands he had visited in his travels where women were often secluded.

Later, in the nineteenth century, the American author and diplomat Henry Adams wrote home from Tahiti that the sexes were too much alike for his taste. "The Polynesian woman," he complained, "seems to me too much like the Polynesian man; the difference is not great enough to admit of sentiment, only of physical divergence" (1930:484). And in the same period, the

French painter Paul Gauguin described the native men as "androgynous," adding that "there is something virile in the women and something feminine in the men" (Gauguin 1957:47).

In the 1960s, when Robert Levy did fieldwork on Tahiti, he found these impressions of sexual indeterminacy still valid. He writes that sex differences are "not strongly marked" in Tahiti but rather are "blurred" or "blended" (Levy 1973:234–35). Men are no more aggressive than women; women do not seem "softer" or more "maternal" than the men. As well as having similar personalities, men and women also have roles so similar as to seem almost indistinguishable. Both perform most of the same tasks, and there are no jobs or skills reserved for either sex by cultural dictate. The men routinely do the cooking (ibid.:233); women do almost everything that men do outside the house. In addition, there is no stress on proving manhood, no pressure on men to appear in any significant way different from women or children. Men have no fear of acting in ways Westerners would consider effeminate. During dances, for instance, adult men will dance together in close bodily contact, rubbing against each other without any anxiety, and most men visit the village homosexual frequently and without shame (the *mahu*, whose ritualized status we will discuss later).

Even where minimal sex differences are noted by Tahitians, frequent "crossovers" in role, as Levy calls them (ibid.:235), take place, especially among the men—a situation that he found surprising (ibid.:234). Men show no discomfort at assuming a female identity, and a typical male informant would often illustrate a point by saying, "Suppose you are the man and I am the woman, and we have an argument." Sometimes in such an example, Levy notes, the informant "would make me the woman and himself the man" (ibid.:235). Levy continues:

> There are many other examples of minute crossovers in role playing by men. Teri'i Tui [a Tahitian informant], for example, demonstrated the traditional method of giving birth to me and to his youngest children by pretending he was pregnant and sitting down on the floor in the proper position. He then asked his oldest sons to pretend to help him with the delivery. Other men, when talking about the

nursing of a baby, showed how it was done by holding an imaginary baby to their own breasts. (Ibid.)

Such male crossovers in role playing are not only very frequent but are also accompanied by no evidence of anxiety whatsoever. Levy was struck by this curious nonchalance and continually questioned the men about it. But the men invariably said that there "are no general differences" between male and female in terms of character, thoughts, moral characteristics, or the difficulty of their lives (ibid.:236). No "strong thought" here! Indeed, "effeminacy" (Levy's term) is generally accepted as the general and ordinary kind of male personality (ibid.:133). Macho types are regarded as foreign and unsavory. Like Gauguin and Henry Adams, Levy concludes, almost plaintively, "the men seemed a little feminine and the women a little masculine" (ibid.:100).

This blurring of sex roles is echoed in the Tahitian language, which does not express gender grammatically. Pronouns do not indicate the sex of the subject or the gender of the object, and gender has no role in any other aspect of grammar. It is in fact possible to listen to someone talking about an interaction with another person for a long time without knowing whether the subject or object is male or female. In addition, most of the traditional Tahitian proper names are applied equally well to either a man or a woman. Although some related peoples, like the New Zealand Maoris, are said to have classified many nonsexual objects in their environment into male and female, there is nothing of this in contemporary Tahiti (ibid.:232–33).

MALE ROLE

Unlike the fiercely protective Trukese, the Tahitians make no effort to protect their women or to fend off foreign intruders. In fact, the opposite is true—much to the shock and delight of Western observers. When the English ship *Dolphin* put in at Tahiti in 1767, the sailors were amazed at their reception: the native women, wrote the ship's captain, "came down and stripped themselves naked and made all the alluring gestures they could to entice them onshore" (cited in Levy 1973:97). Apparently the Tahitian men had not only acquiesced in this behavior but had actually given their blessing to it (ibid.:126). Later the French explorer Bougainville, who rediscovered Tahiti ten months after the *Dolphin's* visit, was so struck by the easy eroticism of the women and the connivance of their menfolk that he named the place *La Nouvelle Cythère,* after the island where Aphrodite, in some versions of her history, first appeared from the sea. Bougainville writes, "Each day our men walked in the country without arms alone or in small groups. They were invited into the houses and fed; but it was no light snack to which the civility of the host is limited here. They offered them their daughters" (1958:128). Compare this behavior to that of the Trukese!

Few demands are made on Tahitian men. They do not hunt. There are no dangerous or strenuous occupations that are considered masculine. There is no warfare or feuding. The colonial French administration was relatively benign, providing welfare assistance for the indigent. The local lagoon supplies plentiful fishing without the need for arduous deep-sea expeditions as in Truk. Arable land is also plentiful: everyone either owns sufficient land or rents it "for a very small sum" (Levy 1973:11–12). Domesticated animals are plentiful as well, and there is no grinding poverty or economic struggle. The economy, rather than promoting competitiveness among men, fosters an unusual degree of cooperation, as families help each other out both in fishing and in harvesting the two major crops, vanilla and taro. Materialistic striving is not only rare among men but, according to Levy, is actually frowned upon as un-Tahitian. The average Tahitian man "refuses to strive" and is content with bare subsistence (ibid.:40). A laconic attitude toward work is considered "traditional, truly Tahitian" (ibid.). Non-Tahitian residents and visitors find the men lazy. One deviant male type was pointed out to the anthropologist. Of mixed Polynesian and Caucasian ancestry, he was brought up by a Chinese-born father to work hard and to make money. He is criticized by other villagers because "he works too hard and plans too much to be an ordinary Tahitian" (ibid.:51).

In conformity with this mild self-image, men are expected not only to be passive and yielding but also to ignore slights. There is no concept of male honor to defend, no "getting even." Men share a cultural value of "timidity" which forbids retaliation, and even when provoked men rarely come to blows (ibid.:285). The remarkable passivity of the men is something that visitors since Cook have noticed with astonishment. One early explorer, John Turnbull, generalized (1812:339), "Their dispositions are gentle to an extreme. . . . I never saw a [Tahitian] out of temper the whole time I was in [Tahiti]."

Prohibitions against aggression go far to exclude thoughts of revenge even when cheated. A French gendarme who administered a Tahitian district in the early 1960s remarked on this with satisfaction. He had worked previously in French Guinea, Algiers, and Morocco. For him the Tahitians were "lambs" in comparison (cited in Levy 1973:276). The French policeman contrasts the Tahitians with the people of Morocco, who were "hot tempered, easily angered." The Tahitians, he writes, are "the other end of the world." What most surprised him was the total lack of a vengeful spirit. "Even when they are cheated by a visitor or a merchant they do not seem to show any anger over this, or any need to get even." The same observation was made in pre-Christian times by the missionary James Wilson (1799:327), who describes the Tahitian men in the following terms: "Their manner [is] affable and engaging; their step easy, firm, and graceful; their behavior free and unguarded; always boundless in generosity to each other, and to strangers, their tempers mild, gentle, and unaffected; slow to take offense, easily pacified, and seldom retaining resentment or revenge, whatever provocation they may have received."

RITES AND MAHUS

Without any behavioral discriminants or markers for a conventional masculinity, the Tahitians do however have a rite of passage ceremony for boys. It consists of a superincision of the penis. Unlike the other circumcision rituals we have seen, this is done for "health" purposes only and has no connotation of testing. It is not looked at as a passage to manhood but simply as a medical procedure. The ritual is simple and unstressful. When old enough, the boy is taken to a secluded place, where the expert performs the brief operation in private. There is no public evaluation of "performance." There is no onus attached to crying out or showing fear, and many of the boys have been known to faint dead away with no scandal at all (Levy 1973:119–20).

A standout feature of Tahitian culture is the figure of the *mahu,* or village homosexual, an ancient tradition often noted by early explorers. Like the famous *berdache* among the North American Plains Indians (W. Williams 1986), or the *xanith* among the Omani Muslims described recently by Wikan (1984), the mahu is apparently a transsexual who elects to be an honorary woman. More than simply tolerated, he is, again like the berdache, often highly respected. One early visitor, James Morrison, gave this account based on observations between 1789 and 1791:

> They have a set of men called Mahoo [mahu]. These men are in some respects like the Eunichs [*sic*] in India but are not castrated. They never cohabit with women but live as they do. They pick their beards out and dress as women, dance and sing with them and are as effeminate in their voice. They are generally excellent hands at making and painting of cloth, making mats and every other women's employment. They are esteemed valuable friends in that way. (Cited in Levy 1973:130)

The mahus are practicing homosexuals, entertaining men and boys by offering sodomy and fellatio. Each village seems to have one of these transsexual characters, and only one, and he is always accepted without opprobrium by his fellows. Most Tahitian men consort openly with the mahu when there are no women available and think nothing of it. Interestingly, unlike the other men we have looked at, the "normal" Tahitian men usually assume the passive role in sex with the mahu, and they are quite open about saying so. Levy (1973:135) reports, "Males describing their relationships with mahu tend to stress their passive participation in the relationship and the lack of symmetry, as the following quotation from Toni [an informant] suggests. 'I was "done" by a mahu in Papeete.'"

Levy is suspicious of his informants' blasé attitude about the mahu, finding the custom problematic psychologically. In his inquiries on the matter, however, his informants told him again and again that the mahu is just a temporary sex object who represents nothing more than a substitute in a pinch for a woman. Like Gregor, Levy is an orthodox Freudian who seems to believe that all men everywhere have masculinity problems as a result of innate oedipal castration fears. In this view, a need to be "masculine" is innate, not socially constructed. Thus an explanation is required when the men show no interest in proving their masculinity both in relation to the mahu and in the culture more generally.

Levy proposes the kind of functional psychosocial explanation (1971) that used to be popular in the culture-and-personality school. He argues that the mahu represents a negative model of masculinity for men. In comparing themselves to the mahu, the latter can assure themselves that they are indeed men: "since we are not mahu we are masculine," they say to themselves, or words to that effect. Otherwise, given their androgynous culture, these men would have no cultural means of corroborating a male identity—which Levy believes to be a psychological necessity. There may be some truth in this, but I find the argument both ethnocentric and forced.

For one thing, from Levy's own account, there is absolutely no evidence that masculinity is itself a matter of any great concern for the Tahitians. They never actually say anything like, "We are manly because we are not mahus," either explicitly or implicitly, and as we have seen, despite probing, Levy never detected any observable sexual anxiety in his informants. On the contrary, they seem to have little use for a manliness that is separate and opposed to femininity. The concept is simply foreign to them. There is no stress on boys to take risks or prove themselves in this way, or to be different in role or personality from their mothers and sisters. I think therefore that it is more in concert with the facts (as Levy presents them) to take the Tahitians at their word: they do not care very much about masculinity, and the mahu is, just as they say, nothing more or less than an alternative sex object. One may conclude that, for whatever reasons in Tahiti (repression, cultural conditioning, ego-ideal), manhood is not an important symbolic or behavioral category. One wonders, however, how a Tahitian man would react if his manhood were questioned in a hostile or provocative way, or if men ever insult each other in this fashion. Unfortunately, I have discovered no reliable source of information on this matter.

THE SEMAI

We now turn to the Semai people of central Malaysia, who are in some subtle ways similar to the Tahitians in their lack of a "gender schema" (Bem 1983). The Semai are one of the aboriginal peoples of Southeast Asia, who live presently in the hills and mountains of the Malay peninsula. They are also called Senoi Semai. The word *Senoi* means "person," hence, "Semai people." Anthropologists use it to refer to those Malayan aborigines who do some primitive farming and who speak one of the peninsula's indigenous languages. These Senoi languages belong to the Austro-Asian family, which also includes Cambodian, the Mon language of Burma, and the languages spoken by some Vietnamese hill people. These peoples are all distantly related and probably represent vestiges of an indigenous pre-Mongoloid south Asian population, possibly including the Dravidians of south India and the Australian aborigines. The present-day Semai are split into two populations divided by topographical barriers: the east Semai and the west Semai. More isolated, the former lead a relatively traditional life; the latter, more accessible to outsiders, are slightly more acculturated to Malay ways.

The Semai are called in the anthropological lingo a "refuge population." This means that they once occupied a much wider geographical area than their present habitat and were displaced by more numerous or more powerful invaders, retreating to the undesirable hinterlands (in this case the central hills). Although we know virtually nothing about the early contacts between the Semai and the invading Malay peoples who have displaced them, ethnologists speculate that this contact was not a happy one for the Semai. Conceivably a series of military defeats at the hands of the more populous and technologically advanced Malays led the aborigines to adopt "a policy of fleeing rather than fighting" (Dentan 1979:2). If true, this might help explain the present Semai emphasis on nonviolence and their tendency to retreat from danger rather than defend themselves. For, as we shall see, the Semai are among the most unaggressive and retiring people on the face of the earth—a remarkable quality that has given rise to a virtual industry of scholarly speculation about whether they have any aggressive impulses at all (see Robarchek 1977; Paul 1978; Robarchek and Dentan 1987).

Physically the Semai are a tiny people. Most east Semai men are slightly under five feet tall. The west Semai are on the average almost a half foot taller. An interesting trait is that all the Semai are racially very mixed, a product of decades of casual miscegenation with Malays, Chinese, and others passing through their forest enclaves. Some Semai people look almost Chinese, with modified epicanthic eye folds; others have the Negrito features and dark chocolate skins of the neighboring Semang people. Many are smooth skinned with little or no body hair; others have heavy body and facial hair. Some are indistinguishable in physiognomy from Malays. So interbred are they that physical anthropologists have difficulty in assigning them to any of the recognized ethnic stocks and have given up in despair. The reason for all this genetic diversity stems from their nonviolent culture. The explanation is as follows.

PUNAN: TABOO

The Semai believe that to resist advances from another person, sexual or otherwise, is equivalent to an aggression against that person. They call such aggressiveness *punan*—a very important concept in their culture, meaning roughly "taboo." Punan is a Semai word for any act, no matter how mild, that denies or frustrates another person. The Semai believe that if you punan someone, his or her "heart becomes heavy" and the affected person may therefore hurt himself or become disoriented and do something inappropriate or even violent. This would place the entire village in jeopardy of punishment by the spirits who forbid untoward behavior. For example, if a confused punaned person in his befuddlement made a loud noise or hit someone, Enku, the mighty monkey god, might send down a violent thundersquall with torrential rains and hurricane winds to wash away the village. To avoid such calamity, Semai always accede mildly to requests and importuning. If a man wants to have sex with a woman, married or not, he simply tells her so and she is supposed to accommodate him without protest by lying down and spreading her legs. The converse is also true. To deny a suitor is *punan* (Dentan 1979:62). By the same token, a man or woman must not nag or "wheedle" another person for sex unduly, for that is also shockingly aggressive. The same is true for requests made for material objects or for other favors. Obviously, the Semai express no sexual jealousy, and adultery is rampant. They say of extramarital affairs, "It's just a loan."

These prohibitions against hurting another person's feelings balance out for the most part, so within Semai villages, sexual behavior is generally conciliatory, guided by these rather extreme rules of civility. Yet for more aggressive outsiders, especially persistent Malays and Chinese, the Semai women are easy marks. "Malay men often get access to west Semai women by wooing, bribing, or threatening them" (ibid.:9). In the past this sexual predation occasionally took violent forms. Until the

1920s, Malay raiders were likely to ambush Semai at any time, killing the unresisting men and taking the women and children away (Dentan, letter to the author, 12 Jan. 1988). Without any conception of male honor or paternal rights to inspire them, the Semai men make no effort to resist this "welter of interbreeding" (1979:11). Nor are there unhappy consequences for the offspring of rape or seduction. Any illegitimate children born of such liaisons are loved and well treated by the Semai, because they cannot "bear to see children neglected" (ibid.:9). In short, the Semai men do not worry about honor, paternity, or social boundaries, and outsiders often find Semai women both attractive and complaisant. Though it sounds odd, this is how their culture works.

For the concept of punan to work, the Semai must cultivate the passive, noncompetitive characteristics upon which such unquestioned compliance is based. The Semai personality is founded on a pervasive and strict nonviolent self-image. But, as Dentan points out, this extreme pacifist self-image is not merely an ideal for which the people strive. It is incorporated—introjected—into personality structure as an unconscious element of the ego-ideal. Thus the Semai do not say "Anger is bad"; they assert, "We never get angry," and an obviously angry man will flatly deny his feelings (ibid.:55). The Semai do not say, "It is good to run away when threatened"; they say, "We run away when threatened." They never hit each other or fight, and even noisy arguments are forbidden because noise "frightens people." If a man feels disgruntled because of the actions of another, he simply walks away or sulks. If disputes cannot be resolved without rancor, one of the antagonists will leave the village.

This staunchly nonaggressive image is the face that the Semai present to the outside world. They are in fact famous in Malaya (and among anthropologists) for their excessive, almost masochistic timidity. Westerners who have lived among them invariably use adjectives such as "weak" and "timid" to describe them (ibid.:56). As noted, there is a self-deprecating aspect to this recessive image. The Semai often speak of their own inferiority and backwardness in comparison to the stronger peoples they know, such as the Malays. A word they use for themselves when speaking to non-Semai is the Malay "Sakai," which means something like "bestial aboriginal" or "slave" (ibid.:1). When spoken to roughly by outsiders, they may attempt to defuse the confrontation by referring to themselves as "just dumb, stupid savages" who mean no harm. Although such linguistic self-effacement may mask deeper feelings of resentment, as is true among some oppressed peoples, we have no evidence of this, and the Semai deny that they harbor any angry feelings. Whenever trouble arises, they either immediately capitulate, or else they disappear into the forest. The east Semai are so afraid of strangers that they sometimes flee from the sound of a motorboat coming upstream into their territory (ibid.:43).

Not surprisingly, the Semai have no sporting competitions or contests that might involve one person losing and feeling bad. No one may give orders to another, for to do so would "frustrate" him. Children also may not be disciplined. Here the interesting concept *bood* comes into play. Bood means, roughly, "not to feel like doing something." If a parent tells his child to do something and the child replies, "I *bood*," the matter is closed. To put pressure on the child is punan and thus unacceptable. As Dentan (a master of understatement) puts it, "The Semai indulge their babies" (ibid.:59). There are no competitive or violent children's games. There is no pressure on boys to act strong or tough. To do so would be incomprehensible to the Semai.

The Semai do not distinguish between a male public and a female private realm. There is no effort to seclude or protect women (as we have seen above), and the Western concept of privacy, domestic or otherwise, is not to be found. For example, to refuse someone admission to your house is considered an act of extreme hostility and is therefore punan. Dentan had some trouble adjusting to this:

> My wife and I had a great deal of trouble getting used to the idea that seeking privacy was aggressive. For example, the east Semai often go to sleep early in the evening. Our house was therefore

relatively empty, and we used the evening to type up field notes. The problem was that around five o'clock in the morning some well rested Semai would decide to drop in for a visit. . . . A person who dropped in by himself might just sit down for a while humming a little tune, or he might rummage through our belongings in hope of turning up something interesting. (Ibid.:29)

There are no social boundaries recognized as such among the Semai and consequently not even the remotest notion of "protecting your own," as the concept "your own" has no meaning to them.

ECONOMY

Semai people put little stress on personal property, individualism, or material ambition. Their economy is based on a subsistence-level slash-and-burn farming. Their main crops are amaranth (the leaves are boiled to make a gruel), maize, rice, and squash. Land is relatively plentiful, and the Semai seem to be under no pressure to intensify or modernize their harvests. Their farming practices are cooperative rather than competitive. There is no private ownership, either of land or of consumer goods. If a man has no land under cultivation, he can simply ask a friend or kinsman for a portion of his land. To refuse such a request would be punan, so the land is cheerfully handed over (ibid.:43). The same is true for tools and other moveable items.

Unlike the Tahitians, the Semai like to hunt. Only the men hunt. The main weapon is a blowpipe seven or eight feet long. The blowpipe is made of two tubes of bamboo, one inside the other so that the weapon will not bend over of its own weight. From this tube the men shoot small, featherless darts, the tips of which are smeared with a sticky poison compounded from the *Strychnos* vine and mixed with other poisons. The dart is notched at the end so that the point with the poison will break off and stay imbedded in the fleeing animal. Hunting is by no means a strenuous or dangerous affair. Only small game is taken, the largest animals being small pigs. The men do not go far into the forest to hunt, usually returning to the village by noon—that is, before the day gets too hot. During the fruit season, most hunters will lie underneath a fruit tree and wait for the prey to come to them. If they encounter danger, they run away and hide without any shame or hesitation.

Hunting, moreover, is not essential: it provides little animal protein and virtually no ceremonial items. Much more game is taken by trapping, at which the Semai are proficient (ibid.:32). The Semai keep some domesticated animals, mainly chickens, but they cannot bear to kill them, so when they are fully grown, they barter or trade them to Malay or Chinese traders. The Semai know that the traders will kill these "pets," but they prefer not to think about it. This respectful attitude toward animals conditions Semai response to dangerous quadrupeds and predators, including elephants and tigers, which are common in the area. When such animals are sighted, the Semai do not confront them, like the Masai, but huddle together fearfully in their longhouse, leaving the animal to its depredations. If caught in the open, the Semai response is to run away and hide. People return to their interrupted chores only when the animal has departed. Neither nasty people nor dangerous animals may be challenged. That would be punan.

Stream fishing is also important to the Semai diet. Both men and women fish, the men using weirs, the women using baskets. Fishing by hand, sometimes with the use of mild fish poisons, is a children's game (ibid.:33). Sometimes men and women cooperate in fishing. A man and his wife, for example, will dam up a small stream with rocks or other debris, leaving a narrow opening in which they place a net. Then they beat an area of the stream above the makeshift dam, take their catch, and run upstream to repeat the process.

GENDER

As one might expect from the above, the Semai place little importance on sex differences either in assigning social role or in assessing temperament. However, unlike Tahitian, their language does distinguish between "male" (*kraal*) and "female" (*krdoor*), and gender is an important feature of Semai kinship terminology, second only to age as a discriminator. But aside from calling all rounded protuberances "breasts," the Semai have little use of gender distinctions in their speech, and they have no gender scheme. Women participate in political affairs as much as men, although they are less frequently local headmen. Men rarely become midwives, but there is no social onus to being one. There are no "invidious contrasts" between men and women (Dentan, letter, 12 Jan. 1988). Few traits are distinctively "masculine" or "feminine." The sexual division of labor is preferential, not prescriptive or proscriptive (Williams-Hunt 1952:51). That is, there are no rigid rules, and a man or woman may choose to do whatever he or she feels suited for without incurring criticism. However, the expectation is that someone skilled at an activity normally preferred by the opposite sex will be particularly good at it. For example, male midwives are especially talented, and female headmen are unusually powerful (ibid.). So few are the recognized differences between the sexes that the one visible sartorial distinction has achieved the status of a classic aphorism: "Men's loincloths are long, Women's loincloths are short." Otherwise, men and women are pretty much the same. No machismo here!

Despite all this sexual overlap, one cryptic statement in Dentan's book merits comment. The men are very solicitous of their blowpipes. No other possession can compete with the blowpipe "on an emotional level" (Dentan 1979:31). They lavish more time on making a blowpipe than on building a house; and after they have finished making it, they spend yet more time polishing and ornamenting it. Semai men, Dentan notes (ibid.), "treat their blowpipes as symbols of virility." Apparently (no other evidence is given) the men are concerned about their sexual potency, and the blowpipe is a phallic symbol. The weapon = penis motif celebrated by the Bushmen and other such gentle people seems universal wherever men hunt. Aside from this symbolism, the Semai seem to follow the Bartleby ("I prefer not to") school of masculinity. Or rather, to use one of their favorite locutions, they prefer to "run away" from all challenges. As an inducement to courageous action, manhood has little use in their frame of reference, and bravado of any sort is antithetical to their moral system. Remember that the blowpipes are never used against people and that the Semai do not judge hunting prowess invidiously.

SUMMARY

One must be careful not to generalize from these two isolated cases. For one thing, neither case is black-and-white. Dentan tells us that the timid Semai men consider their blowpipes symbols of virility, which gives one pause. Whether or not they equate potency to some broader notion of masculinity is moot. Levy notes that Tahitian boys who are *very* effeminate may hear some mild teasing about being the next mahu. Nevertheless, neither society distinguishes a "real man" category with a restricted admissions policy. The Tahitians and the Semai simply do not seem to care much about manhood.

Despite the exiguous data, some reasonable inferences about the lack of a manhood cult in these two societies can be drawn through comparison. There are obvious similarities between them in terms of moral norms, modal personality, and material context. In both, men are relieved from having to prove themselves through taking risks. There is no want of natural resources and thus no economic incentive to strive or to compete, no agonistic ethos, no open market for skills. Because the economy is cooperative, ambition is devalued. There are no serious hazards in the external world that the men are expected to defend against (the Semai run away from dangerous animals and outsiders rather than fight them). Neither society feels threatened by invaders; neither engages in warfare. There is little pressure for worldly success. There is no concept of a secluded private sphere of women and children that men must protect. Men have no interest in defining themselves as different from or superior to women, or as their defenders. In short, there is little basis for an ideology of manhood that motivates men to perform under pressure or to defend boundaries.

Although the correlations between ideology and material context seem clear, one must be cautious in drawing causal arrows here. Taken as givens, these two sets of data, the objective (or material), and the subjective (or ideological), could get us into a "chicken-or-egg" conundrum: which came first, the economy or the androgyny? Moreover, we would be guilty of teleological reasoning if we automatically attributed logical or causal priority to the material-economic conditions that seem to fit the regnant ideology (Giddens 1987:68–69). Although, as I have made abundantly clear above, I favor a materialist stance that awards causal priority to environment and basic economy, there is no way to prove that this stance is correct. Materialism, in all its forms, is still theory, not fact, and one cannot appeal to a theory to prove a hypothesis. For example, from an idealist perspective, one could reasonably argue that the ideology of passivity gave rise to the lack of economic competition rather than the other way around. Nevertheless, moving away from the futile quest for origins, one may at least hypothesize a feedback relationship in which the ideology, once formed, assists in and intensifies a matching adaptation to the environment. If a certain response is favorable to group survival and at the same time reconciles group and individual needs, we can assume that there will be selective pressures to retain it. Trait correlations, then, do not prove causal relations in any linear fashion but suggest the existence of third factors that produce the correlations (ibid.:69).

Both the Tahitians and the Semai have been described as "childlike" in comparison both to Westerners and to other, equally industrious civilizations. Perhaps without a typical manhood ideology, men are permitted the luxury of remaining passive and dependent, rather like stone-age Peter Pans. Because the information we have about their inner thoughts and fantasies is incomplete, we cannot know for sure what psychological processes are going on inside the natives' heads. But it does appear that, in these two cultures (and others like them), there is little or no social pressure to "act like men" and that men feel no driven "inherent" need to act manly. This strongly supports the feminist notion that gender norms are ascribed rather than innate.

Finally, one may look to the larger picture of biological stimulus/response for some guidance here. When confronted with danger, all mammals, man included, excrete the hormone adrenalin (Konner 1982). This primes them for an appropriate survival-enhancing response. Though this hormonal priming is the same from a chemical point of view, the behavioral outcome differs radically from species to species. In the lower mammals the response is determined largely by genetic imprinting, that is, by instinct. Evolutionary pressures have predisposed some animals to fight, others to flee (this is sometimes called the fight/flight syndrome). In man, the behavioral response is conditioned not by instinct but by learning. Those cultures that have a pronounced manhood ideology seem to be the ones that have chosen fight as a survival strategy. Without a genetic imprinting, men in those cultures have to be conditioned to be brave in order to fight. The Semai and the Tahitians, for whatever historical reasons, have elected a strategy of avoiding confrontations. This is probably the explanation for their lack of a manhood ideology: they flee.

❄ ❄ ❄ ❄ ❄ 10

Conclusions

A man can't go out the way he came in,
Ben; a man has got to add up to something!
—Arthur Miller, *Death of a Salesman*

Now that we have descriptions of man-playing from just about every corner of the world, can we answer our original questions? Is there a deep structure of manhood? Is there a global archetype of manliness? Although I began this project with a suspicion that the answer would be yes, I am less sure now. After reviewing the last two cases, I do not think there is a conclusive answer to that question. Perhaps I should give the reader a "definite maybe," as the cartoonist Walt Kelly used to say about the really big questions.

The data above support a number of interpretations. We have seen that many societies espouse a doctrine of a manhood-of-achievement; others, such as the Semai and the Tahitians, are content to let men relax and be passive. I am also sure there are androgynous cases that other anthropologists are aware of and that I shall be hearing about soon. Still, the pressured type of manhood seems to be far more frequent. Manhood is a test in most societies, and there is no doubt that this statistical frequency means something. It is clear that manhood cults are directly related to the degree of hardiness and self-discipline required for the male role. Perhaps what this frequency shows is nothing more complicated than that life in most places is hard and demanding, and that since men are usually given the "dangerous" jobs because of their anatomy, they have to be prodded into action. Manhood ideologies force men to shape up on penalty of being robbed of their identity, a threat apparently worse than death. Until someone comes up with a society in which the male role is strenuous but in which there is no manhood ideology, we may conclude that manhood directly correlates with male-role stress. Again, the causal relationships are hard to untangle, and it is unwise to speculate. However, we can safely say this: when men are conditioned to fight, manhood is important; where men are conditioned to flight, the opposite is true. Just why most societies have chosen fight is beyond the scope of this study but probably is related to the general scarcity of resources and the inability of most societies to run away, like the Semai, into open wilderness.

We may add one corollary, if tentative, observation to the above. This concerns the need for manhood rather than womanhood inspiration. In some ways, of course, women are not different from men. They, too, must be prodded into often self-sacrificing behaviors. Women also need to learn self-control and discipline, sometimes at great personal cost. The difference is this: women are normally under the control of men. Because men usually exercise political or legal authority, and because they are bigger and stronger, they can usually coerce women into compliance by force or by the threat of force, that is, if conventional morality fails to do the job. Men, however, especially in atomistic social contexts, are not always under the domination of others and are therefore harder to control socially. It may be because of this difference that a special moral system ("real manhood") is required to ensure a voluntary acceptance of appropriate behavior in men. It may also be for this reason that manhood ideologies are most pronounced in the competitive egalitarian societies of Samburu, Andalusia, Truk, Sambia, and others, in which men must fight for contestable scarce resources: when formal external constraints are absent, internalized norms must come into play to ensure "performance."

One other observation: authentically neuter or androgynous cultures like the Semai are relatively rare on a global scale. This may point to some evolutionary law of social adaptation, fight being a more successful survival strategy for social groups, or something similar. But these androgynous cultures are more than simply exceptions that prove an inflexible law. Rather than confronting a monolithic code that is either present or absent, we instead seem to have encountered a continuum of manly images and codes, a sliding scale or polychromatic spectrum. Machismo represents one extreme on this scale. Obviously Truk, Spain, the Samburu, the Amhara, the Sambia, and some specialized subgroups such as the Rajputs and American cowboys fall at this macho end of the scale. The Mehinaku, the Chinese, Japanese, and modern urban Americans fall somewhere nearer the middle. Perhaps the Semai, with their minimal concern for virility, and the Tahitians with their mahu, represent the opposite extreme. The Hindus refuse to stay in one place. Often manhood as an ideology becomes caught up in nationalist or other political movements that temporarily magnify its emotive power. Sometimes rules of deference and hierarchy interface with rugged masculinity norms, as in Japan and China, so that the picture is further complicated. Still, we may draw some preliminary conclusions about this manhood continuum and its ramifications.

For one thing, wherever "real" manhood is emphasized, even lightly, and for whatever reasons, three moral injunctions seem to come repeatedly into focus. This imperative triad occurs to varying degrees but is common enough to suggest that manhood is a response to specific structural and psychological deficits. These deficits are textured by the sexual division of labor, which is itself an adaptation to the environment. We encountered these three injunctions first in the Mediterranean region, where they stand out starkly. To be a man in most of the societies we have looked at, one must impregnate women, protect dependents from danger, and provision kith and kin. So although there may be no "Universal Male," we may perhaps speak of a "Ubiquitous Male" based on these criteria of performance. We might call this quasi-global personage something like "Man-the-Impregnator-Protector-Provider." Obviously this threefold image is a function of the criteria of male role-playing, but these data suggest that the male role is somewhat more complicated than the simple breadwinning mythology of Western societies. "Real" men are expected to tame nature in order to recreate and bolster the basic kinship units of their society; that is, to reinvent and perpetuate the social order by will, to create something of value from nothing. Manhood is a kind of male procreation; its heroic quality lies in its self-direction and discipline, its absolute self-reliance—in a word, its agential autonomy. Aggressive sexuality is important here, so one cannot speak of this masculinity as purely a cultural invention, totally separate from and opposed to "nature," as Sherry Ortner (1974) does in her scheme, male:culture::female:nature. It is a little more complicated than that.

In most societies, the three male imperatives are either dangerous or highly competitive. They place men at risk on the battlefield, in the hunt, or in confrontation with their fellows. Because of the universal urge to flee from danger, we may regard "real" manhood as an inducement for high performance in the social struggle for scarce resources, a code of conduct that advances collective interests by overcoming inner inhibitions. In fulfilling their obligations, men stand to lose—a hovering threat that separates them from women and boys. They stand to lose their reputations or their lives; yet their prescribed tasks must be done if the group is to survive and prosper. Because boys must steel themselves to enter into such struggles, they must be prepared by various sorts of tempering and toughening. To be men, most of all, they must accept the fact that they are expendable. This acceptance of expendability constitutes the basis of the manly pose everywhere it is encountered; yet simple acquiescence will not do. To be socially meaningful, the decision for manhood must be characterized by enthusiasm combined with stoic resolve or perhaps "grace." It must show a public demonstration of positive choice, of jubilation even in pain, for it represents a moral commitment to defend the society and its core values against all odds. So manhood is the defeat of a childish narcissism that is not only different from the adult role but antithetical to it.

None of the above is very new: many other authors, both academic and popular, have pointed these things out previously, using either scholarship or intuition. Yet the underlying linkage between manhood imagery and its broader social-psychological implications has not been adequately brought out in the scholarly literature on gender. I think one of the reasons for this is that most of the psychological observers have approached gender puzzles from a perspective of methodological individualism, that is, by focusing on individual self-identity or on intrapsychic processes alone, rather than on the relationship of individual behavior to social context. We see things slightly differently if we start from the point of view that gender ideologies are social facts, collective representations that pressure people into acting in certain ways—ways that are often constraining or sacrificial, but which usually have indirectly adaptive structural consequences, especially, in the case of men, the defense of boundaries. In this sense, we may look at manhood scripts not only as avenues to personal aggrandizement or psychic development but—more importantly—as modes of integrating men into their society, as codes of belonging in a hard, often threatening world.

Although symbolic, manhood codes seem to be derivative rather than arbitrary. The data show a strong connection between the social organization of production and the intensity of the male image. That is, manhood ideologies are adaptations to social environments, not simply autonomous mental projections or psychic fantasies writ large. The harsher the environment and the scarcer the resources, the more manhood is stressed as inspiration and goal. This correlation could not be more clear, concrete, or compelling; and although it does not prove anything about causal relations, it does indicate a systemic relationship in which gender ideology reflects the material conditions of life. The question of origins obviously needs further study by those piqued by such questions.

To endure, all societies confront two basic formal requirements: production and reproduction, that is, economy and rebirth. For a group to maintain itself over time, people must have a minimum number of children and must socialize them properly—not an easy task, as anyone knows who has had a child, known a child, or remembers being a child. At the same time someone must feed and protect children and their mothers, both of whom are too otherwise occupied to hunt or fight wars (Friedl 1975). For anatomical or whatever other reasons, women in most societies are largely responsible for the work of reproduction, men for production (and defense). To a large extent, both women's and men's roles are directed at replicating social structures rather than at some socially neutral or inconsequential path of personal self-fulfillment. Society is a delicate perpetual motion machine that depends upon the replication of its primary structures, the family in particular, because without the family there is no context for socializing children and thus for perpetuating the culture. This requires that enough people make certain minimal sacrifices and contributions.

In most societies, this basic continuity is always threatened, either directly or indirectly. It is threatened in two ways: internally by simple entropy, the process by which matter collapses into free energy and "things fall apart" on their own; externally by dangers inherent in human (and animal) life in general—predators, wild nature, limited resources. As anthropologists have argued for decades, culture is humankind's device for adaptation. The moral codes and norms of culture encourage people (sometimes through psychological rather than material reward and punishment) to pursue social ends at the same time that they follow their own personal desires. This is the genius of culture: to reconcile individual with group goals. Japanese culture exemplifies this most strikingly among industrial civilizations today, but all surviving, prospering cultures do this to degrees.

I think that we can characterize manhood, then, as a mythic confabulation that sanctifies male constructivity, in Walter Pater's terms. Its critical threshold represents the point at which the boy produces more than he consumes and gives more than he takes. Manhood is the social barrier that societies must erect against entropy, human enemies, the forces of nature, time, and all the human weaknesses that endanger group life. I realize that this view could be criticized from a methodological point of view because, in rejecting a narrow analytical individualism, it comes close to slipping into its opposite, methodological holism, or sociocentrism. Yet, as Steven Lukes (1973) and, more recently, Anthony Giddens (1987) have argued, it is by no means necessary to posit these approaches as mutually exclusive and exhaustive analytic possibilities. As Lukes puts it (1973:117), "Just as facts about social phenomena are contingent upon facts about individuals, the reverse is also true." Rather, we can see the present state of conceptual ubiquity of manhood as the result of human strategies that have worked well in aggregate under most extant circumstances; then the apparently variant cases like those of the Tahitians and the Semai become more, rather than less, comprehensible. It has been an underlying thesis of this book that a mutualism, or feedback relationship, exists between a society's material context and its ideology and between individual agency and structural constraint, and that causation is less useful as a concept, epistemologically, in understanding the "problem of order" than synergy, or the combined action of multiple factors.

Finally, I might return to my original theoretical statement by adducing the virtues of a dialectical functionalism at this point. Yet, while embracing a multicausal functionalism of this sort, I suppose one could argue from the other side and say that my viewpoint is "kind of" Marxist, insofar as Marxism, too, is quasi-functional. The affinity to Marx lies not so much in the dialectical label I have chosen to describe my analytical framework;

nor does it lie in the unsupported assumption that social being determines social consciousness. Although I am in sympathy with such basic tenets of materialism, I regard them more as questions than answers—an epistemological ambiguity that most sophisticated Marxists today would probably regard as an empirical problem to be addressed in each case by empirical research.

Instead, there is another, more subtle, reason one might call this view Marxist, or at least consonant with the Marxist tradition. This view is based on a notion of culture that approximates Marx's labor theory of value. Marx argues, most notably in his minor sociological masterpiece, *Critique of the Gotha Program* (1978), that all social value is the product of human labor acting upon the raw materials of nature. I suppose I am espousing this labor theory of value here, or rather a labor theory of cultural value, albeit in a modified form. I see any enduring social formation not as a given but as depending for its continuity and progress upon a sustained level of work, upon human effort constantly drawing order and meaning from the flux of nature. As an organization of values that supports society, culture is nothing more than work, physical and mental: human effort, constantly reproducing the conditions that give it birth. For this work to have value it has to be meaningful in social terms; that is, it has to make a contribution to this general constructivity. Manhood ideals force men to overcome their inherent inertia and fearfulness and to "work," both in the sense of expending energy and in the sense of being efficient or "serviceable" in doing so.

But let us also acknowledge that, like ideology, work itself does not stand alone, for human labor, being human, is also culturally conditioned. What I would add to Marx's labor theory, then, would be an appeal to consider the expressive and moral, as well as economic and political, aspects of culture as part of the "material" context. These also link causes to effects through what cultural anthropologists now call "performance" (Bauman 1977), or, more accurately, "performativity" (the "performative excellence" of the Mediterranean peoples being a case in point, as Herzfeld [1985a] has shown so dramatically in the case of Greece).

The psychological dimension provides the necessary third factor to the manhood equation, aside from ideology and environment. Psychic regression is the major obstacle to the performativity of human labor, the main impediment to its manly constructivity; hence the reaction-formation of an omnicompetent, counterphobic masculinity. Regression is the tendency to return to prior states of development, to evade reality. The wish to escape, to run from danger, to seek solace at mother's side, is probably a universal human tendency. It is present in all people, male and female, old and young. Freud regarded psychic "involution" of development—regression—as an element in all forms of character structure and mental functioning (1905:208). In his later metaphysical musings, such as *Beyond the Pleasure Principle* (1920), Freud even promoted regression to the ontological level of a drive, consonant with his idea of a death wish. For Freud the ever-constant aim of the death wish was regression, that is, to revert from the present state to a stage that existed before it—in the last analysis to a biopsychological quiescence that equals death (Balint 1968:122). At a clinical level, Anna Freud ranked regression first in her enumeration of the defense mechanisms; repression came second (1936). All children, she adds, when threatened, tend to "revert," seeking shelter and protection "in the symbiotic and pre-Oedipal mother-relationship" (1963:139). This childish tendency is "never wholly absent" from adults (ibid.:138). Despite their narrow focus on repression, castration anxiety, and penis envy, most contemporary psychoanalysts acknowledge that regression is a major, if not the major, factor in all mental processes and a "general" or "ubiquitous" tendency of all mental life (Arlow and Brenner 1963:16).

This recognition of the importance of puerile self-involution has, in fact, engendered a whole new psychoanalytic industry on the subject of infantile narcissism, as for example in the work of Heinz Kohut on the "bipolar self," which he offers as an alter-

native to Freud's Oedipus complex. One pole of the self, according to Kohut, is derived from the "maternal self-object," that is,
symbiosis with the mother; the other is the "pole that carries the
masculine ideals" (1977:179, 206). In these Kohutian terms,
then, manhood may be seen as society's inducement to grow
toward the progressive pole and, in growing, to replace the pleasure principle with the reality principle, that is, to accept the
responsibility of work. It is no wonder, then, that the major
avenue of attack on American manhood, at least from liberated
men, is against its hard-edged work ethic (Tolson 1977:48;
Ochberg 1987).

I make one other observation along these lines, which concerns the qualitative nature of the masculine contribution. This
observation may surprise (and perhaps outrage) some of the
more radical feminists, but I think the data show it to be true.
When I started researching this book, I was prepared to re-
discover the old saw that conventional femininity is nurturing
and passive and that masculinity is self-serving, egotistical, and
uncaring. But I did not find this. One of my findings here is that
manhood ideologies always include a criterion of selfless generosity, even to the point of sacrifice. Again and again we find that
"real" men are those who give more than they take; they serve
others. Real men are generous, even to a fault, like the Mehinaku fisherman, the Samburu cattle-herder, or the Sambia or
Dodoth Big Man. Non-men are often those stigmatized as stingy
and unproductive. Manhood therefore is also a nurturing concept, if we define that term as giving, subventing, or other-
directed. It is true that this male giving is different from, and
less demonstrative and more obscure than, the female. It is less
direct, less immediate, more involved with externals; the "other"
involved may be society in general rather than specific persons.

The form of nourishment also differs. Women nurture others directly. They do this with their bodies, with their milk and
their love. This is very sacrificial and generous. But surprisingly,
"real" men nurture, too, although they would perhaps not be
pleased to hear it put this way. Their support is indirect and thus

less easy to conceptualize. Men nurture their society by shedding their blood, their sweat, and their semen, by bringing home food for both child and mother, by producing children, and by dying if necessary in faraway places to provide a safe haven for their people. This, too, is nurturing in the sense of endowing or increasing. However, the necessary personal qualities for this male contribution are paradoxically the exact opposite of what we Westerners normally consider the nurturing personality. To support his family, the man has to be distant, away hunting or fighting wars; to be tender, he must be tough enough to fend off enemies. To be generous, he must be selfish enough to amass goods, often by defeating other men; to be gentle, he must first be strong, even ruthless in confronting enemies; to love he must be aggressive enough to court, seduce, and "win" a wife. What is also important about all this, insofar as it relates to the work that many feminists are now doing, is that it strengthens their basic argument by refuting the sociobiological evocation of male aggressiveness as innate, for I am arguing that men are innately not so very different from women and need motivation to be assertive.

What do the exceptional cases, the gentle Tahitians and the timid Semai, show about masculinity? Most importantly they suggest that, as we surmised early on, manliness is a symbolic script, a cultural construct, endlessly variable and not always necessary. Does this mean, as some feminists and male liberationists insist (Pleck 1981, Brod 1987), that our Western masculinity is a fraud, unnecessary and dispensable? Are we ready to throw it all away? Can we all be playful Peter Pans and devote ourselves to "self-fulfillment" or "sensitivity," whatever these terms may really mean? Or at a higher level, let us say, can we all imitate Proust in his cork-lined room, writing *The Remembrance of Things Past*, spending our lives in beautiful reveries of "infantile amnesia" (Kohut 1977:181)? Or, on the contrary, is there something about our complex, competitive world that demands from most of us the tough disciplines inherent in a manhood ethic? Perhaps. But then we have to ask, Why do we have to be competitive or disciplined at all? Why cannot a modern industrial society exist and progress without an aggressive masculine gender role? Is there something about complex society in a more general sense that demands a manly role? Can we, like the Semai, simply run away from the challenges inherent in modern life?

But these questions are not ours to answer, because we do not make up our roles from scratch. The possibilities are not limitless. So long as there are battles to be fought, wars to be won, heights to be scaled, hard work to be done, some of us will have to "act like men." Then again, why should this injunction exclude women? Why should only males be permitted to be "real men" and to earn the glory of a risk successfully taken? But here we have to stop, for this is a question for the philosopher, not the social scientist.

Bibliography

Abu-Lughod, Lila. 1986. *Veiled Sentiments: Honor and Poetry in a Bedouin Society.* Berkeley: University of California Press.

Adams, Henry. 1930. *Letters of Henry Adams, 1858-1891,* ed. Worthington C. Ford. Boston and New York: Houghton Mifflin Co.

Alston, A. J. 1980. *The Devotional Poems of Mirabai.* Delhi: Motilal Banarsidas.

Ames, Roger T. 1981. Taoism and the androgynous ideal. In *Women in China: Current Directions in Historical Scholarship,* ed. Richard W. Guisso and Stanley Johannesen, pp. 21–45. Youngstown, N.Y.: Philo Press.

Archer, John, and Barbara Lloyd. 1985. *Sex and Gender.* Cambridge: Cambridge University Press.

Arlow, Jacob, and Charles Brenner. 1963. *Psychoanalytic Concepts and the Structural Theory.* New York: International Universities Press.

Asano-Tamanoi, Mariko. 1987. Shame, family, and state in Catalonia and Japan. In *Honor and Shame and the Unity of the Mediterranean,* ed. David D. Gilmore, pp. 104–20. Washington, D.C.: American Anthropological Association, Special Pub. no. 22.

Bakan, David. 1966. *The Duality of Human Existence.* Chicago: University of Chicago Press.

Baker, Susan W. 1980. Biological influences on human sex and gender. *Signs* 6:80–96.

Balint, Michael. 1968. *The Basic Fault: Therapeutic Aspects of Regression.* London: Tavistock.

Barth, Fredrik. 1969. *Ethnic Groups and Boundaries: The Social Organization of Cultural Difference.* London: Allen and Unwin.

———. 1987. *Cosmologies in the Making: A Generative Approach to Cultural Variation in Inner New Guinea.* Cambridge: Cambridge University Press.

Bates, Daniel G. 1974. Normative and alternative systems of marriage among the Yörük of southeastern Turkey. *Anthropological Quarterly* 47:270–87.

Bates, Daniel G., and Amal Rassam. 1983. *Peoples and Cultures of the Middle East.* Englewood Cliffs, N.J.: Prentice-Hall.

Bauman, Richard. 1977. *Verbal Art as Performance.* Rowley, Mass.: Newbury House.

Bednarik, Karl. 1970. *The Male in Crisis,* trans. from German by Helen Sebba. New York: Knopf.

Bell, Rudolf M. 1979. *Fate and Honor, Family and Village: Demographic and Cultural Change in Rural Italy Since 1800.* Chicago: University of Chicago Press.

Bellah, Robert. 1985. *Tokugawa Religion: The Cultural Roots of Modern Japan,* 2d ed. New York: Free Press.

Bem, Sandra L. 1983. Gender schema theory and its implications for child development: Raising gender-aschematic children in a gender-schematic society. *Signs* 8:598–616.

Bernard, H. Russell. 1967. Kalymnian sponge diving. *Human Biology* 39:103–30.

Bettelheim, Bruno, 1955. *Symbolic Wounds: Puberty Rites and the Envious Male.* Glencoe, Ill.: Free Press.

Bhatty, Zarina. 1975. Women in Uttar Pradesh: Social mobility and directions of change. In *Women in Contemporary India,* ed. A. de Souza, pp. 25–36. Delhi: Manohar.

Biller, Henry B., and Lloyd Borstelmann. 1967. Masculine development: An integrative view. *Merrill-Palmer Quarterly* 13:253–94.

Black-Michaud, Jacob. 1975. *Cohesive Force: Feud in the Mediterranean and the Middle East.* Oxford: Oxford University Press.

Blok, Anton. 1981. Rams and billy-goats: a key to the Mediterranean code of honour. *Man* 16:427–40.

Boehm, Christopher. 1984. *Blood Revenge: The Enactment and Management of Conflict in Montenegro and Other Tribal Societies.* Philadelphia: University of Pennsylvania Press.

Bougainville, Louis Antoine de. 1958. *Voyage autour du Monde.* Saverne, France: Club des Libraires de France.

Bourdieu, Pierre. 1965. The sentiment of honour in Kabyle society. In *Honour and Shame: The Values of Mediterranean Society,* ed. J.-G. Peristiany, pp. 191–241. Chicago: University of Chicago Press.

———. 1979a. The sense of honour. In *Algeria 1960: Essays by Pierre Bourdieu.* Cambridge: Cambridge University Press.

———. 1979b. The Kabyle house, or the world reversed. In *Algeria 1960: Essays by Pierre Bourdieu.* Cambridge: Cambridge University Press.

Brandes, Stanley H. 1980. *Metaphors of Masculinity: Sex and Status in Andalusian Folklore*. Philadelphia: University of Pennsylvania Press.

———. 1981. Like wounded stags: male sexual ideology in an Andalusian town. In *Sexual Meanings*, ed. Sherry B. Ortner and Harriet Whitehead, pp. 216–39. Cambridge: Cambridge University Press.

Braudel, Fernand. 1972. *The Mediterranean and the Mediterranean World in the Age of Philip II*. 2 vols. Trans. Siân Reynolds. New York: Harper and Row.

Brod, Harry, ed. 1987. *The Making of Masculinities: The New Men's Studies*. Boston: Allen and Unwin.

Brown, Judith K. 1970. A note on the division of labor by sex. *American Anthropologist* 72:1073–78.

Brown, Paula. 1979. *The People of Highland New Guinea*. Cambridge: Cambridge University Press.

Buruma, Ian. 1984. *Behind the Mask: On Sexual Demons, Sacred Mothers, Transvestites, Gangsters, Drifters and Other Japanese Cultural Heroes*. New York: Pantheon Books.

Campbell, J. K. 1964. *Honour, Family, and Patronage*. Oxford: Clarendon Press.

Campbell, Joseph. 1968. *The Hero with a Thousand Faces*, 2d ed. Princeton: Princeton University Press.

Carstairs, G. Morris. 1958. *The Twice Born*. London: Hogarth Press.

Caughey, John L., III. 1970. Cultural values in Micronesian society. Unpublished Ph.D. dissertation, University of Pennsylvania.

Chandos, John. 1984. *Boys Together: English Public Schools, 1800–1864*. New Haven: Yale University Press.

Chodorow, Nancy. 1978. *The Reproduction of Mothering*. Berkeley: University of California Press.

Chou, Rita J.-A. 1987. Health and Sociocultural Factors Related to Life Satisfaction: A Study of the Elderly in Oakland's Chinese Community. Ph.D. dissertation, State University of New York, Stony Brook.

Cicone, Michael, and Diane Ruble. 1978. Beliefs about males. *Journal of Social Issues* 34:5–16.

Collier, George A. 1987. *The Socialists of Rural Andalusia: Unacknowledged Revolutionaries*. Stanford: Stanford University Press.

Conant, Robert W. 1915. *The Virility of Christ*. Chicago: no publisher.

Cooper, Arnold M. 1986. What men fear: The façade of castration anxiety. In *The Psychology of Men: New Psychoanalytic Perspectives*, ed. Gerald Fogel, F. M. Lane, and R. S. Liebert, pp. 113–30. New York: Basic Books.

Crapanzano, Vincent. 1980. *Tuhami: Portrait of a Moroccan*. Chicago: University of Chicago Press.

Dahlberg, Frances. ed. 1981. *Woman the Gatherer*. New Haven: Yale University Press.

D'Andrade, Roy G. 1974. Sex differences and cultural institutions. In *Culture and Personality: Contemporary Readings*, ed. Robert A. LeVine, pp. 16–39. Chicago: Aldine.

David, Deborah S., and Robert Brannon. 1976. The male sex role: Our culture's viewpoint of manhood, and what it's done for us lately. In *The Forty-Nine Percent Majority*, ed. D. S. David and R. Brannon, pp. 1–45. Reading, Mass.: Addison-Wesley.

Davis, John. 1973. *Land and Family in Pisticci*. London: Athalone Press.

———. 1977. *People of the Mediterranean*. London: Routledge and Kegan Paul.

———. 1987. Family and state in the Mediterranean. In *Honor and Shame and the Unity of the Mediterranean*, ed. David D. Gilmore, pp. 28–34. Washington, D.C.: American Anthropological Association, Special Pub. no. 22.

Denich, Bette. 1974. Sex and power in the Balkans. In *Women, Culture, and Society*, ed. Michelle Rosaldo and Louise Lamphere, pp. 243–62. Stanford: Stanford University Press.

Dentan, Robert K. 1979. *The Semai: A Nonviolent People of Malaya*. New York: Holt, Rinehart and Winston.

DeVos, George. 1973. *Socialization for Achievement*. Berkeley: University of California Press.

Dimrock, George E., Jr. 1967. The name of Odysseus. In *Essays on the Odyssey: Selected Modern Criticism*, ed. Charles H. Taylor, Jr., pp. 54–72. Bloomington, Ind.: Indiana University Press.

Divale, William, and Marvin Harris. 1978. The male supremacist complex: Discovery of a cultural invention. *American Anthropologist* 80:668–71.

Dover, Kenneth J. 1978. *Greek Homosexuality*. Cambridge, Mass.: Harvard University Press.

Dutta, D., H. R. Phookan, and P. D. Das. 1982. The koro epidemic in lower Assam. *Indian Journal of Psychiatry* 24:370–74.

Duvignaud, Jean. 1977. *Change at Shebika: Report from a North African Village*, trans. F. Frenaye. New York: Pantheon.

Dwyer, Daisy. 1978. *Images and Self-Images: Male and Female in Morocco*. New York: Columbia University Press.

Dyck, Noel. 1980. Booze, barrooms and scrapping: Masculinity and violence in a western Canadian town. *Canadian Journal of Anthropology* 1:191–98.

Edwards, James W. 1983. Semen anxiety in South Asian cultures: Cultural and transcultural significance. *Medical Anthropology* 7:51–67.

Ember, Carol R. 1978. Myths about hunter-gatherers. *Ethnology* 18:439–48.

Erikson, Erik. 1950. *Childhood and Society.* New York: Norton.

Estioko-Griffin, Agnes, and P. Bion Griffin. 1981. Woman the hunter: The Agta. In *Woman the Gatherer,* ed. Frances Dahlberg, pp. 121–51. New Haven: Yale University Press.

Fabian, Johannes. 1983. *Time and the Other: How Anthropology Makes Its Object.* New York: Columbia University Press.

Feldman, Saul D. 1975. The presentation of shortness in everyday life—height and heightism in American society. In *Life Styles: Diversity in American Society,* 2d. ed., ed. Saul D. Feldman and Gerald W. Thielbar, pp. 437–42. Boston: Little, Brown.

Fetterly, Judith. 1978. *The Resisting Reader: A Feminist Approach to American Fiction.* Bloomington, Ind.: Indiana University Press.

Fogel, Gerald I. 1986. Introduction: being a man. In *The Psychology of Men: New Psychoanalytic Perspectives,* ed. Gerald Fogel, F. M. Lane, and R. S. Liebert, pp. 3–22. New York: Basic Books.

Forster, John. 1778. *Observations Made During a Voyage Round the World.* London: G. Robinson.

Freeman, Derek. 1983. *Margaret Mead and Samoa: The Making and Unmaking of an Anthropological Myth.* Cambridge, Mass.: Harvard University Press.

Freud, Anna. 1936. *The Ego and the Mechanisms of Defense,* trans. Cecil Baines. London: Hogarth Press.

———. 1963. Regression as a principle in mental development. *Bulletin of the Menninger Clinic* 27:126–39.

Freud, Sigmund. 1905. Three Essays on the Theory of Sexuality, III: The Transformations of Puberty. *Standard Edition,* ed. James Strachey, 7:207–30. London: Hogarth Press (1975).

———. 1914. On narcissism. *Standard Edition,* ed. James Strachey, 14:67–102. London: Hogarth Press (1975).

———. 1920. *Beyond the Pleasure Principle,* trans. James Strachey. New York: Liveright.

———. 1930. *Civilization and Its Discontents,* trans. James Strachey. New York: Norton.

Friedl, Ernestine. 1962. *Vasilika: Village in Modern Greece.* New York: Holt, Rinehart and Winston.

———. 1975. *Women and Men: An Anthropologist's View.* New York: Holt, Rinehart and Winston.

Frye, Northrop. 1976. *The Secular Scripture.* Cambridge, Mass.: Harvard University Press.

Gauguin, Paul. 1957. *Noa Noa.* New York: Noonday Press.

Gay, Peter. 1982. Liberalism and regression. *Psychoanalytic Study of the Child* 37:523–45. New Haven: Yale University Press.

Gearing, Frederick O. 1970. *The Face of the Fox*. Chicago: Aldine.

Geertz, Hildred. 1979. The meanings of family ties. In *Meaning and Order in Moroccan Society*, ed. Clifford Geertz, H. Geertz, and L. Rosen, pp. 315–86. New York: Cambridge University Press.

Giddens, Anthony. 1987. *Social Theory and Modern Sociology*. Stanford: Stanford University Press.

Gilmore, David D. 1980. *The People of the Plain*. New York: Columbia University Press.

———. 1982. Anthropology of the Mediterranean area. *Annual Review of Anthropology* 11:175–205.

Gilmore, Michael T. 1985. *American Romanticism and the Marketplace*. Chicago: University of Chicago Press.

Giovannini, Maureen. 1987. Female chastity codes in the Circum-Mediterranean: comparative perspectives. In *Honor and Shame and the Unity of the Mediterranean*, ed. David D. Gilmore, pp. 61–74. Washington, D.C.: American Anthropological Association, Special Pub. no. 22.

Gladwin, Thomas F. 1953. The role of man and woman on Truk: A problem in personality and culture. Trans. of the New York Academy of Sciences, ser. 2, 15:305–09.

Godelier, Maurice. 1986. *The Making of Great Men*. Cambridge: Cambridge University Press.

Golding, William. 1964. *The Lord of the Flies*, ed. James R. Baker and Arthur P. Ziegler, Jr. Casebook Ed. New York: Putnam.

Goodenough, Ward H. 1949. Premarital freedom on Truk: Theory and practice. *American Anthropologist* 51:615–20.

Gouldner, Alvin W. 1965. *Enter Plato: Classical Greece and the Origins of Social Theory*. New York: Basic Books.

Gregor, Thomas. 1977. *Mehinaku: The Drama of Daily Life in a Brazilian Indian Village*. Chicago: University of Chicago Press.

———. 1985. *Anxious Pleasures: The Sexual Life of an Amazonian People*. Chicago: University of Chicago Press.

Habegger, Alfred. 1982. *Gender, Fantasy, and Realism in American Literature*. New York: Columbia University Press.

Haberstroh, Charles J. 1980. *Melville and Male Identity*. Rutherford, N.J.: Associated Universities Press.

Hallman, Ralph. 1969. The archetypes in Peter Pan. *Journal of Analytic Psychology* 14:65–73.

Hantover, Jeffrey P. 1978. The Boy Scouts and the validation of masculinity. *Journal of Social Issues* 34:184–95.

Hart, David M. 1976. *The Aith Waryaghar of the Moroccan Rif: An Ethnography and History.* Tucson: University of Arizona Press.

Heald, Suzette. 1982. The making of men: The relevance of vernacular psychology to the interpretation of a Gisu ritual. *Africa* 52:15–36.

Helms, Mary W. 1988. *Ulysses' Sail: An Ethnographic Odyssey of Power, Knowledge, and Geographical Distance.* Princeton: Princeton University Press.

Hendry, Joy. 1986. *Becoming Japanese: The World of the Pre-School Child.* Honolulu: University of Hawaii Press.

Herdt, Gilbert H. 1981. *Guardians of the Flutes.* New York: McGraw-Hill.

———. 1982. Fetish and fantasy in Sambia initiation. In *Rituals of Manhood,* ed. Gilbert H. Herdt, pp. 44–98. Berkeley: University of California Press.

Herzfeld, Michael. 1980. Honour and shame: some problems in the comparative analysis of moral systems. *Man* 15:339–51.

———. 1985a. *The Poetics of Manhood: Contest and Identity in a Cretan Mountain Village.* Princeton: Princeton University Press.

———. 1985b. Gender pragmatics: Agency, speech and bride-theft in a Cretan mountain village. *Anthropology* 9:25–44.

———. 1987. *Anthropology Through the Looking-Glass: Critical Ethnography in the Margins of Europe.* Cambridge: Cambridge University Press.

Hezel, Francis X. 1973. The first European visit to Truk. *Guam Recorder* n.s. 3:38–40.

Hill, W. W. 1982. *An Ethnography of Santa Clara Pueblo, New Mexico.,* ed. and annotated by Charles H. Lange. Albuquerque, N. Mex.: University of New Mexico Press.

Hobsbawm, E. J., and Terrance O. Ranger. 1983. *The Invention of Tradition.* Cambridge: Cambridge University Press.

Honig, Emily, and Gail Hershatter. 1988. *Personal Voices: Chinese Women in the 1980s.* Stanford: Stanford University Press.

Hopkins, Gerard M. 1935. *The Correspondence of G. Manley Hopkins and Richard Watson Dixon,* ed. C. G. Abbot. London: Oxford University Press.

Hughes, Thomas. 1879. *The Manliness of Christ.* London: MacMillan.

Jeffery, Patricia. 1979. *Frogs in a Wall.* London: Zed Press.

Jung, Carl. 1926. *Psychological Types.* New York: Harcourt, Brace and Co.

Kakar, Sudhir. 1981. *The Inner World: A Psychoanalytic Study of Childhood and Society in India.* Delhi: Oxford University Press.

Kakar, Sudhir, and John Mundar Ross. 1987. *Tales of Sex, Love and Danger.* Oxford: Basil Blackwell.

Kamarovsky, Mirra. 1976. *Dilemmas of Masculinity: A Study of College Youth.* New York: W. W. Norton.

Katchadourian, Herant A. 1979. The terminology of sex and gender. In *Human Sexuality: Comparative and Developmental Perspectives,* ed. Herant A. Katchadourian, pp. 8–34. Berkeley: University of California Press.

Kay, A. 1974. Population growth in Micronesia. *Micronesian Reporter* 22:13–22.

Keesing, Roger M. 1982. Introduction. In *Rituals of Manhood,* ed. Gilbert H. Herdt, pp. 1–43. Berkeley: University of California Press.

Kelly, Raymond C. 1974. *Etoro Social Structure.* Ann Arbor: University of Michigan Press.

Kinmonth, Earl H. 1981. *The Self-Made Man in Meiji Japanese Thought.* Berkeley: University of California Press.

Kline, Paul. 1972. *Fact and Fantasy in Freudian Theory.* London: Methuen.

Kohut, Heinz. 1977. *The Restoration of the Self.* New York: International Universities Press.

Kondo, Dorinne. 1984. Review of *Behind the Mask,* by Ian Buruma. *New York Times Book Review,* Sept. 16, pp. 13–14.

Konner, Melvin. 1982. *The Tangled Wing: Biological Constraints on the Human Spirit.* New York: Harper Colophon Books.

Kriegel, Leonard. 1979. *On Men and Manhood.* New York: Hawthorn Books.

Kuper, Adam. 1983. *Anthropology and Anthropologists: The Modern British School.* London: Routledge and Kegan Paul.

La Fontaine, Jean. 1986. *Initiation.* Manchester: Manchester University Press.

Leacock, Eleanor. 1978. Women's status in egalitarian society: Implications for social evolution. *Current Anthropology* 19:247–75.

Leary, James P. 1976. Fists and foul mouths: Fights and fight stories in contemporary rural American bars. *Journal of American Folklore* 89:27–39.

Lebra, Takie Sugiyama. 1985. *Japanese Women: Constraint and Fulfillment.* Honolulu: University of Hawaii Press.

Lebra, Takie Sugiyama, and William P. Lebra, eds. 1986. *Japanese Culture and Behavior: Selected Readings,* 2d ed. Honolulu: University of Hawaii Press.

Lee, Richard B. 1979. *The !Kung San: Men, Women, and Work in a Foraging Society.* Cambridge: Cambridge University Press.

Leverenz, David. 1989. *Manhood and the American Renaissance.* Ithaca: Cornell University Press.

Levine, Donald N. 1966. The concept of masculinity in Ethiopian culture. *International Journal of Social Psychiatry* 12:17–23.

LeVine, Robert A. 1973. *Culture, Behavior, and Personality.* Chicago: Aldine.

———. 1979. Anthropology and sex: Developmental aspects. In *Human Sexuality: Comparative and Developmental Perspectives,* ed. Herant A. Katchadourian, pp. 309–31. Berkeley: University of California Press.

Levy, Robert I. 1971. The community function of Tahitian male transvestism: A hypothesis. *Anthropological Quarterly* 44:12–21.

———. 1973. *Tahitians: Mind and Experience in the Society Islands.* Chicago: University of Chicago Press.

Lewis, Oscar. 1961. *The Children of Sanchez.* New York: Random House.

Lidz, Ruth, and Theodore Lidz. 1977. Male menstruation: A ritual alternative to the Oedipal transition. *International Journal of Psycho-Analysis* 58:17–31.

Lindholm, Charles. 1982. *Generosity and Jealousy: The Swat Pakhtun of Northern Pakistan.* New York: Columbia University Press.

Little, Kenneth L. 1967. *The Mende of Sierra Leone: A West African People in Transition.* London: Routledge and Kegan Paul.

Llewelyn-Davies, Melissa. 1981. Women, warriors, and patriarchs. In *Sexual Meanings,* ed. Sherry B. Ortner and Harriet Whitehead, pp. 330–58. Cambridge: Cambridge University Press.

Lockwood, William G. 1974. Bride theft and social maneuverability in western Bosnia. *Anthropological Quarterly* 47:253–69.

Loizos, Peter. 1975. *The Greek Gift.* New York: St. Martin's Press.

Lonner, Walter J. 1980. The search for psychological universals. In *Handbook of Cross-Cultural Psychology,* ed. Harry C. Triandis and William W. Lambert, 1:143–204. Boston: Allyn and Bacon.

Lukes, Steven. 1973. *Individualism.* New York: Harper and Row.

McPherson, James M. 1988. *Battle Cry of Freedom: The Civil War Era.* New York: Oxford University Press.

Mahler, Margaret, et al. 1975. *The Psychological Birth of the Human Infant.* New York: Basic Books.

Mahoney, F. B. 1974. Social and cultural factors relating to the cause and control of alcohol abuse among Micronesian youth. Prepared for the Govt. of the Trust Territory of the Pacific Islands under contract TT 174–8 with James R. Leonard Associates, Inc. (Cited in M. Marshall 1979:160.)

Mailer, Norman. 1968. *Armies of the Night.* New York: New American Library.

Mandelbaum, David G. 1988. *Women's Seclusion and Men's Honor: Sex Roles in North India, Bangladesh, and Pakistan.* Tucson: University of Arizona Press.

Marcus, Michael. 1987. "Horsemen are the fence of the land": Honor and history among the Ghiyata of eastern Morocco. In *Honor and Shame and the Unity of the Mediterranean,* ed. David D. Gilmore, pp. 49–60. Washington, D.C.: American Anthropological Association, Special Pub. no. 22.

Marshall, Lorna. 1976. *The !Kung of Nyae Nyae.* Cambridge, Mass.: Harvard University Press.

Marshall, Mac. 1979. *Weekend Warriors.* Palo Alto, Calif.: Mayfield.

Martinez-Alier, Juan. 1971. *Labourers and Landowners in Southern Spain.* London: St. Martin's Press.

Marx, Karl. 1978. *Critique of the Gotha Program.* In *The Marx-Engels Reader,* ed. Robert C. Tucker, pp. 525–41. New York: W. W. Norton (orig.: 1891).

Mead, Margaret. 1935. *Sex and Temperament in Three Primitive Societies.* New York: New American Library.

Meeker, Michael E. 1979. *Literature and Violence in North Arabia.* Cambridge: Cambridge University Press.

Meggitt, Mervyn J. 1967. The pattern of leadership among the Mae-Enga of New Guinea. *Anthropological Forum* 2:20–35.

Mernissi, Fatima. 1975. *Beyond the Veil.* New York: Schenckman.

Messner, Michael. 1987. The meaning of success: The athletic experience and the development of male identity. In *The Makings of Masculinity,* ed. Harry Brod, pp. 193–210. Boston: Allen and Unwin.

Mitchell, Timothy J. 1988. *Violence and Piety in Spanish Folklore.* Philadelphia: University of Pennsylvania Press.

Morris, Ivan. 1975. *The Nobility of Failure: Tragic Heroes in the History of Japan.* New York: Holt, Rinehart and Winston.

Munroe, Robert L., and Ruth H. Munroe. 1980. Perspectives suggested by anthropological data. In *Handbook of Cross-Cultural Psychology,* ed. Harry C. Triandis and William W. Lambert, 1:253–317. Boston: Allyn and Bacon.

Murdock, George P. 1967. *Ethnographic Atlas.* Pittsburgh: University of Pittsburgh Press.

Murphy, Michael. 1983. Coming of age in Seville: The structuring of a riteless passage to manhood. *Journal of Anthropological Research* 39:376–392.

Nadel, S. F. 1951. *The Foundations of Social Anthropology*. London: Cohen and West.

Nandy, Ashis. 1980. *At the Edge of Psychology: Essays in Politics and Culture*. Delhi: Oxford University Press.

Newman, Philip. 1965. *Knowing the Gururumba*. New York: Holt, Rinehart and Winston.

Newman, Philip, and David J. Boyd. 1982. The making of men: Ritual and meaning in Awa male initiation. In *Rituals of Manhood*, ed. Gilbert H. Herdt, pp. 239–85. Berkeley: University of California Press.

Obeyesekere, Gananath. 1976. The impact of Ayurvedic ideas on the culture and the individual in Sri Lanka. In *Asian Medical Systems: A Comparative Study*, ed. Charles Leslie, pp. 201–26. Berkeley: University of California Press.

Ochberg, Richard L. 1987. The male career and the ideology of role. In *The Making of Masculinities*, ed. Harry Brod, pp. 173–92. Boston: Allen and Unwin.

O'Flaherty, Wendy D. 1980. *Women, Androgynes, and Other Mythical Beasts*. Chicago: University of Chicago Press.

Ortner, Sherry B. 1974. Is female to male as nature is to culture? In *Woman, Culture, and Society*, ed. Michelle Z. Rosaldo and Louise Lamphere, pp. 67–88. Stanford: Stanford University Press.

———. 1981. Gender and sexuality in hierarchical societies: The case of Polynesia and some comparative implications. In *Sexual Meanings*, ed. Sherry B. Ortner and Harriet Whitehead, pp. 359–409. Cambridge: Cambridge University Press.

Otten, Charlotte M. 1985. Genetic effects on male and female development and on the sex ratio. In *Male-Female Differences: A Bio-Cultural Perspective*, ed. Roberta L. Hall, pp. 155–217. New York: Praeger.

Pater, Walter. 1910. *Plato and Platonism: A Series of Lectures*. London: MacMillan.

Paul, Robert A. 1978. Instinctive aggression in man: The Semai case. *Journal of Psychological Anthropology* 1:65–79.

Peristiany, J.-G., ed. 1965. *Honour and Shame: The Values of Mediterranean Society*. London: Weidenfeld and Nicolson.

Pettigrew, Joyce. 1975. *Robber Noblemen: A Study of the Political System of the Sikh Jats*. London: Routledge and Kegan Paul.

Pitt-Rivers, Julian. 1961. *The People of the Sierra*. Chicago: University of Chicago Press.

———. 1965. Honour and social status. In *Honour and Shame*, ed. J.-G. Peristiany, pp. 19–77. London: Weidenfeld and Nicolson.

————. 1977. *The Fate of Shechem*. Cambridge: Cambridge University Press.

————, ed. 1963. *Mediterranean Countrymen*. Paris: Mouton.

Pleck, Joseph. 1981. *The Myth of Masculinity*. Cambridge, Mass.: MIT Press.

Poole, Fitz John P. 1982. The ritual forging of identity: Aspects of person and self in Bimin-Kuskusmin male initiation. In *Rituals of Manhood*, ed. Gilbert H. Herdt, pp. 99–154. Berkeley: University of California Press.

Quinn, Naomi. 1977. Anthropological studies on women's status. *Annual Review of Anthropology* 6:181–225.

Raphael, Ray. 1988. *The Men from the Boys: Rites of Passage in Male America*. Lincoln, Nebr.: University of Nebraska Press.

Read, Kenneth. 1965. *The High Valley*. London: Allen and Unwin.

Reminick, Ronald A. 1976. The symbolic significance of ceremonial defloration among the Amhara of Ethiopia. *American Ethnologist* 3:751–63.

————. 1982. The sport of warriors on the wane: a case of cultural endurance in the face of social change. In *Sport and the Humanities,* ed. William H. Morgan, pp. 31–36. Knoxville, Tenn.: Bureau of Educational Research and Service, University of Tennessee Press.

Rin, Hsien. 1963. Koro: A consideration of Chinese concepts of illness with case illustrations. *Transcultural Psychiatric Research Review* 15:23–30.

————. 1965. A study of the aetiology of koro in respect to the Chinese concept of illness. *International Journal of Social Psychiatry* 11:7–13.

Robarchek, Clayton A. 1977. Frustration, aggression, and the nonviolent Semai. *American Ethnologist* 4:762–69.

Robarchek, Clayton A., and Robert K. Dentan. 1987. Blood drunkenness and the bloodthirsty Semai: Unmaking another anthropological myth. *American Anthropologist* 89:356–65.

Rochlin, Gregory. 1980. *The Masculine Dilemma: A Psychology of Masculinity*. Boston: Little, Brown.

Roland, Alan. 1988. *In Search of Self in India and Japan: Toward a Cross-Cultural Psychology*. Princeton: Princeton University Press.

Roy, Manisha. 1975. *Bengali Women*. Chicago: University of Chicago Press.

Rubin, Gayle. 1975. The traffic in women: Notes toward a political economy of sex. In *Toward an Anthropology of Women,* ed. Rayna Reiter, pp. 157–210. New York: Monthly Review Press.

Sahlins, Marshall. 1984. Poor man, rich man, big man, chief. In

Conformity and Conflict, ed. J. P. Spradley and D. W. McCurdy, pp. 274–288. Boston: Little, Brown.

Saitoti, Tepilit Ole. 1986. *The Worlds of a Maasai Warrior: An Autobiography.* Berkeley: University of California Press.

Salamon, Sonya. 1986. "Male chauvinism" as a manifestation of love in marriage. In *Japanese Culture and Behavior,* ed. Takie Sugiyama Lebra and William P. Lebra, pp. 130–41. Honolulu: University of Hawaii Press.

Salisbury, Richard F. 1965. The Siane of the eastern Highlands. In *Gods, Ghosts, and Men in Melanesia,* ed. P. Lawrence and M. J. Meggitt, pp. 50–77. Melbourne: Oxford University Press.

Sanday, Peggy R. 1973. Toward a theory of the status of women. *American Anthropologist* 75:1682–1700.

———. 1981. *Female Power and Male Dominance: On the Origins of Sexual Inequality.* Cambridge: Cambridge University Press.

Schafer, Roy. 1986. Men who struggle against sentimentality. In *The Psychology of Men: New Psychoanalytic Perspectives,* ed. Gerald I. Fogel, L. M. Lane, and R. S. Liebert, pp. 95–110. New York: Basic Books.

Schieffelin, Edward L. 1982. The *bau a* ceremonial hunting lodge: An alternative to initiation. In *Rituals of Manhood,* ed. Gilbert H. Herdt, pp. 155–200. Berkeley: University of Chicago Press.

Schneider, Jane. 1971. Of vigilance and virgins. *Ethnology* 9:1–24.

Schodt, Frederick. 1983. *Manga! Manga! The World of Japanese Comics.* Tokyo: Kodansha International.

Schwenger, Peter. 1984. *Phallic Critiques: Masculinity and Twentieth-Century Literature.* London: Routledge and Kegan Paul.

Shapiro, Judith. 1979. Cross-cultural perspectives on sexual differentiation. In *Human Sexuality: Comparative and Developmental Perspectives,* ed. Herant A. Katchadourian, pp. 269–308. Berkeley: University of California Press.

Shostak, Marjorie. 1981. *Nisa: The Life and Words of a !Kung Woman.* Cambridge, Mass.: Harvard University Press.

Simic, Andrei. 1969. Management of the male image in Yugoslavia. *Anthropological Quarterly* 42:89–101.

———. 1983. Machismo and cryptomatriarchy: power, affect, and authority in the contemporary Yugoslav family. *Ethos* 11:66–86.

Slater, Philip E. 1968. *The Glory of Hera.* Boston: Beacon Press.

Smith, Robert J. 1983. *Japanese Society: Tradition, Self and the Social Order.* Cambridge: Cambridge University Press.

Smith, Robert J., and Ella L. Wiswell. 1982. *The Women of Suye Mura.* Chicago: University of Chicago Press.

Spence, Janet, and Robert L. Helmreich. 1979. *Masculinity and Feminini-ty: Their Psychological Dimensions, Correlates and Antecedents.* Austin, Tex.: University of Texas Press.

Spencer, Paul. 1965. *The Samburu: A Study of Gerontocracy in a Nomadic Tribe.* Berkeley: University of California Press.

———. 1973. *Nomads in Alliance: Symbiosis and Growth among the Ren-dille and Samburu of Kenya.* London: Oxford University Press.

Spratt, Philip. 1966. *Hindu Culture and Personality.* Bombay: Manaktalas.

Stearns, Peter N. 1979. *Be a Man! Males in Modern Society.* New York: Holmes and Meier.

Stephens, William N. 1967. A cross-cultural study of menstrual taboos. In *Cross-Cultural Approaches,* ed. Clellan S. Ford, pp. 67–94. New Haven: HRAF Press.

Stoller, Robert. 1968. *Sex and Gender.* New York: Science House.

———. 1974. Facts and fancies: An examination of Freud's concept of bisexuality. In *Women and Analysis,* ed. Jean Strouse, pp. 343–64. New York: Dell.

Stoller, Robert, and Gilbert H. Herdt. 1982. The development of mas-culinity: A cross-cultural contribution. *Journal of the American Psycho-analytic Association* 30:29–59.

Strathern, Andrew. 1971. *The Rope of Moka.* Cambridge: Cambridge University Press.

Strathern, Marilyn. 1981. Self-interest and the social good: Some im-plications of Hagen gender imagery. In *Sexual Meanings,* ed. Sherry B. Ortner and Harriet Whitehead, pp. 166–91. Cambridge: Cambridge University Press.

Taylor, Jared. 1983. *Shadows of the Rising Sun: A Critical View of the Japanese Miracle.* New York: Morrow.

Theweleit, Klaus. 1987. *Male Fantasies,* trans. S. Conway, Erica Carter, and Chris Turner. Minneapolis: University of Minnesota Press.

Thomas, Elizabeth Marshall. 1959. *The Harmless People.* New York: Vin-tage Books.

———. 1965. *Warrior Herdsmen.* New York: Knopf.

Thucydides. 1951. *The Complete Writings: The Peloponnesian Wars,* ed. J. H. Finley, Jr., trans. Richard Crawley. New York: Modern Library.

Tierno Galván, Enrique. 1961. Los toros, acontecimiento nacional. In *Desde el Espectáculo a la Trivilización,* pp. 53–77. Madrid: Taurus.

Tiger, Lionel. 1971. *Men in Groups.* New York: Random House.

Tolson, Andrew. 1977. *The Limits of Masculinity: Male Identity and the Liberated Woman.* New York: Harper and Row.

Tseng, W.-S., et al. 1987. A socio-cultural and clinical study of a *koro* epidemic in Guangdong, China. Paper read at a conference of the Society for the Study of Psychiatry and Culture, Quebec, Sept. 16–19, 1987. Abstracted in *Transcultural Psychiatric Research Review* 25:74–77 by R. H. Prince (1988).

Turnbull, Colin M. 1981. Mbuti womanhood. In *Woman the Gatherer*, ed. Frances Dahlberg, pp. 205–19. New Haven: Yale University Press.

Turnbull, John. 1812. *A Voyage Round the World in the Years 1800, 1801, 1802, 1803, and 1804*. London: A. Maxwell.

Tuzin, Donald F. 1980. *The Voice of the Tambaran: Truth and Illusion in Ilahita Arapesh Religion*. Berkeley: University of California Press.

———. 1982. Ritual violence among the Ilahita Arapesh: The dynamics of moral and religious uncertainty. In *Rituals of Manhood*, ed. Gilbert H. Herdt, pp. 321–55. Berkeley: University of California Press.

Van Gennep, Arnold. 1960. *The Rites of Passage*, trans. Monika B. Vizedom and Gabrielle L. Caffe. Chicago: University of Chicago Press (Orig.: 1908).

Vanggaard, Thorkil. 1972. *Phallos*. New York: International Universities Press.

Veyne, Paul. 1985. Homosexuality in ancient Rome. In *Western Sexuality*, ed. Philippe Ariès and André Bejin, trans. Anthony Forster, pp. 26–39. Oxford: Basil Blackwell.

Vivekananda. 1953. *The Yogas and Other Works*, ed. S. Nikhilananda. New York: Ramakrishna-Vivekananda Center.

———. 1970. *Collected Works of Swami Vivekananda*, 8 vols. Calcutta: Advaita Ashrama.

Whiting, John M. W., R. Kluckhohn, and A. Anthony. 1958. The function of male initiation ceremonies at puberty. In *Readings in Social Psychology*, ed. Eleanor E. Maccoby, T. M. Newcomb, and F. L. Hartley, pp. 359–70. New York: Holt, Rinehart and Winston.

Whyte, Martin K. 1978. Cross-cultural codes dealing with the relative status of women. *Ethnology* 17:211–37.

Wikan, Unni. 1984. Shame and honour: A contestable pair. *Man* 19:635–52.

Williams, John E., and Deborah L. Best. 1982. *Measuring Sex Stereotypes: A Thirty-Nation Study*. Beverly Hills: Sage Publs.

Williams, Walter C. 1986. *The Spirit and the Flesh: Sexual Diversity in American Indian Culture*. Boston: Beacon Press.

Williams-Hunt, Peter D. R. 1952. *An Introduction to the Malayan Aborigines*. Kuala Lampur: Government Press.

Wilson, James. 1799. *A Missionary Voyage to the Southern Pacific Ocean in 1796, 1797, 1798*. London: T. Chapman.

Wilson, Peter J. 1988. *The Domestication of the Human Species*. New Haven: Yale University Press.

Wolf, Margery. 1985. *Revolution Postponed: Women in Contemporary China*. Stanford: Stanford University Press.

Wyatt-Brown, Bertram. 1982. *Southern Honor: Ethics and Behavior in the Old South*. New York: Oxford University Press.

Yap, P. M. 1965. Koro—a culture-bound depersonalization syndrome. *British Journal of Psychiatry* 111:43–50.

Young, Frank W. 1965. *Initiation Ceremonies: A Cross-Cultural Study of Status Dramatization*. Indianapolis: Bobbs-Merrill.

Zweig, Ferdynand. 1961. *The Worker in an Affluent Society*. New York: Free Press.

Index